Emotion-Focused Family Therapy

Emotion-Focused Family Therapy

A Transdiagnostic Model for Caregiver-Focused Interventions

ADELE LAFRANCE, KATHERINE A. HENDERSON, AND SHARI MAYMAN

AMERICAN PSYCHOLOGICAL ASSOCIATION
Washington, DC

Published by
American Psychological Association
750 First Street, NE
Washington, DC 20002
https://www.apa.org

Order Department
https://www.apa.org/pubs/books
order@apa.org

In the U.K., Europe, Africa, and the Middle East, copies may be ordered from Eurospan
https://www.eurospanbookstore.com/apa
info@eurospangroup.com

Typeset in Charter by Circle Graphics, Inc., Reisterstown, MD

Printer: Sheridan Books, Chelsea, MI
Cover Designer: Beth Schlenoff Design, Bethesda, MD

Library of Congress Cataloging-in-Publication Data

Names: Lafrance, Adele, author. | Henderson, Katherine A., author. |
    Mayman, Shari, author.
Title: Emotion-focused family therapy : a transdiagnostic model for
    caregiver-focused interventions / Adele Lafrance, Katherine A.
    Henderson, and Shari Mayman.
Description: Washington : American Psychological Association, [2020] |
    Includes bibliographical references and index.
Identifiers: LCCN 2019022631 (print) | LCCN 2019022632 (ebook) |
    ISBN 9781433830853 (paperback) | ISBN 9781433830860 (ebook)
Subjects: LCSH: Emotion-focused therapy. | Family psychotherapy. |
    Mentally ill—Family relationships.
Classification: LCC RC489.F62 L34 2020 (print) | LCC RC489.F62 (ebook) |
    DDC 616.89/156—dc23
LC record available at https://lccn.loc.gov/2019022631
LC ebook record available at https://lccn.loc.gov/2019022632

http://dx.doi.org/10.10370000166-000

Printed in the United States of America

10 9 8 7 6 5 4 3

Contents

Acknowledgments	*vii*
Introduction	*3*
1. Emotion-Focused Family Therapy Explained	11
2. Emotion Coaching	29
3. Behavior Coaching	49
4. Therapeutic Apologies	63
5. Working Through Caregiver Blocks	81
6. Working Through Clinician Blocks	105
7. Emotion-Focused Family Therapy for Eating Disorders	119
8. Frequently Asked Questions and Future Directions	139
Epilogue: Lessons Learned	*147*
Appendix A: The Super-Feeler Explained	*151*
Appendix B: Emotion-Coaching Cheat Sheet	*153*
Appendix C: Behavior Coaching for Cooperation and Collaboration	*155*
Appendix D: Healing Family Wounds via Therapeutic Apology	*157*
Appendix E: Caregiver Styles Self-Reflection Tool	*161*
Appendix F: Caregiver Traps Scale	*163*
Appendix G: Behavior Coaching: Family Safety Plan for Self-Harm and Suicidality	*165*
Appendix H: Relationship Dimensions Scale	*167*
Appendix I: Connecting in Relationships: Validating Silence	*169*
Appendix J: Processing Caregiver Blocks Using Chair Work	*171*

Appendix K: Clinician Traps Scale   *175*
Appendix L: Self-Directed Block Worksheet for Clinicians   *177*
Appendix M: Processing Clinician Blocks Using Chair Work—
       Caregiver Involvement   *181*
Appendix N: Helpful Resources When Caring for a Loved One With
       an Eating Disorder   *185*
References   *187*
Index   *203*
About the Authors   *211*

Acknowledgments

We would first like to acknowledge the many clinicians and researchers who influenced the development and evolution of emotion-focused family therapy (EFFT), either directly or indirectly. They include (in alphabetical order): Jonathon Baylin, Ahmed Boachie, Guy Diamond, John Gottman, Leslie Greenberg, Daniel Hughes, Daniel Le Grange, James Lock, Gabor Maté, Daniel Siegel, and Janet Treasure. Thank you for your wisdom, your vision, and your generosity.

We also thank our EFFT colleagues who reviewed and provided feedback on each of the chapters, as well as those who contributed personal anecdotes based on their clinical experiences: Sarah Penney, Jiabao Gao, Tamara Davidson, Elizabeth Easton, Allen Sabey, Laura Connors, Ashley Skinner, Hien Nguyen, Patricia Nash, and Sarah Jane Norwood. Sincere thanks to Maya Partrick as well for the wonderful images she created for this manual.

Deepest gratitude goes out to Joanne Dolhanty, codeveloper of the model, for the many years of collaboration and camaraderie. We also extend our thanks to the caregivers and their loved ones with whom we've worked. We humbly thank you for teaching us about the extraordinary healing power of families. We particularly want to acknowledge those families who continue to struggle. Know that our ongoing efforts to refine the model are in your honor.

Finally, and perhaps most important, we thank our own families: our parents, Claude, Glenys, Doug, Lou, Phil, and Debby, for instilling in us the power of love; our partners, John, Peter, and Kevin, for believing in us and supporting us in ways that made this book possible; and our children, Kayden, Sydney, Andrew, Isla, Ezra, and Noah, for serving as our guiding lights on this journey (and for their patience when we struggled to practice what we preach!).

> To clinicians thinking about learning EFFT, I'd say just do it. Learn it. Teach it. Share it. This is the opportunity to give us skills. It's like when you give a man a fish, he eats for a day, and when you teach a man to fish, he eats for a lifetime. You're teaching us how to fish. I just feel so much more empowered having gone through this process. I keep getting stronger, and my loved one does too.
> —Quote from a caregiver, when asked for a message
> for clinicians new to the model

Emotion-Focused
Family Therapy

INTRODUCTION

A 30-year-old man moves into his parents' basement after losing his job and separating from his wife. He is suffering from serious depression, rarely leaving his room and refusing to engage socially with anyone. His parents, who oscillate between worry, helplessness, and frustration, contact you for support. You urge them to encourage their son to seek help, and you suggest they set limits, if necessary, but you are left with a nagging feeling that this family needs more. Although you feel deeply for this family, you too feel helpless. Now imagine that you receive this same phone call, but you have at your disposal a set of tools tailor-made for this scenario. You inform the parents that, despite their son's reluctance to connect and access supports, there is much that can be done and you can help them to support their son using interventions from emotion-focused family therapy (EFFT).[1]

---

[1]Emotion-focused family therapy is not to be confused with the similarly titled emotionally focused family therapy. Although they share similar roots, to our knowledge, the latter is a more traditional approach to family therapy, whereas emotion-focused family therapy is primarily focused on equipping caregivers with advanced skills to support their loved one struggling with a behavioral or mental health issues. Techniques from both models can work well together and we encourage readers to benefit from the models' strengths in supporting families.

http://dx.doi.org/10.1037/0000166-001
Emotion-Focused Family Therapy: A Transdiagnostic Model for Caregiver-Focused Interventions, by A. Lafrance, K. A. Henderson, and S. Mayman

EFFT is an innovative transdiagnostic approach to the treatment of mental health issues across the lifespan that involves caregivers for their healing power. EFFT is a flexible approach that can be used to treat many behavior or emotion-based disorders, and specific interventions can be adapted for use in other treatment approaches. Unlike other family therapies that are more systemic in nature, the goal of EFFT is to support parents, partners, and other carers to increase their role in promoting the health and wellness of their loved ones. To do so, EFFT clinicians teach a set of skills to caregivers that allow them to provide emotional and practical support to individuals of all ages and with a wide variety of challenges. In addition, EFFT practitioners attend to and transform the unprocessed or maladaptive emotions that can impede treatment progress, whether their own or those of caregivers, using a variety of techniques for improved outcomes. The EFFT model was designed to be flexible in its implementation with single families, carers only, dyads, and multicaregiver groups. In fact, one of the key strengths of the EFFT approach is that clinicians can guide caregivers to provide home-based support, even when their loved one refuses or is unable to access service. The tools and techniques of EFFT can also be integrated within other treatment modalities and at various levels of care to empower families and clinicians alike.

CORE PRINCIPLES

EFFT is built on a foundation of core principles that guide clinicians and therapists in their work. The first and perhaps most important guiding light is the belief that it is most therapeutically worthwhile for caregivers to implement behavioral and emotional interventions with their loved one. As such, EFFT privileges the caregiver's role as an active agent of healing, regardless of their loved one's age or motivation for change, and even when caregivers present with difficult behaviors or emotional challenges of their own. Second is the emphasis on the role that emotion processing plays in the onset and maintenance of mental health difficulties, given that it is a factor that may be more easily targeted in the service of symptom reduction. It is expected that in supporting their loved ones in these ways, caregivers will require "advanced caregiver skills"—skills not previously acquired or that are not required for "typical" caregiving. As such, a third principle relates to a focus on skill development and experiential practice. EFFT is also guided by the principle of "no blame," meaning that caregivers are not to blame for the development of mental health challenges in their loved ones; they are instead conceptualized within a broader framework of historical and societal influence, intergenerational trauma, and the expression of individual differences. Clinicians also commit to collaborating with caregivers in a manner that is transparent, in particular when it comes to clinical decisions. For example, the clinician does not determine whether the caregiver is capable of engaging in a particular intervention. Rather, they discuss together the risks and benefits of doing so, boosting caregiver empowerment and reducing the likelihood that the clinician will impede treatment progress on the basis of their own unspoken fears or assumptions. The final guiding principle of EFFT lies in the concept of the one-degree effect, in that even small shifts in caregiver attitudes and behaviors can lead to meaningful change in their loved one over time. This principle is meant to encourage EFFT clinicians to brainstorm ways to include caregivers who initially present as "incapable" or who may have previously been excluded from treatment due to limited resources or capacities.

DEFINITION OF KEY TERMS

Throughout this manual, the individual delivering EFFT is referred to as the *clinician* unless the technique being described is psychotherapeutic in nature and therefore reserved to those authorized to practice psychotherapy. In these cases, the term *therapist* is used. In the context of the model, we also use the terms *loved ones* and *caregivers*. The term *loved one* is defined as an individual who is affected by a behavioral or mental health issue, including a diagnosed mental disorder. A *caregiver* (also referred to as *carer* throughout this text) is an adult who cares about the welfare of the identified individual and who, in the context of their relationship, engages in caregiving to various degrees. Within this framework, caregivers can refer to parents or guardians, stepparents, grandparents, or other extended family members. A caregiver can also be a spouse, partner, or friend. Depending on the nature of the relationship, the caregiver's involvement may differ in its intensity, and additional factors may be considered. For example, in parent–child dyads, there is a strong attachment within a hierarchical relationship, making it such that there is an expectation they will care for their child, and more so than other family members or important others. The extent to which they actively provide caregiving may change over time as a function of their child's increased need or independence, their living situation, their relationship status, and the severity of their issues, but not simply because of their age. With respect to romantic partnerships, although there is an expectation of caring for one another, there is also an expectation of reciprocity, which requires consideration to maintain the health of the union.

When family members, significant others, or close friends are available on a limited basis or altogether unavailable, personal support and group home staff or nursing home attendants can also be recruited as caregivers, but this within the parameters of their employment.

PURPOSE OF THE MANUAL

This book serves as a clinical manual for the delivery of EFFT in the treatment of behavioral and mental health issues. It is intended to provide a comprehensive introduction to the model for those who are new to EFFT and a deepened understanding of its theory and application for those already familiar with the stance and its interventions. Throughout the book, we provide theory, research evidence, treatment protocols, and clinical examples of the application of EFFT across the lifespan in the context of different caregiving relationships, and across diagnoses.[2] We also provide an in-depth description of its application in the context of eating disorders as an example of the therapeutic process that clinicians can apply to other disorders.

INTENDED AUDIENCE

It is our hope that this clinical manual will appeal to a wide range of health care professionals. Clinicians and students in the fields of psychology, social work, psychotherapy, and family counseling, including divinity counseling, will find this manual useful whether they adopt EFFT as a primary approach or as an adjunct to other approaches. We also hope to inspire our colleagues rooted in other therapeutic modalities to explore the amalgamation of theory, principles, and techniques of EFFT within their current work. In fact, we believe that whether someone is trained in cognitive and/or behavioral techniques, process experiential modalities, or structural family therapy, this book will build on existing clinician strengths and add significantly to one's skill set in working with caregivers of individuals struggling with mental health issues. We also believe that clinicians working with children, adolescents, or adults can benefit from this manual to supplement individual interventions. We have found that doing so can offer hope to individuals and families who are suffering, especially when standard approaches have not yielded expected outcomes. Others who may benefit from this text include

---

[2]Client information in the case examples has been disguised to protect confidentiality.

those in community public health and nursing, allied health (e.g., dietitians, physiotherapists, occupational therapists) education (e.g., teachers, professors, guidance counselors), and child and youth work. The skills in this book can help to navigate difficult conversations, improve treatment engagement and cooperation, and guide caregivers to support their loved one's health and wellness in various contexts.

CHAPTER OUTLINE

The five modules in EFFT include (a) emotion coaching, (b) behavior coaching, (c) therapeutic apologies, (d) caregiver blocks, and (e) clinician blocks. In the first three modules, caregivers are equipped with tools to support their loved one to process overt and underlying emotions fueling problematic behaviors, interrupt symptoms and increase health-focused behaviors, and heal relational injuries to strengthen the power of their efforts. The remaining modules are clinician-led and involve techniques to address the emotional states fueling therapy-interfering attitudes and behaviors in caregivers and clinicians that arise throughout treatment.

Chapter 1, "Emotion-Focused Family Therapy Explained," provides an in-depth exploration of the development and application of EFFT, including an elaboration of core principles and modalities of treatment delivery.

Chapter 2, "Emotion Coaching," introduces theory and research supporting the focus on emotions and emotion processing, followed by a practical introduction to the model of emotion coaching. Commonly encountered challenges faced by caregivers and the clinicians who support them are also presented.

Chapter 3, "Behavior Coaching," provides a framework for empowering and supporting caregivers to lead behavioral interventions in the home setting. Clinical scenarios and sample scripts are provided.

Chapter 4, "Therapeutic Apologies," introduces the module on this topic and guides the reader through the theory, principles, and intervention techniques to relieve self-blame and strengthen family relationships—and therefore the impact of caregiver supportive efforts. The ingredients of a skilled therapeutic apology are also highlighted through clinical vignettes.

Chapter 5, "Working Through Caregiver Blocks," introduces the reader to the model's conceptualization of problematic caregiver attitudes and behaviors as stemming from unprocessed or maladaptive emotion. Building on this theoretical foundation, the chapter then describes various tools and techniques for clinicians to use in supporting caregivers to work through such blocks.

Chapter 6, "Working Through Clinician Blocks," extends the theory of blocks to clinicians and treatment teams. The reader is guided to engage in self-reflection or guided supervision activities to work through emotional reactions that can affect treatment decisions and therapeutic outcomes.

Chapter 7, "Emotion-Focused Family Therapy for Eating Disorders," provides a detailed example of the model's application in the context of a specific mental disorder. This chapter provides examples of the ways in which each of the modules in EFFT can be integrated in the treatment of eating disorders with clinical examples and vignettes. Although this chapter reviews symptoms and strategies that are specific to eating disorders, such as meal support to promote normalized eating, the underlying principles of EFFT are emphasized throughout the chapter, illustrating a general process that can be adapted to other behavior and emotion-based disorders.

Chapter 8, "Frequently Asked Questions and Future Directions," reviews the answers to questions that are most frequently asked during EFFT trainings and supervision. We also introduce extensions of the model for those individuals who struggle with an eating disorder and a comorbid substance use disorder, as well as emotion-focused applications in school settings and in health care more broadly.

The reader will note that each chapter begins with a quote from a caregiver and ends with a testimonial from a clinician. We share their enthusiasm and gratitude with readers to provide inspiration to integrate these teachings into practice, even if they reflect a shift in practice corresponding to a single degree. The epilogue includes personal reflections from the authors about the impact of EFFT on their personal and professional lives, followed by appendices that include supplemental materials to support the implementation of skills outlined throughout the book, including caregiver handouts and other therapeutic tools.[3]

NEXT STEPS

This manual is meant to serve as an introduction to the model and a guide for implementation. In fact, we encourage readers to integrate these tools and techniques into their work with clients knowing that they can rely on their existing clinical or psychotherapeutic skills should they encounter challenges with implementation. That being said, the interventions presented

---

[3]The handouts in the appendices are also available online at this book's companion website so that clinicians can download and distribute them to their clients (http://pubs.apa.org/books/supp/lafrance/).

do require a minimum level of training when a clinician is working with a mental health disorder, especially given that competence is an essential element of ethical practice, as stated in Section 2: Competence of the *Ethical Principles of Psychologists and Code of Conduct* (American Psychological Association [APA], 2017a). We also strongly recommend obtaining supervision to ensure implementation adherence. Those interested in deepening their knowledge of EFFT are encouraged to view the the this book's companion video where the first author (AL) demonstrates the use of caregiver block chair work in a live demonstration, followed by a discussion of the theoretical underpinnings of the approach more generally.[4] Readers may also be interested in attending one of the many online and in-person trainings recognized by the International Institute for Emotion-Focused Family Therapy. These core and advanced trainings are offered by highly skilled facilitators who provide standardized training opportunities to interested educators, clinicians, and therapists worldwide. Certified facilitators commit to ongoing personal and professional development, as well as the embodiment of EFFT principles in their personal and professional lives. Certification pathways are available for clinicians (e.g., nurses, dietitians) and therapists (e.g., psychologists, psychotherapists, social workers) committed to the practice of EFFT and involve minimum training and supervision requirements. For more information on training opportunities and certification requirements, visit the International Institute for Emotion-Focused Family Therapy's website (https://efftinternational.org).

Finally, although outside of this book's scope, clinicians must consider cultural factors that influence familial structures and behaviors in the implementation of EFFT. Although the model has been shown to be applicable worldwide (including in Europe, Central and South America, and Asia), systematic research is required to clarify the nuances in its application across cultures. Until then, we direct readers to APA's (2017b) recently updated *Multicultural Guidelines* for guidance and inspiration.

---

[4]This book's companion video is available online (https://www.apa.org/pubs/videos/4310012).

1

EMOTION-FOCUSED FAMILY THERAPY EXPLAINED

*This approach changed my outlook and mind-set and gave me the tools
I needed to support my child, and with confidence.*

—Caregiver

Codeveloped by psychologists Adele Lafrance and Joanne Dolhanty, the essence of emotion-focused family therapy (EFFT) is to empower caregivers to take on an active role in the healing of their loved one's mental health issues. The recruitment of caregivers extends beyond childhood and adolescence to the full lifespan, and the foci of interventions are both behaviorally based and emotion focused. Specifically, the EFFT clinician is tasked with supporting caregivers to support their loved one with the interruption of symptoms and the increase of health-focused behaviors, the processing of overt and underlying emotions fueling problematic behaviors and symptoms, and the repair of relational injuries to strengthen the power of their efforts. Throughout treatment, the EFFT clinician also seeks to transform emotion blocks in caregivers who struggle to support their loved one. Such

http://dx.doi.org/10.1037/0000166-002
*Emotion-Focused Family Therapy: A Transdiagnostic Model for Caregiver-Focused
Interventions*, by A. Lafrance, K. A. Henderson, and S. Mayman

emotion blocks are also identified and processed in clinicians as they implement these interventions.

This focus on the engagement of caregivers as an extension of the treatment team can represent a departure from conventional methods, particularly when clients are adults. However, given the dearth of services available to those struggling—whether due to psychological or financial barriers—the model offers the possibility of filling important gaps in the mental health care system. More important, given that outcomes are improved for all involved in treatment efforts, EFFT offers the possibility of healing that extends far beyond the identified client.

THE SIX PILLARS OF EFFT

The pillars of EFFT were elaborated to clarify the therapeutic stance of the model for families, clinicians, and policymakers, enabling them to make an informed decision about engagement. They serve as guideposts in the integration of EFFT theory and interventions within one's practice, and, when grounded in the spirit of the model, clinicians can navigate tricky scenarios with increased confidence. Over time and with more experience, EFFT clinicians can also bring creativity and flexibility to their application of the techniques, knowing that these reference points maintain their alignment with the core therapeutic values.

Caregiver Empowerment and Involvement

The first and perhaps most important pillar of EFFT relates to the recruitment of caregivers as active agents of healing. Caregivers represent an often-untapped resource for enhancing change in individuals who struggle with mental health issues. As we often state to caregivers in the initial stages of therapy, caregivers know their loved ones best and love them the most; therefore, we can harness the power of their bond for healing. Caregiver efforts are also thought to be more neurologically powerful than those of a stranger, including a trained clinician, and even when those efforts are imperfect or of lesser intensity (Bartels & Zeki, 2004; Cassidy & Shaver, 2002; Hughes & Baylin, 2012; Siegel, 2010). There are other practical reasons for the involvement of carers. First, those who struggle with behavioral or mental health issues often live at home, with a spouse or partner, or are dependent on their families in some way. Therefore, it is sensible to equip these individuals with evidence-based skills for use in day-to-day interactions. When caregivers can offer support in the real-world settings where their loved one is most likely to struggle, outcomes also improve (Gordon, Arbuthnot, Gustafson, & McGreen, 1988; Henggeler et al., 1999). Finally, some caregivers report tremendous frustration with mental health systems that are underresourced and therefore ill-equipped to meet their loved one's needs. They often find themselves on the outskirts of treatment when they could be utilized to fill in these systemic gaps. Providing caregivers with an active role in the service of their loved one's healing also decreases their feelings of powerlessness and paralysis, which can lead to burnout, relationship strain, and problematic behavior patterns (Sepulveda, Lopez, Todd, Whitaker, & Treasure, 2008). Finally, it is sometimes the case that individuals who seek out their own therapy for significant mental health issues terminate service when their pain begins to surface. This leaves the clinician without avenues to reengage the client, especially if they are considered high risk. If caregivers are involved in some way, even peripherally, they can continue to receive services on behalf of their loved one as surrogate healer.

There are some cases in which the recruitment of a caregiver may prove challenging. Some carers initially refuse to be involved or insist on individual therapy for their loved one. Clinicians may also determine that caregiver involvement is inappropriate or potentially harmful, or they do not feel equipped to work with the parents or caregivers of their clients. In these instances, EFFT provides a framework for working through such impasses to facilitate or increase the involvement of caregivers in a manner that is developmentally sensitive. In fact, one of the core beliefs in EFFT is that regardless of their age, people want to be supported by their carers, and carers want to support their loved ones in healing. Filtered through the EFFT lens, resistance to carer involvement in treatment (on the part of the caregiver, the loved one, or the clinician) is believed to be rooted in fears about the potential negative outcomes related to such involvement or fueled by other unprocessed emotional states (e.g., hurt, resentment) that can be targeted and transformed.

Focus on Emotion Processing

Within the EFFT perspective, it is theorized that problematic emotion processing plays a key role in the onset and maintenance of behavioral problems and mental health issues (e.g., depression, anxiety). Emotional avoidance (i.e., suppressing or ignoring emotions) is also considered a maladaptive coping strategy that drives a variety of symptoms. Although numerous factors (e.g., genetics, culture, trauma) can contribute to the development of a mental health disorder, the ways in which individuals and their families attend to and process emotions can actually be targeted and transformed.

Thus, the EFFT clinician supports carers to support their loved one with emotion processing. By doing so, loved ones will be more likely to turn to their caregiver in times of overwhelm, rather than to symptoms or problematic behaviors, to cope. Over time, this support will also lead to the internalization of the loved one's capacity to manage emotions in healthier ways.

Focus on Skill Development

While a respect for the capacity of carers to activate their own internal resources to support their loved one is inherent in the EFFT approach, so too is the provision of skill training. These skills are referred to as *advanced caregiving skills* because they are not required under typical circumstances and their absence does not trigger the development of mental health issues. One parent captured the spirit perfectly when she realized that "not using these skills didn't get us here, but using them can get us out." When teaching these skills, repeated experiential practice is essential for caregivers to develop the capacity to override default modes of responding to their loved one, and instead draw on their newly acquired skills when needed.

Foundation of No Blame

EFFT is an approach that takes a firm and explicit stance of "no blame." In part philosophical and in part spiritual, this stance is supported by various lines of research relating to myriad factors that contribute to mental health issues (and the complex relationships among them; Uher, 2014; Uher & Zwicker, 2017) as well as the evidence for the generational echo of trauma (Dias & Ressler, 2014; Schickedanz, Halfon, Sastry, & Chung, 2018). In fact, one of the primary foci of intervention is to support caregivers to release their narratives of self-blame. It is our experience that caregivers often blame themselves, whether overtly or covertly, when their loved one struggles with mental illness. Their self-blame can lead to the experience of deep pain, potentially problematic interactional cycles, and an overall sense that "I can't be the solution if I caused the problem." As such, when caregivers share with us their shortcomings or the "mistakes" they've made, however serious, the EFFT clinician guides them to widen their lens of interpretation to understand at a much deeper level that they did their best with the internal and external resources to which they had access. With this wider lens, the notion of blame becomes irrelevant, and its effect on caregivers is diminished. When the EFFT clinician takes time to explore and actively work through caregivers' self-blame with structured interventions, he or she also supports them in rewriting the narrative of the family's life in a way that is more compassionate.

Collaboration and Transparency

Within EFFT, the relationship between the clinician and the caregiver is collaborative and transparent. Caregivers are the experts on their loved one and the one most available to effect change, while the clinician is the expert on mental health issues. Clinicians do not make decisions about the appropriateness of caregiver involvement nor do they establish the treatment goals without caregiver input. The clinician uses a genuine and transparent approach in sessions, providing the caregiver with the same information as any other member of the treatment team. When the clinician is concerned about the caregiver's capacity to engage in a task, the clinician brings these concerns to session for discussion. For example, should a therapist worry about a caregiver's capacity to engage in caregiver block chair work, she would be honest in communicating her concerns and work with the caregiver to determine whether it is in fact an appropriate intervention, and if so, whether the timing is right. This level of transparency boosts rapport and enhances caregiver empowerment. Perhaps equal in importance is the effect that this transparent approach has on the clinician. This way of being with clients serves to protect clinicians from their own fears or clinician blocks, including making incorrect assumptions about a caregiver's capacity to engage in specific ways.

The One-Degree Effect

The final pillar of EFFT lies in the concept of the one-degree effect. Consider the following: If a plane flew from Toronto to Chicago and its navigation was off by a single degree, it would travel 92 feet off course for every mile flown—a slightly different trajectory with a vastly different outcome. For this reason, when clinicians ask us how best to determine a caregiver's capacity to engage in EFFT, the simple answer is: "We don't." Clinicians aim to engage carers as much as possible. In situations where a caregiver is underresourced or severely limited (e.g., in hospital, incarcerated, or struggling with severe mental health issues) and members of the treatment team feel discouraged or hopeless about their capacity for involvement, the goal is to work toward a change in the caregiver's interactional style that corresponds to a single degree. Clinicians do so knowing that it can be the beginning of a significant shift over time, even though they may not see the results during the course of treatment. We have personally observed tremendously positive outcomes of the one-degree effect, even when carers presented initially as resistant, in denial, critical, dismissive, hopeless or suffering from physical or mental illness or a personality disorder. This uncovering of caregiver capacity is a central task within EFFT and one that can only be achieved when the clinician holds a deep belief in caregivers' abilities to contribute to their loved one's recovery, even in seemingly minor ways. In fact, we take seriously the notion that a little can go a long way. The guiding principles of EFFT, listed in Exhibit 1.1, embody the heart of the approach and are considered the clinical "guiding lights," especially when clinicians recognize the emergence of their own blocks.

EFFT MODULES

There are five modules in EFFT. Three of these involve the empowerment of caregivers to actively support their loved one via emotion coaching, behavior coaching, and the initiation of therapeutic apologies, if relevant. Skills and strategies related to each of these modules are taught to caregivers for implementation in family sessions, dyad sessions, or outside of the office. The remaining modules, those of identifying and working through caregiver and clinician blocks, are clinician-led and involve tools and techniques to address therapy-interfering attitudes or behaviors in carers and clinicians that are expected to emerge throughout treatment.

EXHIBIT 1.1. Guiding Principles of Emotion-Focused Family Therapy

Loved ones yearn for the support of their caregivers, even when they try to convince the clinician or therapist otherwise.

Caregivers are motivated to support their loved ones to heal, even when they try to convince us otherwise.

Carers struggling with mental health issues themselves do not require extensive psychotherapy to engage in EFFT in meaningful ways.

Even when severely underresourced, caregivers can make small yet significant contributions to their loved one's mental health.

With targeted support, carers can move through emotion blocks that may be keeping them paralyzed or stuck in unhelpful patterns of relating to their loved ones.

Caregivers need to be empowered and provided with skills and opportunities for experiential practice to support the realization of their potential.

Clinicians are not immune to the influence of emotion blocks. They can work through these blocks to help the family get on track with wellness, even in dire circumstances.

Emotion Coaching

Carers are equipped with advanced skills to support their loved one with emotions. In doing so, they aid in the transformation of the loved one's inner world, addressing problematic patterns of emotion processing that fuel mental health issues. To lay the foundation for the emotion-coaching framework, the EFFT clinician teaches caregivers about the nature of emotion, as well as its role in the onset and maintenance of mental health issues. Caregivers then learn the steps of emotion coaching, derived from the theory of emotion processing in emotion-focused therapy (EFT; Greenberg, 2015, 2017) and influenced by Gottman (Gottman, Katz, & Hooven, 1996). The emotion-coaching module includes a comprehensive five-step model of emotion coaching and a brief two-step model. The two-step model was developed in response to caregivers who required a simplified approach that could be effective in the face of emotions, thoughts, urges, and behaviors, although both versions can be used to enhance the implementation of other EFFT interventions as well as to strengthen relationships.

Behavior Coaching

Mental health issues often involve behavioral symptoms. Caregivers are encouraged to support the interruption of these symptoms as well as the development of health-focused behaviors. The ways in which caregivers can support their loved one in doing so will vary according to their symptom profile. For instance, caregivers with a loved one suffering from an eating disorder will be taught strategies for meal support as well as tools to interrupt related behaviors such as purging and compulsive exercising (refer to Chapter 7 for more information). A caregiver with a loved one suffering from anxiety will be coached to codevelop a fear hierarchy followed by the facilitation of graduated exposures in real-world settings. Regardless of the symptoms targeted, caregivers are encouraged to combine the skills of this module with the strategies of emotion coaching to maximize effectiveness.

Therapeutic Apology

Inspired by the facilitation of forgiveness in EFT for couples (Greenberg, Warwar, & Malcolm, 2010; Meneses & Greenberg, 2011, 2014), the *therapeutic apology* intervention is a psychotherapeutic technique that involves the delivery of a specifically constructed apology to support the resolution of old pain and strengthen the caregiver–loved one relationship, given that it is the vehicle for the behavioral and emotional interventions. This intervention can also lead to relationship reconciliation or releasing the loved one, caregiver, or both from maladaptive self-blame. This is a powerful mechanism for strengthening family bonds, and many caregivers find it helpful across a broad range of circumstances; it is perhaps the most potent of the EFFT interventions.

Caregiver and Clinician Blocks

Within the context of family-based treatment, it is expected that unprocessed or maladaptive emotion will negatively affect carers as they make attempts to understand and support their loved one. For example, when the caregiver presents as unmotivated, unwilling, or uncaring, EFFT theory posits that these clinical presentations are merely symptoms of an emotion "block" in need of processing. Within this fourth module, the most common emotion blocks include fear, shame, hopelessness, helplessness, and resentment. The clinician is encouraged to use various tools and techniques to support the caregiver in working through the emotion block driving the problematic attitudes or behaviors. Strategies to work through these blocks include increasing awareness of common blocks and their emotional drivers as well as engaging in experiential exercises (i.e., role-play, two-chair dialogues) to transform them.

Clinician Blocks

Emotion blocks can also occur in clinicians and teams as they support caregivers and their loved ones. As such, the model includes a fifth and final module related to the resolution of such blocks. Similar to caregiver emotion blocks, EFFT clinicians identify and work through their own emotional reactions that arise as they provide treatment through self-guided, peer- or hierarchical "emotion-focused" supervision. For example, we've observed that clinicians can be less likely to engage carers who present with high expressed emotion, who engage in overt criticism of the loved one, or who display symptoms of a mental health issue or personality disorder, particularly when the client is an adult. Although there may be valid concerns about involving certain caregivers in treatment, attending to the emotions evoked in such cases can open new avenues for clinicians to work with them in some manner and, in some cases, guided by the principle of the one-degree effect.

Integrating EFFT Modules in Other Treatment Settings

Clinicians can use most of the tools and techniques within each of the modules to support clients and their families at various levels of care. Those involved in care may include medical professionals, psychologists, social workers, nurses, dietitians, educators, and others who interact with individuals, parents, and families in the service of physical and mental health. The exceptions include the psychotherapeutic strategies involved in therapeutic apologies and caregiver block chair work, which are reserved for those with specific training and credentials for the delivery of psychotherapy.

EFFT IN PRACTICE

Guided by the principles underlying EFFT and supported by the tools and techniques, clinicians can work with families in various ways. The most common methods of delivery include variations of caregiver-focused, family-based and dyadic applications, multicaregiver workshops, and the integration of tools and techniques within other evidence-based treatment modalities.

Caregiver-Led EFFT

Caregiver-led EFFT is one of the more common approaches to implementing the model. Within this method of delivery, the therapeutic work occurs primarily with a caregiver or cocaregivers. These sessions can occur weekly over the course of several months as in traditional models, or they can occur in the context of an intensive piece of work. An intensive piece of work involves a focus on one or two identified goals to increase caregivers' capacity to support their loved one in specific ways. This short-term application usually consists of three to six sessions of 2 hours, every 2 to 3 weeks, to ensure opportunities for integration and practice of learned skills. Before participation, parents and caregivers are invited to review online EFFT resources as a primer. Once engaged in the treatment, the clinician and caregivers establish a set of goals to guide the integration of the modules. For example, the parents of an anxious child who is unable to sleep in her own bed may choose to focus on the integration of emotion-coaching skills to support behavioral exposure exercises. Should one of the caregivers hesitate to follow through on the agreed-on interventions (e.g., fearing the intervention will cause the child too much distress), the emotional states fueling this resistance are processed to resume working on the targeted behavior. Therapeutic apologies are integrated as necessary—whether to strengthen the relationship, to increase the power of the caregiver's efforts, or to release the caregiver or the loved one of self-blame. Table 1.1 outlines an example of a short-term framework developed to support the parents of

TABLE 1.1. Short-Term Application of Parent-Led Emotion-Focused Family Therapy (EFFT)

Number of sessions	Concepts to cover	Resources to provide
1-2	Validate parents' experience seeking treatment.	Super-feeler handout
	Collaborate on the identification of clear goals for the piece of work.	Caregiver Traps Scale
	Introduce contributing factors to behavioral and mental health issues, including their loved one's status as a super-feeler, if relevant.	Relationship Dimensions Scale Animal Metaphors Handout
	Reframe their loved one's symptoms as maladaptive coping strategies to manage stress and emotional pain.	Tree Metaphor Handout
	Introduce the New Maudsley method's animal metaphors; provide psychoeducation and identify polarizations, if relevant.	Website link: http://www.emotionfocusedfamilytherapy.org
	Introduce the caregiver block framework, including the paper-and-pencil tools to facilitate the identification of potential blocks.	
	Introduce the skills of emotion coaching (brief version) with in-session opportunities for targeted practice relating to goals.	
	Set behavioral and emotion coaching goals related to presenting problem.	
	Encourage carers to share with their loved one what they learned in the session, excluding specifics relating to caregiver blocks.	
	Invite coparents to support one another with emotion coaching when faced with challenges, if relevant.	
1-2	Review parents' attempts at meeting behavioral and emotion coaching goals in the home setting.	Relationship Repair worksheet (if relevant)
	Highlight successes and challenges, including the manifestation of caregiver blocks.	
	Engage in caregiver block chair work related to identified blocks in the implementation of home-based interventions.	
	Introduce and practice a therapeutic apology, if appropriate.	
	Set behavioral and emotion coaching goals related to presenting problem.	
	Set therapeutic apology goals, if relevant.	
	Prepare for the end of the piece of work.	

TABLE 1.1. (*Continued*)

Number of sessions	Concepts to cover	Resources to provide
1–2	Review behavior, emotion coaching, and therapeutic apology goals. Process caregiver blocks using emotion coaching and chair work, if necessary. Review the guiding principles of EFFT. Set short and long-term behavioral and emotion-coaching goals related to the presenting problem. Set short and long-term goals for a therapeutic apology, if relevant. Bring closure to the piece of work and plan for next steps.	Website link for caregiver videos and resources: http://www.mentalhealth foundations.ca/resources
Next steps	Depending on the severity of the situation, next steps may include regular boosters to support the work, or carers may be encouraged to take a treatment break to practice their skills. Treatment breaks are typically 2 to 3 months in duration. Parents are also encouraged to refer to online EFFT resources between sessions.	Website link for online parenting series: http://www.mentalhealth foundations.ca/parent-coaching
Considerations for separated and blended families	When working with parents who are separated, you may discuss the benefits of meeting in the same session or in separate sessions. We also recommend the involvement of stepparents and extended family members significantly involved in caregiving. It is important to acknowledge some of the challenging dynamics that can arise with separated and/or blended families, including the ways in which they can reinforce problematic caregiving styles.	

a child struggling with a behavioral or emotional issue. This framework can be used with other dyads across the lifespan as well.

Family-based EFFT

The EFFT clinician can also work with parents and their children, spouses, or caregivers and their loved ones in the same session, introducing the modules of the model, developing home-based treatment plans and facilitating emotional or relational work in vivo. For example, the clinician may support the development of behavioral protocols, assist carers to engage with their loved one using the skills of emotion or facilitate a therapeutic apology, if relevant. The clinician may also support the caregivers to meet their loved ones' needs for security or identity development (Greenberg & Goldman, 2008). In high-conflict scenarios, it may be helpful for the clinician to support the identification of negative cycles of interaction between the caregiver and their loved one or between coparents (Greenberg & Johnson, 1988; Johnson, 2004). Doing so increases awareness of vicious cycles, deescalates conflict, and develops new narratives for the family.

Throughout treatment, when caregiver blocks emerge, the EFFT clinician attends to family members affected by the block and supports the caregiver to move through the stuck point with psychoeducation, emotion coaching, or a combination of these. Should the carer remain blocked, the EFFT clinician may choose to meet with the caregiver on his or her own for a few sessions, as an adjunct to the family work. The clinician may also identify dyads within the family most in need of attention and structure a targeted piece of work to address potentially problematic dynamics.

Two-Day EFFT Caregiver Workshop

Based on the principles of EFFT, a structured, manualized intervention was developed first for parents of individuals with eating disorders and then extended for delivery among carers of loved ones with a variety of presenting problems. The initial format involved a weekly multicaregiver group format with eight to 10 participants to address the needs of a regional outpatient eating disorder program. Although caregiver feedback was positive and research findings demonstrated encouraging outcomes (Kosmerly et al., 2013), many parents and caregivers struggled to attend each of the eight sessions. In response to this observation, a 1-day intervention was developed and piloted with three groups of 15 to 20 caregivers in treatment or on a wait list. Throughout the day, material from each of the EFFT modules was presented, with techniques practiced in the context of role-plays. As a result of caregiver feedback, the intervention was expanded and delivered over the course of 2 days to offer participants more opportunities to work with the different modules, and in particular those relating to emotion coaching and caregiver blocks. Over time, the main goals of the intervention were to educate and support caregivers in mastering the skills involved in emotion coaching, behavior coaching, and working through emotion blocks to effective support, with opportunities for skills practice (Lafrance Robinson, Dolhanty, Stillar, Henderson, & Mayman, 2016). Parents and caregivers also streamed in by video from up to three additional rural sites, where clinicians were present to support the uptake of the intervention. Lafrance, Henderson, and Mayman then manualized the 2-day caregiver workshop to study caregiver outcomes across eating disorder programs in Canada (Strahan et al., 2017). From there, it was adapted for use more broadly, and it is now regarded as a transdiagnostic intervention for emotion-based disorders.

Currently, the 2-day workshop is administered by two certified facilitators and delivered to carers in a workshop setting. The group-based setting allows for vicarious learning and mutual support as participants work through various experiential activities related to each of the modules together. Some caregivers engage in the workshop as an adjunct to treatment, whereas others derive benefit as a primary treatment, including repeat attendance or additional one-to-one sessions to refine their skills. Today, many certified facilitators are providing this intervention throughout the world in community-based settings for prevention and early intervention, as a wait-list intervention in outpatient mental health, or as a part of the treatment curriculum in higher levels of care. Organizations have also adopted this intervention to replace the traditional "family and friends" support groups in line with a shift in affording caregivers a more active role in their loved one's health and wellness. The 2-day EFFT caregiver workshop continues to evolve based on parent and caregiver feedback and multiple research projects are in progress.

Adjunctive to Other Treatment Models

EFFT is perhaps best known for its integration within other well-established treatment models. Many clinicians and therapists who attend EFFT trainings are already rooted in a therapy modality with which they feel well aligned. In these instances, it is not practical, nor is it necessary, for experienced clinicians to abandon what they have learned. Rather, EFFT was developed for integration within other modalities to harness the strengths of each approach. The following are examples of the integration of EFFT modules within established treatments.

Supplementing Interventions With Individual Clients

Modules of EFFT can supplement individually focused interventions to increase the structured involvement of carers. When individually focused interventions are primary, parents and caregivers can be recruited separately to learn skills consistent with the treatment approach to support their loved one's efforts in the home setting. For instance, cognitive behavior therapists may teach parents and caregivers to lead activities to address their loved one's cognitive distortions, facilitate interoceptive exposures, and support the practice of progressive muscle relaxation. They may also integrate the skills of emotion coaching to address resistance and increase the positive impact of their supportive efforts.

Processing Caregiver Blocks in Family-Based Therapies

Caregiver block interventions can increase the potency of family-based therapies for those who do not respond to standard care. Regardless of the family therapy orientation, the Relationship Dimensions Scale described in Chapter 5, this volume, can be used with each of the family members. Doing so can illuminate new paths for healing by identifying relational vulnerabilities and polarizations within systems and subsystems. Caregiver block chair work (see Chapter 5) can also be integrated within adjunctive sessions of family therapy when carers become stuck in patterns of criticism, hopelessness, or problematic patterns of engagement. Currently, a working group is exploring the integration of emotion coaching and caregiver block chair work within family-based treatment for eating disorders. These modules would be introduced to parents and caregivers whose loved one has not gained sufficient weight within the first few weeks of treatment, a critical target that can predict treatment outcome.

Processing Clinician Blocks in All Forms of Treatment

The clinician blocks module can provide a framework for working through clinician or team blocks, regardless of therapeutic modality or treatment setting. Perhaps the most straightforward to integrate within clinical settings, the Clinician Traps Scale, described in Chapter 6, can be used to quickly identify potentially problematic reactions to individual clients, couples, or families. Likewise, the clinician block chair work can be used to explore and move through problematic attitudes or behaviors or assist in decision-making processes to increase clinical objectivity. For example, an adult inpatient psychiatry team uses this framework during monthly team meetings, during which a clinician who is reacting negatively to one of the patients will volunteer to engage in experiential chair work facilitated by a colleague. Team members observe the process, benefiting from the vicarious processing of their own potential blocks. They then engage in a practice of debriefing, allowing the experience to inform care practices. Doing so also creates a culture on the unit where clinician blocks are regarded as normal and where their processing allows for improved team dynamics by revealing shared vulnerabilities.

There are numerous other examples of the integration of EFFT principles, tools, and techniques within existing treatments. The current state of mental health interventions reflects a need for new and innovative treatments, and we believe that working together across various modalities can lead to promising developments. As such, we hope to inspire readers to explore the amalgamation of theory, principles, and techniques from cognitive behavior, emotion-focused, somatic, experiential, and other approaches.

The Role of Individual Therapy in EFFT

EFFT was developed for use primarily with families, dyads, and parents and caregivers. As such, EFFT therapists tend to prioritize caregiver involvement over the delivery of classic individual therapies, if at all possible, especially when the affected individual is a child or an adolescent. However, this work does not need to be at the exclusion of individual treatment plans that are often helpful and necessary. As such, it is our belief that when EFFT clinicians are guided by the therapeutic principles, and hold on to the deep belief in the healing power of families, they can skillfully navigate the provision of service to individuals and their caregivers, as necessary. For example, adjunctive individual work is likely appropriate if the client's symptoms are deeply entrenched, as are their caregiver's emotion blocks. The therapist then serves to support both the individual and his or her carer(s), in separate sessions, building an emotional bridge between them. It is also appropriate with clients with more long-standing or challenging issues who require more intensive support.

When EFFT therapists engage clients in individual psychotherapy as a primary or adjunctive mode of treatment, they hold in mind certain considerations to maximize benefit. First, when clients develop a therapeutic alliance with an individual therapist, without careful management, it can become a competing emotional attachment, leading to a distancing from parents, caregivers, or relationship partners. Therefore, when working with clients individually, EFFT therapists are careful to preserve healthy attachment with caregivers to avoid this problematic shift and promote the strengthening of these bonds as part of the therapeutic goals. Second, in an effort to validate their client's suffering, some well-intentioned therapists can place too much emphasis on the shortcoming of their client's significant relationships without cultivating in them a belief that they are loved and that their carers are doing their best. The risk increases when clinicians have strained or estranged relationships with significant others themselves because this unfinished business can cloud their judgment and limit their belief in others. In these instances, EFFT therapists ensure they engage in regular experiential supervision to mitigate this potential, knowing that for the deepest healing to occur, clients must feel validated in their pain and have the capacity to hold anger, hurt, *and* love toward their loved ones.

EFFT RESEARCH

Research on EFFT was first conducted in the context of eating disorder treatment across the lifespan. Qualitative outcomes of an 8-week parent group of transitional age adults with an eating disorder revealed that participation in the intervention led to decreases in caregiver shame and guilt and increases in self-confidence, motivation, and hope (Kosmerly et al., 2013). Participants reported improved family functioning in general and specific to the relationship with their loved one. They also felt the module on emotion coaching was the "missing piece" in family-based treatment. Finally, parents involved in the study were more aware of their emotion blocks and had a better understanding of the nature of the illness, including the ways in which symptoms and their underlying emotions could be addressed in the home setting (Kosmerly et al., 2013).

Quantitative research on the application of EFFT for eating disorders within a 2-day workshop setting also revealed positive outcomes for caregivers (Davidson, Stillar, Hirschfeld, Jago, & Lafrance Robinson, 2014; Hirschfeld, Stillar, Davidson, Jago, & Lafrance Robinson, 2014; Lafrance Robinson, Dolhanty, Stillar, Henderson, & Mayman, 2016). A pilot study of a 2-day EFFT intervention for parents of adolescent and adult children (mean age of 18 years) with ED led to healthier attitudes with respect to their children's emotions and their role as emotion coach. Parents also reported increased parental self-efficacy, a reduction in the fears associated with their involvement in treatment, and a decrease in self-blame. With respect to their active role in their loved one's recovery, parents reported greater intentions to implement strategies that were consistent with the targeted treatment domains. Levels of satisfaction with the intervention were also high (Lafrance Robinson et al., 2016).

Process research has been conducted to explore the theoretical underpinnings of EFFT. Relationships were explored between common emotion blocks and caregiver outcomes among a sample of 137 carers (parents, stepparents, relatives, and partners) of a loved one diagnosed with an eating disorder. Specifically, results revealed that caregiver fear and self-blame were predictive of lower levels of caregiver self-efficacy and increased engagement in accommodating and enabling behaviors (Stillar et al., 2016). An EFFT process model was then tested in the context of a 2-day EFFT intervention for parents of loved ones with an eating disorder across various treatment sites. The results showed that the intervention was effective in decreasing parental fear and self-blame, which subsequently led to an increase in parental self-efficacy and an increase in positive intentions to engage in treatment-enhancing behaviors (Strahan et al., 2017). These results underscore the importance of transforming parental fear and low self-efficacy to support carers to become positive and active agents of healing in their loved one's treatment.

The application of EFFT has also been researched in the context of parenting and mental health. A Norwegian study of EFFT (Bøyum & Stige, 2017) revealed that 2 to 4 months after a 2-day parenting workshop, parents who were interviewed reported feeling more secure in their parenting role and more confident in their abilities. They also reported an increase in their understanding of their child, increased focus on emotions in relationships, and improved communication. Parents shared that despite how challenging the work, they continued to make efforts to implement their new skills with positive results.

Most recently, a large-scale study examined the long-term outcomes of a 2-day EFFT caregiver intervention for general mental health (Foroughe et al., 2018). Parents of children, adolescents, and young adults were the target of the interventions, and their children suffered from a variety of issues, including neurodevelopmental disorders, anxiety disorders, mood disorders, disruptive disorders, feeding and eating disorders, substance-related disorders, and other emotional, social, or relationship difficulties warranting clinical attention. One hundred and twenty-nine parents completed the intervention and provided data a week before intervention, postintervention, and at 4-month follow-up. Among other outcomes, participant parents experienced reductions in fears and increased self-efficacy regarding their role in their child's recovery, and their children experienced reductions in symptoms that were sustained over time.

A number of additional research projects are also in progress. These include a qualitative and quantitative follow-up of caregiver and client outcomes following EFFT interventions, as well as the qualitative study of clinician perceptions of clinician blocks. Task analysis research is also underway to examine the processes through which therapeutic change occurs via the caregiver block chair work intervention. Preliminary data suggest that outcomes are best when therapists can support parents to connect with their deepest fears related to their involvement, in tandem with the pure love they hold for their child.

CLINICIAN'S CORNER

In the past year, we've introduced the EFFT 2-day caregiver workshop within our mental health and addictions services in a large pediatric hospital. Currently, we run the workshops as part of a research pilot, evaluating its effectiveness. Preliminary findings are significant, and parent feedback has been exceptional. Three themes that we hear consistently from caregivers after a workshop are that the work is incredibly difficult but definitely worth it, that they wish they had this opportunity sooner in their lives, and that all parents should have access to this knowledge and these skills. As an EFFT therapist, supervisor, and trainer, I practice EFFT with individual families and lead the workshop, and my preference is definitely in leading the workshop. There is something extremely powerful about the model's application in a group setting. In the very first moments of the workshop, there are often significant expressions of vulnerability, including tears, which I attribute to the power of the experiential components of the therapy. Not unlike other group therapy settings, we've also observed the positive impact on caregivers when they hear others share similar struggles, including feelings of guilt, shame, and feelings of isolation, which are often targeted over the 2 days. Facilitating the workshop does require advanced EFFT skills on behalf of facilitators, given the care required to support caregivers who share their greatest vulnerabilities or work through blocks in front of others. That said, as a clinician, it is an incredibly rewarding process to witness, and we always reflect to caregivers what a gift and honor it is to have supported them through these challenging 2 days. It is especially rewarding to witness transformation in families who have been engaged in service for many years, with limited results. In fact, most caregivers in our program report beginning the workshop feeling stuck, hopeless, and frustrated, then moving to a place of increased self-efficacy and hopefulness, reporting new shifts in themselves and their loved ones.

—Psychologist and supervisor

2 EMOTION COACHING

I wish we had this sooner, before anything else, because it's all about emotions. All of the other interventions were about behavior, and yet the emotion coaching helped me understand so much more. I thought my job as a parent was just to tell my kids "what," "when," and "how." Now I see that one of the most important jobs I have is to be their emotion coach.

—Caregiver

One of the primary treatment goals in emotion-focused family therapy (EFFT) is to equip caregivers with advanced skills to respond to their loved one's emotions in a manner that is health focused. The rationale for doing so relates to a wealth of research indicating that emotion processing is an important variable in the development and maintenance of mental health issues (Berking & Wupperman, 2012; Keenan, 2000; Kret & Ploeger, 2015). Specifically, difficulties with emotion processing and styles of avoidance are thought to contribute to states of overwhelm or the adoption of problematic symptoms to cope with stress and distress (Aldao, Nolen-Hoeksema,

http://dx.doi.org/10.1037/0000166-003
Emotion-Focused Family Therapy: A Transdiagnostic Model for Caregiver-Focused Interventions, by A. Lafrance, K. A. Henderson, and S. Mayman

& Schweizer, 2010; Gross, 2002; Salters-Pedneault, Steenkamp, & Litz, 2010; Sloan et al., 2017). Difficulties with emotion regulation have also been related to incidence of relapse across various disorders (Berking & Wupperman, 2012). As a result, in recent years, significant attention has been paid to emotion-processing skills as a treatment target in various individual therapies (Berking et al., 2008; Gratz, Weiss, & Tull, 2015). Furthermore, although numerous other factors are implicated in the onset and course of mental illness such as genetics, sociocultural influences, and adverse early experiences, they are not modifiable. We can, however, help caregivers to support their loved one to increase their skill and confidence in mastering their emotional world. In addition, emerging research suggests that the skills are acquired most effectively through interactions with close others, including parents, partners, and relatives. Morris and colleagues elaborated a tripartite model to explain the role of family factors in the development of emotion-regulation skills in children and adolescents (Morris, Silk, Steinberg, Myers, & Robinson, 2007). First, the authors posited that children learn about regulation through observational learning, modeling, and social referencing. They then stipulated that the emotional climate of the family via parenting style, the attachment relationship, family expressiveness, and the marital relationship can also play a role in the development of these skills. Finally, they considered the importance of parenting practices specifically related to emotion expression and emotion management, including coregulation.

From a neurobiological perspective, when parents attend to their distressed child in a caring and compassionate way, their nonverbal signals (e.g., facial expression, tone of voice) are processed in their child's limbic system as signals of security and approachability, which leads to a buffering effect (Hughes & Baylin, 2012; Joseph, 1999). Chemically, this process is activated in part via the oxytocin system. For example, these caring gestures trigger the release of oxytocin from the child's hypothalamus, sending safety signals to their sensory processing systems and to the limbic system, leading to a calming effect (Hughes & Baylin, 2012). In other words, the parent's presence coregulates the child's stress response by deactivating their biological alarm system and inducing a state of *safe brain*, allowing the child to navigate the world with increased ease. Nurturing relationships have also been shown to activate growth-enhancing brain chemistry. This means that when caregivers connect with their loved one in an emotionally attuned manner, it not only creates a short-term calming effect but also promotes the growth of synaptic connections between the limbic regions of the brain and the frontal lobe, a bridge responsible for emotion regulation (Balbernie,

2001; Hughes & Baylin, 2012). Given that these are neurobiological processes, they are not considered culture-bound or restricted by age, and so it is possible to leverage the neurological power of caregivers in these ways across the life span, and in the context of parental, spousal, and other significant relationships.

EMOTION COACHING

Influenced by the work of Haim Ginott (1965) and developed by John Gottman (1998), *emotion coaching* is a widely accepted form of supported processing to promote healthy emotional development in the context of *prevention parenting* as well as in response to risk for or expression of mental health issues. Gottman (1998) studied parents and children in detailed laboratory observations and followed the development of these children over time. These studies led to an important discovery: The children of parents who engaged in emotion coaching differed in their developmental trajectories from those who did not use this style of emotional communication. "Coached" children were better able to regulate their own emotional states, engage in self-soothing, and regulate their physiological reactions (Goleman, 1995). The children who benefited from emotion coaching also demonstrated increased abilities to focus attention, relate to others, work through difficult social situations and perform academically (Gottman, Katz, & Hooven, 1996). In a study of children whose parents were experiencing marital conflict (Gottman et al., 1996), those who had emotion-coaching parents fared better than those who did not with regard to aggression, academics, and peer relationships. An evaluation of a community-based program designed to improve emotion socialization practices in parents of preschool children also revealed that children of parents who were taught emotion-coaching skills exhibited greater emotional knowledge and reduced behavioral difficulties than wait-list controls at 6 months postintervention (Havighurst, Wilson, Harley, Prior, & Kehoe, 2010). The importance of emotional mastery or intelligence extends beyond childhood.

There is strong evidence to suggest that emotional intelligence (which includes emotion management, emotion perception, and emotion utilization) moderates the relationship between stress and mental health concerns in adolescents and adults, including depression, hopelessness, and suicidal ideation (Ciarrochi, Deane, & Anderson, 2002; Extremera & Fernández-Berrocal, 2006). Taken together, these studies suggest that a focus on the development and refinement of emotion processing and regulation can serve to buffer against the experience of life stressors. For these reasons, the EFFT clinician also works with caregivers to equip them with the skills of emotion coaching to support their loved one's wellness. Over time, their loved one develops self-efficacy with emotion processing—that is, the capacity and confidence to experience, tolerate, regulate, and be guided by their emotions without need of maladaptive coping strategies. In addition to supporting in the moment emotion processing and the development of the capacity to self-regulate, emotion-coaching skills enhance treatment in various ways. As caregivers adopt this new style of relating to their loved one, their relationship will strengthen and their efforts to support their loved one with behavioral symptoms will be more effective and better received. As symptoms decrease, caregivers can also support their loved one to manage the flood of emotions that sometimes follow. This work will also provide loved ones with evidence of their caregiver's capacity and willingness to support them with their emotional pain, making it more likely that they will turn to the caregiver for support in times of stress.

SUPER-FEELERS AND EMOTION PROCESSING

Temperamental sensitivity, or sensory processing sensitivity, was a construct first introduced by Aron and Aron (1997) and refers to an individual's tendency to process information, including emotions, with more intensity than others (Aron, Aron, & Jagiellowicz, 2012). Although controversy remains as to the unidimensionality of the construct (Evans & Rothbart, 2008; Smolewska, McCabe, & Woody, 2006), there is growing evidence from evolutionary biology that personality and temperamental differences exist with respect to responsiveness, reactivity, flexibility, and sensitivity to the environment (Aron et al., 2012). A highly sensitive temperament has been associated with various negative outcomes including stress and ill health (Benham, 2006), anxiety and avoidance in romantic relationships (Jerome & Liss, 2005), and overall depression and anxiety (Liss, Mailloux, & Erchull, 2008; Liss, Timmel, Baxley, & Killingsworth, 2005). In EFFT, and because the word *sensitive* can be associated with negative connotations, we use the term *super-feeler* (see Appendix A for client handout). A super-feeler is a person who has a keen sense for emotions in his or her environment and who experiences emotions intensely. Being a super-feeler can be a burden and a gift. These individuals' radar for emotion makes it such that they have more empathy for others and can cultivate meaningful interpersonal relationships more easily. However, it is more difficult for super-feelers to regulate experiences of stress and distress in themselves and felt from others. As such, it is posited that super-feelers are at greater risk of developing emotion avoidance strategies, including maladaptive behaviors, in an attempt to manage their often-overwhelming experiences of emotions. Furthermore, super-feelers are more likely to feel misunderstood by others who aren't likely to appreciate the depth of their feelings because only 10% to 15% of the population fall within this category (Aron & Aron, 1997). Others may regard super-feelers as too sensitive, dramatic, or attention-seeking, further reinforcing super-feelers' attempts to deny or try to bury their emotions. Super-feeling is most intense in childhood and adolescence when the parts of the brain that down-regulate emotion are not yet fully developed. This means that super-feeling children and adolescents will benefit from even more support from parents and caregivers to promote the development of healthy emotion-regulation skills.

TEACHING EMOTION COACHING TO CAREGIVERS

When teaching the skill of emotion coaching to caregivers, the clinician begins with a review of the rationales for its use. In the short term, emotion-coaching strategies increase cooperation, reduce the likelihood of emotional escalations, and deescalate intense emotional experiences. Over the long term, when carers engage with their loved ones using these skills, they will internalize healthy emotion processing and regulation, therefore making symptoms less necessary to cope with stress or distress. The clinician emphasizes to caregivers that these skills are considered *advanced caregiving skills*. In other words, the teaching of these skills is not in response to a deficit on their part, nor would it be expected that these skills had been previously acquired.

Emotion Basics

The clinician then introduces the caregiver to the theoretical basics of emotion (Niedenthal & Ric, 2017). Emotions are described as fundamentally adaptive signals that provide individuals with information about themselves and the world. They are also described as having neurological primacy in that we tend to "feel before we think." The principal components of emotion are also presented: Every emotion has a bodily felt sense, a label, a need, and an action tendency. Caregivers learn that the bodily felt sense of an emotion provides the signpost for understanding the experience because there is a distinct feeling within the body for each of the core emotions. Caregivers also learn their corresponding needs and associated action tendencies, with a focus on fear, sadness, and anger for illustrative purposes.

Caregivers are then provided with psychoeducation to better understand the nature of more complex emotions and emotional states, including anxiety and shame, as they are so often encountered in those struggling with mental illness. For example, it can be useful to help caregivers differentiate fear from anxiety because they may inadvertently reinforce anxiety through accommodation. We explain that whereas fear is an adaptive response to the presence of actual danger, anxiety is a "brain trick" that evokes a signal in response to the *anticipation* of threat. Therefore, one needs to feel safe to face one's anxieties, as avoidance tends to reinforce and maintain them. Likewise, it can be helpful to support caregivers to distinguish remorse from maladaptive shame. Remorse is an adaptive experience in that it incites individuals to adapt their behavior in accordance with societal rules and therefore maintain social bonds. This is contrast to maladaptive shame, which involves a devaluation of the self. This distinction can be summarized as "I have done something bad" (remorse) versus "I am bad" (maladaptive shame). Shame is one of the most difficult emotions for caregivers to attend to and label for their loved one, likely due to the pain evoked when those closest to them struggle to see themselves as worthy and loveable. However, like other emotions, it does require processing, and we encourage caregivers to lean in to shame as they would other feelings and emotions using the framework provided in what follows.

Emotion Coaching

Informed by the works of Gottman (1998) and Greenberg (2002, Chapter 12; 2011), two models of emotion coaching have been developed—a comprehensive five-step model to respond to emotion and a brief two-step model to respond to emotions, thoughts, and urges. The comprehensive model can serve as a foundation for the application of the brief model in day-to-day interactions. Both models are presented next, beginning with the comprehensive model. Regardless of which model is used, it is helpful to alert carers that although the steps seem simple at first glance, they are likely to be challenging when first attempted. It is also important to alert the caregiver that, given the emotion-coaching framework goes against societal norms regarding the response to emotional pain (e.g., reassurance and problem-solving), it is normal for them to have reservations about its use. Therefore, we do recommend providing ample time to introduce the model for the first time, reminding carers that learning to use the framework requires practice, similar to learning any other new skill or a new language.

The Five-Step Model of Emotion Coaching

Step 1: Attend

This first step of emotion coaching is perhaps the most straightforward in that caregivers are instructed to pay attention to their loved one's emotional cues. Caregivers are taught to notice and pay attention to subtle or overt signals in their loved one that may be of high or low intensity (e.g., tension in the body, downcast eyes, tears). Attending to emotion is in contrast to the more conditioned responses of overlooking or ignoring displays of emotion due to a lack of caregiver self-confidence or skill, feelings of guilt or resentment, or fears of reinforcing what are regarded as inappropriate reactions.

Step 2: Label

The second step is to put into words the emotional label that caregivers believe corresponds with their loved one's emotional experience. In the words of Daniel Siegel (2010), "to name it [the emotion] is to tame it." For many, this will be a moment of "speaking the unspoken" as doing so is often in contrast to family or cultural norms with regard to emotional expression. Although difficult at times, when carers label their loved one's emotional experiences, it supports the organization of the internal experience and provides a road map for meeting the emotional need. When caregivers are unsure of their loved one's internal experience, they are encouraged to make educated guesses rather than asking their loved one to tell them how they are feeling. It is not that there is something inherently wrong with asking them to describe their inner world; it is that often, their loved ones will either be confused themselves, or they will feel ashamed about how they are feeling. As such, when the caregiver takes the lead in voicing the possible label, it reduces the pressure on the loved one, helps to clarify potentially confused states, communicates acceptance of the emotional experience, and begins the process of coregulation. Examples are provided in Table 2.1.

When making attempts to label their loved one's experience, it can be worthwhile for caregivers to match their loved one's nonverbal cues, such as tone of voice and body language. In Example A, a caregiver would match the heightened energy of her loved one's anger with a raised voice (but not angry): "You are really angry with me"; in Example B, a caregiver would

TABLE 2.1. Labeling Displays of Emotion

Presentation	Response (labeling the emotion)
Example A Loud yelling voice with a harsh tone and tense body: "I hate you!"	Example A "Wow, you are really angry with me!"
Example B Somber, with an expressionless face	Example B "I've noticed you've been really quiet this afternoon. I've been thinking that maybe you are feeling sad."

connect with his loved one using a quiet voice, a gentle presence, and a tentative style: "I've been thinking that maybe you are feeling sad." Caregivers continue to be guided by this principle of "matching" as they navigate the remaining steps.

Parents and other caregivers are warned to beware of emotional *miscues*. A miscue is a verbal or behavioral expression that masks true feelings. The expression of anger, for instance, is often a secondary reaction to primary fear, shame, or loneliness. The drive to mask, hide, or avoid true feelings can be fueled by many sources, including an internalization of cultural ideals around emotion. For example, in some cultures, individuals who are strong, capable, and independent are highly regarded, making it such that the expression of vulnerability is considered to be a weakness. In this context, the function of their loved one's miscue is to protect from feeling shame and perhaps to avoid disappointing others. In fact, it is important for clinicians to inform caregivers that many who struggle with emotion regulation also struggle in the face of their caregivers' painful emotional states. Thus, they will be further motivated to avoid expressing themselves if they expect the caregiver might respond with anger, disappointment, or other emotions that are considered "negative." For example, a loved one who suspects that her family members will worry if she shares with them the true depth of her hopelessness may assure them that she is "just fine" so as not to take on their worry as well. As such, the clinician explains that while the message embedded within the miscue is often "I'm fine," the underlying feelings likely reflect: "I'm struggling and I need you, but I'm afraid that I will hurt you and that would be too much to bear." In these and other instances, we encourage caregivers to use imaginary "message-translating headphones" when interpreting their loved one's verbal and nonverbal communication. With these imagined headphones, they can hear the underlying messages, so that "I hate you" becomes "I love you, but I am mad and am overwhelmed by my feelings."

Step 3: Validate

Validation is the cornerstone of emotion coaching and perhaps the most difficult of the steps. It involves conveying understanding of the other's experience rather than providing reassurance or possible solutions to the problem. To pivot from these common impulses, once carers have attended to and labeled their loved one's emotional experience, we invite them to replace the word *but*, which often follows the labeling of emotions or states, with the word *because*. For example, clinicians model moving from this conditioned response: "I can understand you might feel sad about missing out *but* there will be other opportunities" to the validating response of "I understand that you feel sad *because* you were really looking forward to seeing your friends today." Some carers will also struggle with the skill of validation when their loved one presents with experiences that they do not understand or with which they do not agree. In these instances, experiential practice can support caregivers to differentiate validation from agreement to increase their comfort in responding to such scenarios. To do so, it can be helpful to illustrate the difference using more extreme examples (see Table 2.2).

It is also common for caregivers to be drawn to going for the "bright side" or to use logic to explain an alternative viewpoint. Although encouragement and reassurance can be helpful, these supportive efforts must be preceded by validation to be effective. Again, it can be helpful to use examples to demonstrate the importance of validation, no matter how painful the loved one's experience (see Table 2.3).

There are a few strategies that are helpful to share with caregivers to refine their validation efforts. First, it is recommended that they avoid sentence starters such as "I understand" or "I know" if their loved one is sensitive to feeling misunderstood. Although the point of emotion coaching

TABLE 2.2. Differentiating Validation from Agreement

Loved one's experience	Agreement with content	Validation of the emotional experience
I'm a loser.	I agree. You are a loser.	I imagine that you feel really lonely. Everyone wants to have friends, and that sounds really hard.
I will never get better.	I agree. You will never get better.	Sounds like you feel pretty hopeless about your recovery. When I put myself in your shoes, I can imagine you'd feel discouraged because you've been in treatment for a while now and you're still feeling so badly.

TABLE 2.3. Contrasting Validation With Reassurance

Experience	Going for the "bright side" (Reassurance)	Validation of the emotional experience
I'm devastated. My partner had an affair.	At least now you have an opportunity to meet new people.	Oh no, that's terrible! I can imagine you might feel incredibly hurt and angry by the breach of trust. You have been through so much together.
I'm heartbroken. I had a miscarriage this week.	At least you know you can get pregnant!	I can only imagine the depth of your grief. I know how excited you were to meet your little one.

is to convey a sense of understanding, stating the words "I understand" or "I know" can lead a loved one who is sensitive to perceived intrusions to react with anger and dismiss the caregiver's attempts for connection. Where applicable, clinicians can offer caregivers alternatives such as, "I can imagine you'd feel _____ because _____"; "I wouldn't blame you for feeling _____ because _____"; and "It seems like you might be feeling _____ because_____" (see Appendix B for carer handout).

It is also possible that loved ones will rebuff their carers' efforts to validate their feelings or respond with suspicion, even disdain. In these instances, clinicians first validate caregivers' pain or frustration at having their vulnerable attempts for connection rejected and then provide reassurance that these types of responses are normal and to be expected, especially when this style of communication is new to the family. Caregivers are then coached to validate their loved one's reaction to move through the layers of pain one at a time: "I don't blame you for rejecting my attempts to validate your experience because I don't usually respond to you in this way, and I can imagine you might doubt the sincerity of my words."

Step 4: Meet the Emotional Need
Once caregivers have attended to, labeled, and validated their loved one's experience, the fourth step of emotion coaching involves meeting the emotional need. With reference to the emotion basics previously discussed, caregivers are taught to respond to their loved one's sadness, fear, anger, anxiety, and shame with actions that correspond to the promotion of emotional health (see Table 2.4).

It is helpful to discuss with carers that although the theoretical need associated with each of the emotional experiences is relatively straightforward,

TABLE 2.4. Emotions and Needs

Emotional experience	Need
Sadness	Comfort and soothing
Fear/anxiety	Safety (from threat/to approach)
Anger	Space, boundaries, feeling heard
Shame	Reassurance of the self

its enactment may need to be tailored according to their loved one's personality or sensitivities. A hug may meet the need for comfort for some, while this display of affection may be uncomfortable for others. It is also important to remind caregivers about the difference between fear and anxiety because their associated needs are opposite. In the case of fear in response to danger, caregivers are coached to meet their loved one's need for physical safety, whereas in the context of anxiety, caregivers are coached to meet their loved one's need for safety to approach the object of their distress. With respect to anger, although it may not seem so on the surface, one of the needs is to feel heard and understood. Anger may also signal the need for a boundary—whether physical or emotional. If a loved one's anger is directed toward a friend or colleague, caregivers can support her to assert herself in that relationship, share what it is she needs, or set and enforce a boundary as appropriate. If the loved one's anger is directed toward the caregiver, the caregiver can simply validate the anger (to meet the loved one's need to feel heard) and propose a boundary on her behalf or encourage her to take some space. Finally, the expression of shame signals the need for reassurance that is grounded in truth. For example, if a teenager with social skills deficits is struggling with peers, parents provide reassurance to their child that he is loveable all the same and that with time, and their support, he will learn more of the nuances of adolescent social interaction.

Step 5: Problem Solve

The fifth and final step of emotion coaching involves collaborative problem-solving. This final step supports the completion of the emotional experience, from bodily felt sense, to emotion processing, to action if needed.[1] For example, a child who is upset because her teacher is not following her

---

[1]It is worth noting that, in some cases, once caregivers have attended, labeled, and validated their loved one's emotion, and they have made an attempt to meet their emotional need, loved ones may spontaneously identify their own solutions to the problems they face, making this step unnecessary.

individualized education plan may require more than emotional support. The caregiver may need to step in to help resolve the issue. Similarly, an adolescent who is being repeatedly bullied at school will require practical strategies and perhaps external intervention to address the problem. It is also in this step that caregivers are guided to provide their loved one with practical support to tolerate the waves of emotional pain often associated with symptom interruption. In the case of a client struggling with addiction, once his urges are validated, his carer might engage him in distraction strategies, such as playing a game, watching a television show, or going for a walk together.

It is important to emphasize to carers that although it is tempting to skip ahead to this step (and we are conditioned to do so), it loses its efficacy if not preceded by Steps 1 through 4. In fact, most caregivers express the most comfort with Step 5, perhaps because it allows them to act on their impulse to "fix the problem." As such, it can be helpful to remind caregivers that "you've got to feel it to heal it" and that "what you resist persists," even though attending to, naming, and validating their loved one's stress and distress can be intimidating at times.

Emotion Coaching: The Brief Model

Carers have shared with us that the comprehensive model helps to lay the foundation for the acquisition of the skill, while the brief version is most useful when they are using this new style of communication for the first time. The brief model can also be helpful for caregivers whose loved ones are more resistant to emotional validation or whose emotions lie beneath the surface of secondary feelings, thoughts, or urges. The brief model of emotion coaching includes only two steps: validation and support, where support involves both emotional and practical strategies to meet the loved one's needs. The following is an excerpt from a carer handout we developed to support caregivers in the use of the brief model of emotion coaching.

Step 1: Learning to Validate

The first skill of emotion coaching is to validate your loved one's experience—whether it be an emotional experience, an attitude, or an urge. You can do so by transforming *but* to *because*. For example, when your loved one tells you she feels angry about a perceived betrayal from a friend, rather than leading with a typical response such as:

- "I can understand why you might feel angry *but* at least now you know who you can trust."

You would first imagine *why* it would make sense for her to feel angry and then convey your understanding using the word *because* such as

- "I can understand why you might feel angry *because* it feels like a violation of your friendship."

The same strategy can be used with urges to engage with symptoms. For example:

- "I can imagine why you'd want to engage with symptoms, *but* you know that ultimately you are just hurting yourself" becomes

- "I can imagine why you'd want to engage with symptoms *because* you've been under a lot of stress this past week."

Validating the loved one's experience—even if you don't personally agree—will have a calming effect. In fact, validation statements are most effective when they include more than one *because* as they convey a deeper level of understanding.

Step 2: Emotional and Practical Support

Once you've validated her experience, you can then offer your loved one support. If she feels angry, help her to communicate what it is she needs (e.g., space, a boundary, to feel heard). If she feels shame or anxiety, you can now offer reassurance or encouragement. Once you've validated and offered emotional support, it's time to offer practical support to your loved one, if necessary. You can offer advice, distraction, or redirection if appropriate. You can also take over or set limits if necessary. It is important to note, though, that providing support without validation is ineffective, despite how often we feel pulled to do so. That said, when preceded by deep validation, efforts to provide emotional and practical support are much more likely to yield the desired outcomes.

The Good House–Bad House Metaphor

Once the carer understands the framework for emotion coaching, the clinician then presents the metaphor of the "bad house" and the "good house" (D. Zuccarini, personal communication, January, 2013) as a point of reference in its application. All parents know what it feels like to doubt themselves, to wonder whether they have harmed their child in some way, or to feel responsible for their child's suffering. It doesn't help that there continue to be myths around the causes of mental health issues, including a long history of parent-blame and self-stigma (in particular, in the context of schizophrenia, autism spectrum disorder, eating disorders, and certain anxiety disorders; Eaton, Ohan, Stritzke, & Corrigan, 2016; Jensen, 2018; Waltz, 2015). These and other experiences can place caregivers squarely in their "bad house." It is incredibly difficult for caregivers to support their loved one from a place of doubt, worry, shame, and self-blame. If they feel like they have failed as caregivers, when faced with their loved one's pain, they are more likely to become defensive or overwhelmed by their own sadness, guilt, and shame. These reactions then become barriers to their capacity to offer support. In contrast, in the good house, caregivers believe that overall, across time and space, they are capable and "good." From this place of goodness, or their "good house," they feel confident in themselves and in the approach. Caregivers can remember to pivot from their bad house to their good house using this metaphor as an anchor. Following is a case example illustrating the successful use of emotion coaching to respond to resistance to parental involvement from the "good house."

> Hena is a 21-year-old woman who has returned from college due to a resurgence of symptoms of anxiety and depression. She attempted individual treatment while on campus, but she did not find relief. She is now home with her parents, who want to support her to move through this relapse. Hena insists she does not want their help. Her parents are torn between respecting her wishes and trusting their gut that she is exhibiting a miscue. They believe that deep down, their daughter wants and needs their support but is ashamed of her mental status and worried about being a burden. The clinician encourages them to trust their instincts and respond to her help-refusal using the steps of emotion coaching. They initiate a conversation after dinner one evening:
>
> DAD: (in a calm, caring voice) Mom and I have been talking. We are worried about you and we want to help you to move through this.
>
> HENA: (scowling) I told you many times already, I don't want your help. This is something I need to deal with on my own.
>
> DAD: (raising the volume of her voice to match his daughter's energy) I can see it's frustrating when I start to talk about helping you to feel better. I can imagine it feels like I'm not listening to you.
>
> HENA: (firing back) Exactly. Leave me alone!
>
> DAD: (again, with energy) I would bet that when we talk about wanting to help, you might think we don't believe you can handle it on your own. And that must feel pretty awful—to feel like your own parents don't believe in you.
>
> HENA: (softening her tone) I'm 21. I should be able to do it on my own.
>
> DAD: (matching his daughter's tone) No doubt this is a really hard situation. And there is probably some shame that somehow you didn't get it right this past year. When we offer help, I could imagine that it might bring that pain to the surface.

HENA: (in tears) I did fail, I wasn't able to do it. What self-respecting 21-year-old needs their parents to help them get out of bed in the morning? It's ridiculous!

DAD: Feeling like a failure is the worst.

HENA: (sobbing) It is unbearable. I am a failure. And the last thing I want to do is hijack your life too. I can't handle it when you're put out because of me.

DAD: (gently placing his hand on Hena's back) There's so much going on inside. And on top of it all, you are worrying about us too. I can only imagine the burden you are feeling. That if somehow, we burned out, it would be your fault and then you really wouldn't be able to live with yourself. Sweetheart, you need to know that your mom and I want nothing more than to support you in all of the ways that we can. We will never stop being your parents, and we love you too much to let you face this alone. We've got way more strength than you will ever know. How about we start with a plan—one that we create together—and we'll take it day by day. Sound good?

HENA: (through tears) Okay, Dad. I will try.

DAD: (holding Hena in a hug) Let's start with a morning routine. Baby steps. We'll get through this.

In this case example, the caregiver begins to validate his loved one's experience starting with what's on the surface (frustration), matching tone and energy. He then follows the organic emergence of vulnerability (shame and fear), taking care to validate these emotional experiences before offering emotional (reassurance) and practical support (collaborative problem-solving).

Skills Practice

We cannot emphasize strongly enough how important it is for caregivers to practice the steps of emotion coaching using a range of scenarios, whether in session or in the context of a workshop. Repeated experiential practice allows caregivers to become accustomed to this new skill and to forge new neurological pathways to override their conditioned "default mode" when responding to their loved one's pain (discussed further in Chapter 5, this volume). Role-plays can be conducted one on one with an EFFT clinician, in groups (usually made up of eight–10 caregivers), or in caregiver workshops (usually made up of 20–30 carers), in which smaller groups can be created to maximize the opportunities for participation and feedback. In groups and workshops, role-plays are best introduced with a warm-up exercise and a bit of humor to increase caregiver comfort. It is also important to acknowledge the potential awkwardness associated with experiential activities and validate resistance to participation.

Regardless of the setting, to promote skill development during the role-play, the clinician pays attention to the words spoken as well as to the nonverbal cues and the unspoken messages, molding the caregiver's approach as necessary. A caregiver who delivers the right words but with an angry tone or with body language that conveys a lack of confidence will require some gentle redirection to ensure consistency across nonverbal and verbal messages. When redirecting caregivers and providing feedback, it is important to do so in a way that does not intensify their shame. As such, we encourage clinicians to pause the exercise as soon as they suspect the caregiver may be struggling and suggest an alternate strategy or script. We also recommend that the clinician stop and start frequently to invite the caregiver (and observing members of the group if applicable) to reflect on his or her own emotional experience in the role or as observers. This can be especially helpful before and after the clinician suggests adjustments. Observing members can also provide feedback to support the carer to fine-tune his or her efforts.

When facilitating experiential exercises, no matter the setting, we recommend that clinicians support carers to practice scenarios that have proved most difficult in the past, as well as situations that they expect to encounter in the future. We've found that doing so allows caregivers to increase their feelings of self-efficacy with emotion coaching, particularly when the clinician takes care to use a scaffolding approach to skill development. For example, the clinician and caregiver may work together to brainstorm possible "becauses" before practicing in the context of role-play. We especially encourage clinicians to create opportunities for caregivers to brainstorm possible emotion-coaching scripts to practice in response to their loved one's anger, shame, hopelessness, or silence because these tend to be the states most difficult to respond to in a constructive manner.

Once scripts are developed, clinicians encourage caregivers to practice both the delivery of emotion-coaching strategies with their loved one (played by another member of the group or the clinician) and experience what it's like to be supported in this way while another carer practices the use of the technique. It is our experience that caregivers gain the most insight and skill development when they are able to experience both roles. Specifically, when practicing their skills, caregivers tend to feel uncomfortable and ineffective. When they take on the role of their loved one, they often experience it quite differently and report feeling supported and more willing to engage (despite perhaps outwardly conveying the opposite). The juxtaposition of these different experiences encourages carers to continue to provide emotional and practical support to their loved one, even when they feel their efforts are awkward or even unproductive.

EMOTION COACHING IN FAMILY SESSIONS

When clients and their carer(s) attend sessions together, the clinician models these skills with each member of the family, acting like a conduit between them. When an opportunity arises in session, the clinician may also support caregivers to validate their loved one's feelings with gentle prompts and redirection if necessary. If required, the clinician may speak for both caregiver and the loved one to help interpret interactions as the family engages in this new way of relating to one another. Before doing so, however, it is important for the EFFT clinician to clearly explain to the family, couple, or dyad that they will leverage these opportunities in session, interrupting and guiding interactions to facilitate deeper connections. It may also be helpful to provide an opportunity for caregivers to process any anxieties or resentments before engaging in the work because doing so will reduce the likelihood that they will react to their loved one's disclosures with surprise, defensiveness, shame, or self-blame. The following example demonstrates the interventions that can be used by clinicians when a client and his or her carer(s) attend a session together.

> At the beginning of a session with a mother and her teenage daughter, the therapist notices the child shift her gaze as her mother reports on the challenges they encountered the previous week. The therapist stops the flow of the session to express curiosity about this observation.
>
> THERAPIST: (looking at the adolescent) I noticed that something happened just there as you were listening to your mom report on your week.
>
> CHILD: I feel bad.
>
> THERAPIST: (looking to mom) Let's slow this down and use the emotion-coaching framework that we've been talking about.
>
> CHILD: It's really okay.
>
> THERAPIST: (looking to client) I can imagine it's uncomfortable to be on the spot. It might also feel like we're making a big deal out of nothing. Let's just take a minute to check it out. Can we give it a try? [Therapist models the skill by validating the child's resistance to being attended to in this way.]
>
> CHILD: Okay.
>
> THERAPIST: (speaking to mom) I want you to replay Sydney's words and notice her body language. See if you can get a sense of how she

	might be feeling right now. [Therapist supports the caregiver to narrow her focus on relevant emotional cues.]
PARENT:	I would guess that she's feeling sad or like she's screwed up.
THERAPIST:	Okay . . . now let's validate these possible reactions. Why might it make sense for her to feel like that? [Therapist guides the caregiver to validate the emotional experience of her loved one.]
PARENT:	I'm not sure, because I'm not actually angry.
THERAPIST:	Yes, okay. Thank you, that's good for her to know. Even if you might not be feeling angry, could you imagine or even guess why she might feel sad right now? [Therapist redirects the caregiver to access child's perspective.]
PARENT:	Well . . . it would be awful to think that your mom is angry or even disappointed in you. Moms are supposed to love you no matter what.
THERAPIST:	Great, can you tell her that? Start with what you imagine she is feeling, and then you can guess as to the reasons why. [Therapist acts as a conduit between parent and child.]
PARENT:	I'm not sure.
THERAPIST:	(Prompting) I imagine . . . [Therapist provides scaffolding to support the process.]
PARENT:	I imagine that you might feel sad and maybe not good enough because I'm focusing on the tough stuff.
THERAPIST:	(Prompting) And thinking that I'm angry or disappointed . . . [Therapist prompts with script.]
PARENT:	Thinking that I'm angry or disappointed must feel pretty bad because I am the one person who is meant to be there for you no matter what and because you've been working so hard on your recovery.
THERAPIST:	(turning toward Sydney) Sydney, can you connect with anything your mom said? [Therapist again acts as a conduit between parent and child.]
CHILD:	Well, yeah. Hearing her talk about the bad stuff makes me feel like she's disappointed that things haven't been better and that's hard. I guess I do feel sad, and scared too. I don't want to upset any of you, and I'm doing the best I can.
THERAPIST:	(turning toward mom) Mom, do you remember the different emotional needs we talked about? The ones that go with sadness and this kind of fear? [Therapist prompts caregiver to identify the emotional needs.]
PARENT:	(spontaneously turning toward Sydney) I'm thinking you could use reassurance and comfort. Sydney, I'll always be in your

corner, even if sometimes I'm tired or having a bad day myself. I'm serious. And I really see how hard you are working. In fact, I'm really so proud of you! Will you let me give you a hug? (Hugs her daughter) From now on, I'm going to make a point of telling you how proud I am of you so that when we talk about the tough stuff, it doesn't feel so imbalanced. Sound good?

CHILD: (holding back tears) Thanks, Mom. That does sound good.

POTENTIAL PITFALLS

When we introduce caregivers to the concept of validation as a core skill within the emotion-coaching framework, many will share that they "already do this." We believe this is because there are many definitions in popular culture of what it means to validate another person, and unfortunately most are inconsistent with the definition in the context of EFFT. For example, a simple web search will lead to a popular cartoon where a lot attendant "validates" a client's parking by saying what a great job he's done staying within the lines. As such, the EFFT clinician takes time to establish a shared definition of validation as a foundation on which to build.

In our experience, it is also common for carers new to this style of communication to report that when they tried out their new skills at home, their efforts simply "didn't work." When we probe further, sometimes we find that there was an issue with the implementation of the skill as intended, warranting further practice. In these instances, the EFFT clinician validates the caregiver's frustration or disappointment, offers reassurance that it's never too late to circle back and try again, and provides additional opportunities for practice with a focus on the nuances thought to be most relevant (e.g., tone, volume, body language). Should the difficulties faced relate to fears of rejection or feeling shame or to negative beliefs related to the approach, the EFFT clinician can use the tools and techniques of block work to support the caregiver (see Chapter 5).

In other instances, the caregiver has done a good job with implementation, but the loved one did not respond in a way that felt constructive. When this occurs, it can be worthwhile for the clinician to validate caregivers' disappointment and reassure them that although these skills can often lead to immediate results (e.g., deescalating and regulating their loved one's emotion and increasing cooperation), some of the desired outcomes (e.g., greater self-efficacy with emotion and strengthening of the relationship) can take time. The benefits related to emotion-coaching skills can be likened to a long-term investment fund to which caregivers are contributing in the service of their loved one's health and wellness. They make small and frequent deposits but don't always see the "payoff" until later. In fact, we often tell caregivers that the best measure of success is whether or not the skills were attempted.

SUMMARY

In EFFT, we equip carers with advanced skills to support their loved one with their feelings. In doing so, caregivers aid in the transformation of their loved one's inner world, addressing the emotion-processing deficits and related avoidance strategies fueling their mental health issues. These skills can also increase the effectiveness of behavioral interventions and are an integral component of the module relating to therapeutic apologies. With repeated exposure, the affected individual will eventually internalize the skills of emotion coaching, increasing his or her capacity for self-regulation and making symptoms unnecessary to cope with pain. The hope is that this newfound confidence with managing emotions will also reduce the likelihood of relapse in those suffering from mental health issues. Although the acquisition of emotion-coaching skills takes time and repeated practice, as carers develop this new style of relating to their loved ones, it becomes a second language, or as one parent described it, "our new normal." Not only can these skills enhance treatment efforts for those suffering from mental health issues, it is a framework recognized for its universality, including in the context of *prevention parenting*.

CLINICIAN'S CORNER

In my experience, it can be quite difficult for parents and therapists to stay focused on the underlying emotions instead of getting hooked by thoughts and storylines. Time and time again, parents have shared with me that the simple skills of emotion coaching have literally transformed the way they relate to their child. They hear what their child is saying in a different way and feel far less helpless when faced with their pain. As a therapist, I too try to remember that, when in doubt or unsure how to proceed, it's time to breathe and then to validate. Then I keep up with the validation longer than I think is needed, and I teach parents to do the same. Learning and integrating this framework has actually brought me back to my roots as a therapist. The essence of EFFT reminds me that the simple gift of authentic validation can break down barriers, quiet the noise, and empower change.

—Psychologist and clinical director

3

BEHAVIOR COACHING

For me, being part of her treatment just made sense. She is an adult, but she lives with me. It didn't make sense to me to hand it all over to someone else when she is living in our home. This gave me concrete techniques and skills to help us cope on a day-to-day basis with the challenges she is facing.

—Caregiver

The behavior coaching module in emotion-focused family therapy (EFFT) involves the recruitment of caregivers to use behavioral techniques to support a reduction in frequency of problematic behaviors and mental health symptoms with which their loved ones struggle (e.g., self-harm, school avoidance, rituals) and cultivate an increase in health-focused behaviors (e.g., social outings, mindfulness activities, good sleep hygiene). The EFFT clinician assumes three primary roles when supporting caregivers to provide their loved one with this type of behavioral support. The first is to empower them to engage in this active role, the second is to brainstorm behavioral strategies specific to their loved one's needs, and the third is to practice these skills experientially, bringing in elements of emotion coaching. These

http://dx.doi.org/10.1037/0000166-004
Emotion-Focused Family Therapy: A Transdiagnostic Model for Caregiver-Focused Interventions, by A. Lafrance, K. A. Henderson, and S. Mayman

goals are achieved in a manner that is truly collaborative. The clinician is the expert with respect to the behavioral techniques, and the caregiver is the expert with respect to implementation of the techniques in the home setting. Together, they leverage their strengths to create a treatment plan to respond to the loved one's unique needs.

In addition to the healing power of their relational bond, there are practical reasons to empower carers as behavioral treatment allies for their loved ones. They can benefit from learning evidence-based interventions to support their loved one and, in doing so, reduce the frequency of potentially problematic strategies. They also have more opportunities to engage with their loved one outside of the therapy office, and their support can occur in real time and in settings where their loved one is most likely to engage in symptoms. Their efforts truly have the potential to supplement and even outweigh the influence of weekly 1-hour sessions with a mental health professional. Thus, the EFFT practitioner "unlocks" behavioral interventions from the clinical domain and transfers them to caregivers for use in the home. To do so, EFFT clinicians share their knowledge of evidence-based strategies with caregivers, including related resources, such as readings, websites, and applications. The clinician also empowers the caregiver to identify behavioral targets using their own knowledge and instincts, instructing them to consider what their loved one "needs to do more of and less of" to be on a path toward health and wellness. Following is an example of behavior coaching in action, in the context of a caregiver session with an EFFT therapist. Note that the skills of emotion coaching are integrated to create a foundation of emotional attunement on which to build.

Sameena and Ash have an 18-year-old daughter, Keya, who struggles with obsessive–compulsive disorder (OCD) and can't seem to complete her therapy homework (exposure and response prevention). The rituals are frequent and time-consuming and have been affecting Keya's social life and academics. After receiving guidance from their therapist, Sameena and Ash take turns enacting the interventions in both roles (playing themselves and their daughter).

THERAPIST: Okay, Sameena. We have agreed that targeting the morning rituals is too big of a leap right now. So let's practice supporting Keya with the bedtime rituals. We're going to have you practice using the emotion-coaching framework to help Keya—played by Ash—to resist going back to the bathroom to wash up more than once. We'll start and stop as often as we need so that you can feel good about the plan, and then we'll switch roles.

SAMEENA: Okay. (Turns toward Ash playing the role of Keya) Sweetheart, I know that you are feeling embarrassed about getting our help with the rituals. But I also know you want to have a bit more freedom from the OCD, so I'm going to help you make some small steps to get there.

THERAPIST: Okay, Sameena, that was a good start. I like how you let her know right away that your goal is to make it manageable. Let's ask Ash how it felt, as Keya.

ASH: I don't know. I just felt like my walls went up. Like she doesn't get why I do it.

THERAPIST: Right. Like maybe Sameena needs to spend more time showing she gets how hard it is to resist the temptation?

SAMEENA: You're right—I used "but" right away.

THERAPIST: That's why we practice! Let's try it again with a "because" statement. Maybe related to the relief the rituals give her?

SAMEENA: Sweetheart, it makes sense to me that you'd want to engage with the rituals. They can provide you with instant relief from the thoughts and urges.

THERAPIST: Great! Let's do a couple more "becauses."

SAMEENA: And I can imagine that you might be scared about what might happen if you didn't go back to the bathroom. Like washing your hands is such a simple act if it could somehow reduce the chances that something bad might happen.

THERAPIST: Ash, how is this feeling as Keya?

ASH: It's like I can feel myself relaxing a bit, but I don't really want to admit it.

THERAPIST: That's a really important thing to note for Sameena. Keya might be responding to your efforts without necessarily showing it. Try to remember that when you get blocked by the feeling that "it's not working."

SAMEENA: It's true; I get stuck there sometimes.

THERAPIST: That was great validation. I also thought your tone was spot on— you sounded confident and also calm. You really conveyed how much you care. Okay, let's keep going. Let's introduce the plan.

SAMEENA: I also know that as much as it provides you with relief, the OCD isn't always a friend to you, and it takes up a lot of time. As your mom, I can't let you deal with that on your own anymore. We're going to start taking small steps to decrease those bedtime rituals, starting with the bathroom use.

ASH: (out of role) Can we pause for a second? I had a bit of a reaction to the "friend" thing. Maybe leave that out? I think it might also be helpful to get her input on which part of the bedtime rituals we should tackle first.

SAMEENA: (out of role) Got it. Okay, rewind. (back in role) I also know that as much as it provides you with relief, the OCD takes up a lot of time. As your mom, I just can't sit back and let you deal with it all on your own. We're going to start taking small steps to decrease those bedtime rituals, maybe starting with fewer visits to the bathroom?

ASH: (out of role) Yes—the tentativeness feels better. Good job, honey! Okay—back in role.

SAMEENA: Okay, starting tonight, we're going to hang out in the evening so that you can be distracted. We'll play cards, and we'll tuck you into bed. I'll even lay with you for a bit like we used to when you were younger, so we can ride the wave together.

THERAPIST: Okay, Sameena—what's the verdict? How did it feel?

SAMEENA: If felt good, actually. I think the toughest part will be how to deal with her response. I think she'll probably fight it a bit.

THERAPIST: It's important to listen to your instincts about that. This could be a good time to switch roles to practice this part of the delivery, just in case. Ash—are you up for a turn?

BEHAVIOR-COACHING TARGETS

Within EFFT, the carer is regarded as a partner in the development of the treatment strategy as well as an extension of the behavioral support team. Once the behavioral focus is established, the clinician and carer work together to individualize a plan to meet the needs of the loved one. This collaboration bolsters the consistent implementation of these interventions outside of the clinician's office, and in a way best suited to the needs of the affected individual. For example, parents of an anxious child would be supported to create a personalized hierarchy of fears with their child followed by the facilitation of exposure exercises in the home. The parent of an adult child struggling with problematic substance use would offer appropriate distractions to manage urges to use substances. The spouse of an individual suffering from depression would be encouraged to engage her partner in previously enjoyed activities in the service of behavioral activation. Behavior coaching can also be used to decrease eating disorder symptomatology (discussed further in Chapter 7, this volume) and self-harm behaviors, and increase cooperation with everyday expectations, including attending therapy or medical appointments. This process is supported by the clinician with expertise in the relevant domains and shared in a manner that respects the fact that most caregivers do not have background in mental health interventions. In other words, the clinician and caregiver work together to identify strategies that are most relevant, taking into consideration the loved one's struggles and the caregiver's capacity and level of comfort. Although not exhaustive, Table 3.1 lists a variety of strategies that can be taught to caregivers to help them to support their loved one with behavior change, keeping in mind the power of the one-degree effect.

Integrating Emotion Coaching With Behavior Coaching

It is safe to assume that before seeking professional help, carers will have already attempted any number of strategies to support their loved one with behavior change. Some caregivers will have researched and attempted various techniques, such as positive and negative reinforcement; others may have attempted to use logic, punishment, or coercion in desperate attempts to effect change in their loved one. It is important to recognize that some of these caregivers may now present as disengaged (e.g., "I can't help him unless he wants to help himself"), fueled by a history of failed attempts to offer behavioral support. In these instances, the EFFT clinician encourages carers to "try again," but this time with the integration of the skills of emotion coaching (elaborated in Chapter 2) within the behavior-coaching framework. First, an emotion-focused approach to behavioral support leads to a calming effect in their loved one and therefore increases cooperation and engagement. Second, some individuals lack trust in their caregiver's intentions or their ability to offer ongoing support in the face of their resistance. They may need to believe that their caregiver appreciates and has empathy for the extent to which they are suffering or are reluctant to change. Carers are taught how the skills of emotion coaching—and in particular, the skill of validation—can do just that. Third, for many, behavior change can lead to the loss of emotion-avoidance strategies, necessitating emotional support to manage the eruption of emotion that may arise as a result. In fact, regardless of circumstance, caregivers are typically equipped with the skills of emotion coaching before learning the module on behavior coaching to promote a supportive style that is both firm and compassionate, therefore increasing the effectiveness of their efforts. The reader may also refer to Appendix C for a caregiver handout to support cooperation and collaboration with everyday expectations using the integration of these skills.

Preparing for the Eruption of Emotion

When carers support their loved one with behavior change in the context of a mental health disorder, it is likely that strong emotions will emerge,

TABLE 3.1. Behavioral Strategies for Various Mental Health Issues

Presenting problem	Sample tools/strategies
Anxiety disorders	Engaging in progressive muscle relaxation
	Engaging in relaxed breathing and meditation
	Facilitating exposure exercises
Obsessive-compulsive disorder	Reducing frequency of caregiver-assisted rituals
	Changing or delaying rituals
	Facilitating exposures and response prevention
	Cultivating detachment from intrusive thoughts
Major depressive disorder	Facilitating activities of daily living (e.g., dressing, showering, leaving the house)
	Scheduling leisure activities (e.g., board games, social outings)
	Supporting socialization, return to school, return to work
	Encouraging good sleep hygiene
	Engaging in regular exercise
Feeding and eating disorders	Providing meal support
	Reintroducing feared foods
	Providing supervision postmeals to interrupt purging
	Interrupting overexercise
Attention-deficit/ hyperactivity disorder	Establishing routines
	Creating checklists
	Developing organizational systems
	Planning for moments of overwhelm
	Engaging in regular exercise
Substance use disorders	Supporting stimulus control
	Reinforcing positive behaviors
	Supporting urge surfing
	Increasing opportunities for connection and family-based activities
	Engaging in mindfulness to manage urges
	Teaching distress tolerance
	Providing distraction
	Creating substance-free spaces
Disruptive, impulse-control, and conduct disorders	Increasing opportunities for connection (e.g., playing a game)
	Reinforcing positive behaviors
	Planning for moments of overwhelm
	Addressing sensory needs (e.g., weighted blanket)
	Providing realistic opportunities for leadership

including conduct that may be quite out of character. This pattern of reactivity is most often observed in the symptom interruption of substance use disorders, eating disorders, and anxiety disorders. The clinician must prepare caregivers for the potential for such outbursts, validate caregivers' emergent fears, and reassure them that working through these reactions will increase the potential for long-term behavior change. The following example demonstrates the way in which we prepare carers for this eruption:

> As you support your husband with his addiction, he may sometimes react to your efforts with strong negative emotion. It may even feel like you have just caused a volcano to erupt. All the feelings that he has been pushing away will rise to the surface because we are interrupting his use of the coping strategies that have long kept them at bay. At times, you may even doubt the appropriateness of these interventions, or you may wish to back off completely for fear that your efforts are actually making things worse. It is important to remember that this is a challenging yet necessary part of the process. Once he can move through those big feelings, it is much less likely that he will turn to symptoms to cope, especially if he can turn to you for emotional support when the urges are strongest.

Skills Practice

As with all practical components of EFFT, a didactic approach to skill acquisition is viewed as necessary but insufficient. As such, once the treatment plan elaborated, it is beneficial to refer to behavior coaching as a set of skills to be learned that require regular practice. Clinicians share that all mental health workers receive training in these skills, conveying to caregivers that, with time, they too can lead these interventions. It can also be helpful to remind carers that clinicians require ongoing support from peers and supervisors to increase the effectiveness of their efforts. When caregivers approach this module with that mind-set, they are more likely to feel empowered to continue with their efforts and to ask for help when they struggle or feel stuck.

When engaging in experiential practice with carers, as with the skills of emotion coaching, it is important for clinicians to set a tone of nonjudgment and to acknowledge that practicing these skills, especially with the most triggering scenarios, can be extremely difficult. When frustrations arise, clinicians validate the caregiver's reaction and provide reassurance that many others have experienced the same when learning to use these skills. In fact, these experiential opportunities for practice are typically one of the most helpful caregiver interventions, especially in a group setting. Again, in the context of role-plays, caregivers should be encouraged to alternate between taking the role of their loved one and their own role because important learning happens in both positions. In the caregiver role, the technical skills are learned, as is the process of managing one's own emotional reactions when moving through the technique. Throughout the exercise, the clinician actively provides feedback, shaping the caregiver's attempts in a way that is compassionate, kind, and even lighthearted, attending to voice, tone, and body language, as well as the actual words being used. This often involves frequent starting and stopping of the activity to offer suggestions to prevent the caregiver from feeling discouraged or from stumbling without a safety net. As with the skills of emotion coaching, targeted caregiver block work is recommended (see Chapter 5) should thoughts or feelings arise that block the caregiver from skill acquisition.

Additional Strategies to Enhance the Effectiveness of Behavioral Supports

In addition to the integration of emotion-coaching skills, there are general principles that can guide carers to support their loved ones with behaviors. The first is the importance of increasing opportunities for success for both parties. To do so, the EFFT clinician and caregiver set relevant behavioral goals to work toward in a gradual, stepwise fashion. Once the goal is identified, it can also be helpful for EFFT clinicians to guide caregivers to break down target behaviors into manageable steps as illustrated in the following example:

> Sarah is motivated to support her loved one (Austin) who is struggling with depression. She believes that if she can get him out of the house and engaged with his friends, his mood will improve. However, she feels stuck with where to begin because, most of the day, he lays in bed watching movies. With Austin's input, Sarah works with the clinician to outline a series of steps to work through to eventually reach the goal of increasing social engagement.
>
> Goal 1: Supporting him to get out of bed for three 1-hour increments per day.
> Goal 2: Supporting him to take a shower and get dressed during one of these daily increments.
> Goal 3: Supporting him to text a friend every other day.
> Goal 4: Supporting him to make a plan for a social outing.
> Goal 5: Supporting him to follow through on the social plan.

In some cases, it is possible that carers will struggle with the overwhelming number of behaviors requiring intervention. In such situations, they can be guided to create a hierarchy of target behaviors to prioritize those that are most important for their loved one's mental health and wellness. With input from the clinician, parents and caregivers are invited to list their loved one's most problematic patterns of behavior. Once these lists are populated, the caregiver and clinician identify as many potential behavioral strategies as possible. They then consider which behaviors to target first, informed by the loved one's level of impairment and evidenced-based clinical practices. For instance, when supporting those with serious self-injurious behaviors, the highest risk behaviors would be prioritized, whereas with anxiety disorders or obsessive-compulsive disorder, the least anxiety-provoking symptoms might be tackled first.[1]

Other tools that can be useful to maximize the effectiveness of carer-led behavioral interventions include the use of *externalizing* and *normalizing* language to describe symptoms. The externalization of symptoms is an approach most common to narrative therapy (Madigan, 2013). It involves separating the person from his or her behaviors or symptoms. Using this approach, a carer might say to his or her loved one, "I can see that your *anxiety* is telling you that it is too scary to go to school right now," rather than stating, "You're too anxious to go to school right now." This subtle shift in language serves to reduce shame and increase a sense of agency within the affected individual. The language used can also be adjusted according to age and developmental level to maximize the effectiveness of the technique. Young children, for example, often benefit from choosing a name for their anxiety, such as a "worry bug." Using externalizing language has benefits for the caregivers as well because it decreases frustration and fosters compassion for the loved one, who is seen as overtaken by the urge or symptom as opposed to being unmotivated, unwilling, or defiant. It is important to note, however, that the use of externalizing language will not always be helpful or welcome by those struggling. Should the loved one experience this use of language as condescending or invalidating, the caregiver is encouraged to explore alternative strategies (e.g., "There is part of you that feels really scared right now"). Sometimes people simply aren't ready to talk about their symptoms in this way, and therefore it can be worthwhile to reintroduce the technique later in treatment.

Normalizing language can also serve to decrease feelings of shame, isolation, and hopelessness—emotional states that can become barriers to change. Carers may share with their loved ones that everyone experiences some level of anxiety and that, at times, it can be harnessed for one's benefit (e.g., anxiety can optimize performance and support thoughtful decision-making). It can also be helpful for caregivers to lift their loved ones' shame by reassuring them that nearly half the population will suffer from a mental health issue in their lifetime and that nobody chooses to suffer in these ways, much like no one asks for the flu or other physical illnesses. The stigma around mental

---

[1]It is important to note that when mental health symptoms are severe or risky, caregivers are not expected to be their loved one's sole providers of support but rather part of a team that may also include an individual therapist.

illness leaves many individuals feeling broken or to blame for the family burden. Normalizing their experiences can help alleviate these feelings, even if only temporarily.

THE CASE OF ELIZABETH AND TAMARA: AN EXAMPLE OF THE INTEGRATION OF EMOTION COACHING AND BEHAVIOR COACHING IN THE TREATMENT OF CHILDHOOD ANXIETY

Tamara was a bright, 7-year-old girl in second grade. Although she had always been a somewhat anxious child, she usually managed well in the day-to-day. Tamara's mother (Elizabeth) became worried when her daughter's anxiety began to manifest as school refusal. According to Elizabeth and her husband, Leo, Tamara refused to attend school after she became the target of relational aggression that occurred most often during unstructured times of the day. She was especially anxious about lunch periods and assemblies. It wasn't uncommon for her to have crying fits in the morning, and in these instances, Elizabeth and Leo sometimes allowed Tamara to stay home. They sought guidance from the teachers at school, as well as a local mental health clinician, but they received conflicting advice. Elizabeth and Leo were then referred to a therapist, who introduced them to the principles of EFFT. Over a few sessions, they were taught the basics of behavior coaching for school anxiety, as well as emotion-coaching strategies to support their efforts. Along with Tamara, they created a plan involving graduated exposures to school, first accompanied by her mother and then on her own. Collaboratively, they developed a set of goals along with rewards to reinforce success. Guided by the therapist, Elizabeth also taught Tamara several behavioral strategies to respond to future episodes of bullying, including a plan for adult intervention if needed. Elizabeth was empowered by these consultations and then proceeded to help her daughter to face her fears on her own. Once Tamara resumed regular school attendance, Elizabeth sent a letter to the therapist describing her experiences with the model (some details have been modified to ensure anonymity):

> Initially, when Tamara's anxiety emerged and she began to refuse to go to school, I truly felt helpless and exasperated. I didn't know what to do to handle the situation. I had a million thoughts running through my head. I was trying different things but felt I was lacking a clear sense of direction. In our initial discussion, you shared a few key principles that really helped to anchor things for me and give me the direction and support I needed. Here are some of the big "aha moments" that really stuck with me and helped us get through this difficult time:

The importance of emotion coaching. I always thought of myself as a very nurturing parent who listened to and validated my children's feelings. But this experience taught me what it really means to validate someone. I recognized that I often said things like "I know it's hard, but it'll be okay" or "you can do it." With your guidance, I learned how to truly validate Tamara's feelings and fears. I also learned the importance of validating without qualifiers and without the "but." As soon as we shifted our style, she opened up so much more. Overall, this was a great parenting principle and a skill that we'll use in all ongoing interactions with both of our kids.

Focus on the underlying issue. It's a lot harder to treat school anxiety without addressing the triggers. In Tamara's case, her anxiety was made worse by episodes of bullying that had been escalating for some time. That meant we needed to address her anxiety and equip her with skills, but we also needed to work with the school to address and remedy the situation.

Consistency is critical. You reminded me how critical it was to be consistent. We really worked hard with the school to make sure that there was a plan in place throughout the day. We had to keep going with the plan even when it was difficult to see Tamara going through tough emotions, and even when we felt overwhelmed. The consistency and predictability of the plan played a big role in Tamara's ability to trust that she was going to be well supported no matter what happened.

Minimize avoidance at all costs. Initially, it was hard to get Tamara to school when she adamantly refused to go. Before the therapy, there were days when we just let her stay home because we didn't know what else to do or how to "force" her to go (or whether that was even the right thing to do). The real turning point for me was when you suggested I stay at school with Tamara until she felt safe. Initially, I stayed with her for a good part of the day and then gradually she became comfortable engaging in regular school activities on her own, just knowing that I was somewhere else in the building. I know that people thought I was crazy (and wrong!) for staying at the school all of that time. They worried that I was creating a harmful dependency, and in all honesty, there were moments when I also questioned whether I was doing the right thing. It was also extremely trying and logistically difficult to be in school for all of that time. As you know, I kept going and with time, there was significant progress. I began to know deep down that I was doing the right thing. And once she truly started to feel safe at school, it didn't take long (and wasn't as hard as I feared) to leave her on her own. Now that we're on the other side of things and seeing how far Tamara has come, I'm so grateful that we stayed the course.

Anxiety can be overcome (or at least greatly reduced). Your encouragement and reassurance that kids can overcome anxiety meant a lot to me and helped get me through the really tough moments. It's really not something they have to learn to deal with forever and that's such a relief.

Tamara's case is a beautiful example of the role carers can adopt in the management of behavioral and emotional issues. Elizabeth and Leo knew that Tamara initially needed their support to face her fears, and they were guided by their instincts in the implementation of the strategies offered to them. Using the emotion-coaching framework as a foundation, her parents employed a combination of behavioral strategies in addition to those outlined in this chapter, including rewards and reinforcement, cognitive strategies (challenging distorted thoughts), and relaxation techniques (deep breathing). They also adopted an advocacy role with the school staff. Tamara's parents were able to carry out a plan that was more comprehensive than any clinician could have done in the context of a course of weekly therapy. Engaging Tamara's parents increased the likelihood of treatment success and cultivated within each of the family members a sense of confidence in their ability to overcome challenges together. Furthermore, the skills and experience they acquired will carry forward, making them better equipped to deal with difficulties in the future.

SUMMARY

Whether in the context of everyday expectations or serious mental health symptoms, the essence of this module is to support caregivers to support their loved one to achieve behavioral change. Most often, this involves the adaptation of evidence-based techniques for implementation in the home environment. As such, caregivers are empowered to believe in their role on the treatment team and use the behavior-coaching skills with regularity outside the office. When supporting them to do so, the EFFT clinician must emphasize that although learning these new skills and strategies can be challenging, they can be acquired with practice over time. For this reason, clinicians must take great care to provide a nurturing atmosphere to facilitate the acquisition and eventual mastery of these skills. We also believe these carer-led interventions are most effective when coupled with the skills of emotion coaching outlined in the previous chapter. Thus, most often, the practice of behavior coaching involves a delicate balance of validating a loved one's emotional distress and resistance to change while working toward a sequence of behavioral goals, maintaining limits when necessary. Should the caregiver express anxiety about taking on this role, the EFFT clinician can engage the tools and techniques outlined in the Chapter 5 on caregiver blocks so that progress can continue.

Finally, it is important to note that teaching caregivers the skills of EFFT and supporting them to take on the role of behavior coach can be critical for the recovery of their loved one from mental health issues. In fact, their involvement can be lifesaving when their loved one is struggling with serious symptoms (e.g., eating disorder, substance misuse), especially if they are unable or unwilling to engage in treatment. In these instances, carers may be the only link between their loved one and health care professionals and evidence-based care. We do wish to acknowledge, however, that caregiver involvement of this nature may represent a departure from conventional methods, especially when working with adult clients. In some clinical settings, policies and procedures will require adjusting (e.g., charting, use of billing codes), especially when the loved one isn't present or even a participant in the program. Staff may also require additional training to engage with parents and caregivers in these ways. That being said, we have found that these are worthwhile investments to support our most vulnerable populations to access evidence-based supports via their caregivers.

CLINICIAN'S CORNER

For me, behavior coaching is where the rubber meets the road for many parents. It also allows me to use my knowledge of various interventions to collaborate with them on equal ground. Instead of intervening with the client directly, I'd rather their caregivers do the work because they will always have more influence and they get to own the positive results. It can make the work more challenging initially, but in my experience, most caregivers want to be involved, and they appreciate concrete suggestions to get them started. For example, I'd been working with Joel, a dad whose teenage son presented with symptoms of anxiety and depression. Unsure what to do, Joel allowed his son to stay home from school, and he soon became preoccupied with video games until they consumed his life. Joel came to me for help in setting some behavioral expectations to help get his son out of this rut. I knew this was going to be a challenge for everyone, myself included, because it would interrupt his son's coping behaviors, and therefore Joel would likely face some major resistance. Joel also didn't trust himself to keep his cool if disrespected. I validated his concerns, and we practiced the ways he could communicate the limits using the skills of emotion coaching. To help Joel get it experientially, I acted like his son and reacted with anger as often as needed until he felt ready to do it "for real." Joel shared how this practice gave him the confidence to hold firm to his limits without backing down or lashing out. I'm continuing to work with Joel to help him interrupt other behaviors that are getting in the way of his son's well-being, and little by little, it's making a difference for them both.

—Licensed marriage and family therapist

4
THERAPEUTIC APOLOGIES

I was always someone who held a lot of self-blame, and this showed me that it wasn't actually my fault. It also showed me how to work with those feelings when they came up, like tame them back, so that I could better connect with my child.

—Caregiver

Healing family wounds via a therapeutic apology is perhaps the most powerful of the emotion-focused family therapy (EFFT) interventions, and it is one that requires considerable skill on the part of the therapist.[1] The intervention involves a structured apology from the caregiver to the loved one, whether delivered in person or in the context of an imagined exercise. The purpose of the caregiver-led apology is to relieve caregiver self-blame, strengthen the caregiver–loved one relationship, and share the burden of the loved one's pain. *This apology does not imply blame.* We can't emphasize this point

---

[1]Unlike the tools and techniques of emotion and behavior coaching, the relationship repair intervention is considered a psychotherapeutic technique to be delivered by a therapist trained in the model.

http://dx.doi.org/10.1037/0000166-005
Emotion-Focused Family Therapy: A Transdiagnostic Model for Caregiver-Focused Interventions, by A. Lafrance, K. A. Henderson, and S. Mayman

strongly enough. In fact, throughout this intervention, the primary role of the therapist is to support the caregiver to remain rooted in the truth that mental health issues are complex and multifactorial (Evans-Lacko et al., 2017; Gottesman, Laursen, Bertelsen, & Mortensen, 2010; Hancock, Mitrou, Shipley, Lawrence, & Zubrick, 2013; Rasic, Hajek, Alda, & Uher, 2014; Starr, Hammen, Conway, Raposa, & Brennan, 2014; Uher, 2014; Uher & Zwicker, 2017), and that they—the caregivers—did their best to respond to life's challenges. In fact, this technique must only be initiated within both a non-blaming framework and a belief in the power of caregivers—two of the central pillars of EFFT.

Three common markers indicate that this type of apology could be therapeutic: (a) caregivers blame themselves for the loved one's suffering, (b) the caregiver–loved one relationship is strained or estranged, or (c) loved ones blame themselves for their mental health issues and their impact on others. The EFFT apology can be enacted in session with an empty chair and then delivered in the home setting, or the EFFT therapist can facilitate the intervention in the context of a dyad session with the caregiver and loved one. As with each module of EFFT, should thoughts or feelings arise that block the caregiver from implementing the intervention from a position of no blame, targeted caregiver block work is recommended (see Chapter 5, this volume).

THERAPEUTIC APOLOGY TO PROCESS CAREGIVER SELF-BLAME

Most parents and caregivers supporting a loved one struggling with physical, behavioral, or emotional issues carry within them a powerful narrative of self-blame (Moses, 2010; Nixon & Singer, 1993; Stillar et al., 2016). This phenomenon is observed across the age span and across settings, from the neonatal intensive care to sectors across the mental health system (Barr, 2015; Fernández & Arcia, 2004; Moses, 2010; Stillar et al., 2016; Tennen, Affleck, & Gershman, 1986). Although it is true that caregiver factors and family dynamics can contribute to the development and maintenance of mental health issues, as discussed earlier in the manual, these relationships are not causal (Meiser et al., 2007; Phelan, Yang, & Cruz-Rojas, 2006; Uher, 2014; Uher & Zwicker, 2017). Despite this, research has shown that caregivers of loved ones suffering from mental health issues blame themselves for ineffective caregiving, lack of oversight of their loved one's mental health, passing on "bad genes," and having a negative family environment (Moses, 2010). Although self-blame narratives can emerge as an active coping strategy for perceived control over recurrence (Tennen et al., 1986) and a defense against a state of helplessness (Greenberg, 2011), caregiver self-blame is related to a host of negative outcomes, such as lower levels of self-esteem and resilience and poorer health outcomes (Eaton, Ohan, Stritzke, & Corrigan, 2019; Paleari, Compare, Melli, Zarbo, & Grossi, 2015). It predicts low levels of caregiver empowerment and higher rates of accommodating and enabling behaviors (Stillar et al., 2016; Strahan et al., 2017) and can manifest as other-blame (Tennen & Affleck, 1990), which brings an additional set of challenges.[2] For these reasons, it is critical to engage caregivers in moving from self-blame to self-forgiveness in an active manner.

Paradoxically, one of the most potent ways of facilitating the evocation, processing, and transformation of caregivers' shame or self-blame is to help them to fully express their pain in the presence of a supportive other. Doing so reduces its intensity and begins the process of healing. In other words, simply writing down and sharing an imagined apology in an individual session with a therapist can support a caregiver to move from a state of self-blame to a state of self-compassion and healthy empowerment. Although this may seem simple, it is actually quite a departure from typical responses to caregiver self-blame. We've often heard from caregivers that when they share whispers of self-blame with friends, family, even some clinicians, they are met with expressions of reassurance and comfort. As we know from emotion theory, reassurance can bring temporary relief but not transformation. In fact, we've found that when self-blame is moderate to severe, it can be immune to the well-intentioned efforts of supportive others. As such, the EFFT therapist is committed to guiding caregivers to shine a light on the depths of their guilt, shame and self-blame—regardless of how irrational—to begin the process of letting go.

To do so, caregivers are invited to identify any events they perceive to have influenced their loved one's mental health trajectory and for which they carry the most guilt, shame or self-blame. Next, caregiver and therapist coconstruct an apology (using the framework described later in the chapter), with the therapist taking great care to validate the evoked pain in the caregiver as it arises. Then the caregiver is supported to deliver an apology to his or her "loved one" in an empty chair. Once expressed, the caregiver switches to the empty chair for impact, voicing the imagined response that arises when taking the role of the loved one. This offers the

---

[2]In EFFT, other-blame is regarded as a projection of self-blame that serves as regulatory or soothing function, albeit temporary and potentially damaging. This conceptualization of other-blame is held regardless of its source, be it from the caregivers, their loved one, or the clinical team.

opportunity to respond to the "loved one" using the structure provided by the therapist (see Appendix D for the therapist script). Not only does this experience of unearthing and moving through self-blame increase caregivers' self-compassion and self-forgiveness, freed from the burden of their shame, they often regain access to their healthy caregiving instincts.

THERAPEUTIC APOLOGY TO HEAL A STRAINED OR ESTRANGED RELATIONSHIP

Some caregivers hoping to actively support their loved ones have felt helpless to do so in the context of a strained or estranged relationship. It can be quite difficult for older adolescents and adults to accept behavioral or emotional support from caregivers when they share a history of unresolved conflict (Bowen, 1978, 1982; Scharp & Thomas, 2016; Titelman, 2003). Just as close relationships buffer against illness (Chen, Brody, & Miller, 2017), unexpressed resentment and "unforgiveness" of what was painful during childhood and adolescence—regardless of its perceived validity—can have negative consequences on one's physical and mental health (Luecken, Kraft, & Hagan, 2009; Toussaint, Worthington, & Williams, 2015) and can lead to a complete rejection of caregivers' supportive efforts (Carr, Holman, Abetz, Kellas, & Vagnoni, 2015; Scharp & Thomas, 2016). This is a unique and significant problem in the context of EFFT and other family-oriented therapies given the role of caregivers as primary agents of change. In these instances, the EFFT therapist can support caregivers to attend to and help to heal unresolved hurt, anger, or feelings of betrayal in their loved one using this relationship repair framework.

To begin the process, the EFFT therapist takes time in treatment to explore with caregivers the impact of challenging life events that *they perceive* to have contributed to the relational strain. EFFT therapists empower caregivers to trust their instincts or emotional experiences as a compass to guide them in this process. The therapist then assists caregivers to create an apology where they take responsibility for their part in the breakdown of the relationship. Then, the therapist guides caregivers to engage in an empty-chair apology as described earlier. Doing so affords caregivers an opportunity to release maladaptive self-blame and prepares them for the eventual sharing of the apology with their loved one in the home setting. After having practiced in session, caregivers are invited to deliver the apology to their loved one and initiate the healing process. Should caregivers feel they need additional support, the therapist can help to facilitate this relationship repair intervention with the loved one in a dyad session.

Many loved ones and their caregivers have shared profoundly healing experiences following this type of therapeutic caregiver-led apology. In our own practices and those of our supervisees and trainees, parents of estranged adult children have reported heartfelt repairs—and in a matter of days or weeks—which isn't entirely surprising given that children long to forgive their parents and are wired to do so. The steps of the apology were developed to provide a structure to facilitate this natural process. The intervention also increases the possibility for caregivers to take on the role of behavior and emotion coach now that the relationship is stronger and their loved one is more likely to be receptive to their supportive efforts.

THERAPEUTIC APOLOGY TO RELIEVE SELF-BLAME IN LOVED ONE

Shame and self-blame in those struggling with mental health issues can be debilitating. Research among persons with mental illness indicates that many internalize social stigma and experience diminished self-esteem and self-efficacy (Watson, Corrigan, Larson, & Sells, 2007). We've encountered numerous clinical scenarios in which individuals in treatment blamed themselves for their symptoms (due to lack of willpower or poor choices), as well as the emotional or financial impact of their treatment on family members. Those who blame themselves for their mental health issues are also less likely to accept help or seek treatment (Larkings, Brown, & Scholz, 2017; Wrigley, Jackson, Judd, & Komiti, 2005). In fact, self-blame can become so acute that some clients choose to withdraw from treatment or alienate themselves to lessen the burden they believe they place on friends and family. When faced with their loved one's expression of self-blame, as noted earlier, many well-meaning caregivers and clinicians will also attempt to lift this burden via reassurance, but to no avail. Instead, when their loved one is burdened by self-blame, the EFFT therapist invites caregivers to share this burden with their loved one. Doing so provides loved ones with relief from feeling broken and ashamed for what they feel they are "putting their family through."

Once a therapeutic apology is identified as a treatment goal to support the release of self-blame in their loved one, similar to the preceding example, the therapist invites caregivers to join in the coconstruction of an apology. Within the apology, caregivers take responsibility and apologize for the family factors that *they perceive* could have influenced the development and maintenance of their loved one's struggles. Again, caregivers may enact the delivery of the apology in session with the therapist to ease their own self-blame and increase their confidence before engaging with their loved one at home or in the therapist's office. A mother who went through this process likened it to "taking the chemotherapy" to free her daughter from the "cancer of her self-blame" that created a shift from placing blame (on anyone) to a sense of togetherness and shared empowerment in the journey toward mental health (R. Warren, Smeets, & Neff, 2016).[3]

FACILITATING THERAPEUTIC APOLOGIES

When preparing caregivers to engage with this module, whether to bring healing to the relationship with their loved one or to release self-blame, it is vital that therapists be explicit that they will be conveying seemingly contradictory beliefs in that caregivers are not the cause of their loved one's difficulties and a therapeutic apology can lead to deep healing for both parties. It is often useful to define and explain the concept of the dialectic as a synthesis or integration of opposites (Greenberg, 2011, 2015; Lynch, Chapman, Rosenthal, Kuo, & Linehan, 2006) and invite caregivers to hold this concept in mind throughout the process. Balancing these perspectives requires some capacity for self-compassion on the part of caregivers, and thus in its absence, this work can be introduced first (Greenberg, 2015). Cultivating self-compassion in caregivers will also promote the growth of emotional intelligence (Neff & Germer, 2017) as well as increase their capacity to lead the resolution of conflict with family members (Yarnell & Neff, 2013), including strengthening relationships (Breines & Chen, 2013).

Influenced from the empirical model of forgiveness in emotion-focused therapy for couples in the service of relationship reconciliation (Greenberg & Goldman, 2008; Greenberg, Warwar, & Malcolm, 2008), the therapeutic apology intervention consists of five steps (outlined shortly). Each of these steps will be outlined and illustrated using the following clinical scenarios:

> Scenario 1: Jennifer is 16 years old and suffers from depressed mood. She sometimes engages in self-harm behaviors. She reports that her symptoms emerged when she was 12 years old, shortly after her father was offered a promotion and the family relocated to a new city. Jennifer denies it, but her father is certain that she attributes her difficulties, at least in part, to the fact that she left behind her best friends and struggled to form new friendships. Her father also remembers having encouraged Jennifer to look at the move as an adventure. He feels terrible about having done so, given that it didn't work out the way he had hoped. He recalled that Jennifer often seemed sad but didn't ever want to talk about it, and so he gave her the space he thought she wanted.

---

[3]This technique is equally powerful in the event the loved one's self-blame manifests as other-blame.

Scenario 2: Simon is 32 years old. He is recently divorced and suffers from tremendous shame associated with the breakdown of his marriage. He turned to drugs to cope with the pain, and he is now in treatment. Although family therapy isn't a formal component of program, his mother is desperate to support her son in some way. She sees how deeply he is suffering, and she wants to help relieve his self-blame. Secretly, she feels terrible shame for having separated from his father when Simon was 5 years old. It was a difficult divorce, and custody battles went on until he was a teenager. Her self-blame is deep, and she believes that had they provided Simon with an example of a healthy marriage and a stable home, he would be less likely to be in this situation today.

Step 1: Identify the Event and Its Unique Impact

The first step of the apology begins with identifying a healing opportunity for the family. To do so, the EFFT therapist supports the caregiver to reflect on and identify any patterns of caregiver, events, or series of events for which the loved one has expressed resentment or for which the caregiver or loved one carries guilt, shame, or self-blame. Once the pattern, event, or series of events is identified, the therapist and caregiver work closely to develop an understanding of its unique impact on the loved one to increase the power of the apology. For example, when working with a set of parents who identified a move or divorce as an injury, the therapist may ask them why that life event may have been particularly challenging for the identified child versus their other children. It could involve their age, the stability of their peer group, or even their status as a super-feeler. Caregivers are also encouraged to acknowledge the insufficient emotional support related to the family processing of such event(s) if relevant, and in the unique context identified. For instance, some caregivers who were overwhelmed themselves with the challenges of life may have struggled to attend sufficiently to the experience of their loved one, especially a super-feeling loved one.

Scenario 1: "Jennifer, I want to acknowledge how painful it was for you when we moved, especially since you left behind such a tight-knit group of friends [unique impact]. It makes sense that you would not have come to me with your pain because I often encouraged you to look on the bright side. I see now that I didn't invite you to share with me how upsetting it must have been [insufficient emotional support]."

Scenario 2: "Simon, I want to acknowledge how painful it was for you when your dad and I separated, especially that it came as a shock to you. Your world fell apart in an instant, and what's worse is that dad and I weren't very nice to each other after the fact [unique impact]. I see now that we weren't available to you in the ways that you needed [insufficient emotional support]. You didn't learn the skills you needed to cope, so it would make sense that you turned to alcohol and drugs to distract from the pain you feel now."

Step 2: Label and Validate the Painful Emotions Associated With the Event

Once caregivers identify both the injurious event and its unique impact, they are then coached to use the skills of emotion coaching to label and validate their loved one's experience at that time. They also validate how difficult it would have been in the absence of sufficient support, if relevant. It can be useful to use emotion labels rather than nonspecified descriptors such as *hard* or *difficult* to increase the specificity of the emotional attunement.

> Scenario 1: "Jennifer, I can imagine how sad you would have felt to leave your home, your school, and your peer group. Especially since you've always been a creature of comfort [labeling and validation—sadness]. I could imagine you might have also felt really scared about starting over in case it didn't go well [labeling and validation—anxiety]. In your shoes, I probably would have been furious with mom and me for uprooting the family, no matter the reason [labeling and validation—anger]. And how lonely it must have been for you to carry that pain alone [labeling and validation—insufficient support]."

> Scenario 2: "Simon, I can imagine that you felt like your world fell apart when we divorced—what with the loss of security and stability of our family unit. How scary it must have been [labeling and validation—fear]. I imagine you would have felt really sad, and probably really angry too—that we didn't find a way to make it work and that your life would be forever affected by the conflict you witnessed during our custody battles [labeling and validation—sadness/anger]. And how lonely it must have been for you to be carrying this pain all of these years without the kind of emotional support you needed from me [insufficient support]."

When appropriate, it is important to validate the pain associated with the lack of support with sufficient depth. Although there is no doubt that the life events themselves were painful, the inability of the loved one to express the complex feelings associated with the events may have deepened the wounds.

Step 3: Communicate a Sincere Apology

The next step in the process involves the communication of an apology free from caregiver guilt, shame, or self-blame. To guide them in doing so, caregivers are once again encouraged to use the metaphor of the *good house–bad house* described in Chapter 2. In this context, the bad house is represented by a rundown shack symbolizing the belief that the caregiver is fundamentally flawed and is solely responsible for the loved one's pain. An apology from the bad house can be unproductive, even wounding. The good house, on the other hand, is a sturdy, beautiful home representing the belief caregivers have of being inherently good, holding the best of intentions and having done their best given the circumstances. An apology from the good house maximizes its healing power. It is delivered with an overall tone of confidence that invites the loved one to share with caregivers the depth of their feelings related to the issue. The loved one is also more likely to accept the apology without worry for the parent or caregiver. This is especially relevant if loved ones are super-feelers because they may be very sensitive and subsequently reactive to hints of their caregiver's pain.[4] In fact, the experience becomes one through which caregivers actively demonstrate the ability to shoulder some of their loved one's pain. It is also from within the good house that the caregiver's own pain begins to transform. In some cases, it can require a significant amount of therapeutic work to support caregivers to find this place, but for the reasons already noted, it is time well-spent for all involved.

> Scenarios 1 and 2: "Jennifer/Simon, I am deeply sorry for the pain this caused you. I really am."

Step 4: State What Could Have Been Done Instead and What Will Change

Caregivers are then invited to share what they could have done differently to ease their loved one's suffering, holding the truth that they did their best and sometimes life unfolds in unpredictable ways. One way to support caregivers to move through this step involves an imaginal exercise. For example, parents are invited to imagine that at the time of their child's birth, they were given a crystal ball.[5] This crystal ball showed them exactly how the family's life would unfold, including how their loved one would react to struggles along the way. They are also invited to imagine that in these moments, they had access to sufficient financial resources and social support from which to draw. Only then are they invited to identify different choices that they would have made in an attempt to redirect the course of their loved one's life or ease his or her suffering (whether these choices would have actually had this effect or been realistic at that time is irrelevant). Doing so is an expression of deep validation and a way for caregivers to convey to their loved one that they are willing and able to share the burden of their pain. Next, caregivers commit to engaging in a new behavior and sets a goal that is specific, measurable, achievable, realistic, and involves a specific time

---

[4]Should the caregiver show signs of empathic pain (welling of tears, for example), the caregiver is coached to reassure the loved one that this display of emotion is rooted in healthy compassion.

[5]If a spouse or partner is the caregiver, we invite the individual to imagine having a crystal ball on the day they committed to one another.

frame (Doran, 1981). Most often, this goal involves a change in caregivers' manner of attending to their loved one's emotion in the present.

> Scenario 1: "Jennifer, I realize now that I should have created opportunities for you to share with me just how hard it was for you, so that I could have given you the kind of support you needed and deserved. Starting today, I am going to check in with you about how you are feeling, and I am really going to listen, without trying to make your feelings go away. In fact, we're going to face them together. No more Mr. Look on the Bright Side—at least not at first!"

> Scenario 2: "Simon, I realize that I should have found a way to prepare you for what was to come. I should have gone to counseling myself so that I could have worked better with your father. And most importantly, I should have proved to you that I could handle the truth of how you really felt. Starting today, I'm going to show you that I am available and able to hold your pain. I am really going to listen, and without trying to make your feelings go away. In fact, we're going to face them together."

Step 5: Validate the Reaction and Repeat Steps 3 and 4

Although each of the steps is necessary to ensure the success of the intervention, the fifth and final step is perhaps the most important. Once caregivers have delivered the apology, we've found that most often their loved one will react in one of three ways: with anger (which we have coined the *blast*), with denial, or by reassuring their caregiver that no apology is necessary. As such, it is critical that the EFFT therapist prepare the parent or caregiver to respond to each of these possible outcomes in a way that is most productive.

The Blast

The first possible outcome, and the most promising of the three possibilities, is the blast, which occurs when loved ones take this opportunity to release even more old pain, usually in the form of anger. They may even criticize the way their caregivers offered the apology, the time it took for them to do so, or bring to the table numerous other ways in which they feel their caregiver has "failed them." They may give them the silent treatment, otherwise known as the *silent blast*. It is crucial that EFFT therapists prepare caregivers for the various manifestations of the blast because it is not cause for alarm. If unprepared, caregivers may fall into the trap of responding with defensiveness or with anger themselves, especially given that they have initiated a very vulnerable process in the service of the loved one's healing and they did their best with the resources to which they had access at the time. Caregivers are taught that the blast is to be celebrated. It is an indication that the loved one feels heard and trusts in the capacity of the caregiver to hold his or her pain. In response, the caregiver is instructed to first validate the reaction to the apology (the angry or silent blast) and then repeat Steps 3 and 4 of the intervention to support a process of further unburdening of old hurt, anger or shame.

> Scenario 2: "Simon, of course you are angry—I should have apologized a long time ago. It probably feels like "too little, too late" and I am so very sorry. I should have heard you when you shared how hard it was. I should not have let you carry your burdens alone. And from now on, I am going to be there for you in a better way. We're in this together."

Denial

It may be that the loved one responds to the apology with denial: "I don't really remember that" or "It really wasn't that bad." In this case, the caregiver is instructed to assume an authoritative stance (e.g., upright body posture, locked eye contact) and with a firm, compassionate voice, state,

> Scenario 1: "Jennifer, I don't blame you for minimizing the impact of the move. We are not in the habit of talking about the tough stuff, no matter how long ago. And it doesn't actually matter whether you remember it all, I know it happened, and I know it hurt you. I remember the nights you spent alone in your room, and I am so very sorry. I should have seen the signs. And from now on, I am going to be there for you in a better way."

Although it is possible that in some cases the loved one truly wasn't as affected by the event, it is our experience that this type of response is more often related to a desire to minimize or avoid the pain, and therefore if the caregiver is unsure, it is best to err on the side of caution by interpreting these types of responses as denial. In fact, we've found that, either way, loved ones still appreciate caregiver acknowledgment of the pain they may have felt, even if they do not connect with it at this time. It is also an opportunity for caregivers to demonstrate that they are in fact willing and able to unearth old pain, making the loved one more likely to trust that the caregiver can handle other injuries that are perhaps more salient. We have also experienced that, in some cases, loved ones who initially responded with denial were later able to share with their caregivers their recollections of the event, including the pain they experienced.

Reassurance

The third most common response to this therapeutic apology is for loved ones to offer their caregivers reassurance that they "did their best" and that "there is no need to apologize." Although offering the apology from the "good house" should minimize the chances that a loved one will respond in this way, those who are highly sensitive or have a long-standing pattern of trying to protect others from pain may still attempt to do so. They may even express gratitude for all of the support the caregiver did provide (e.g., "I am so grateful for all that you did! I can't imagine how life would have turned out without you!"). This style of response can pose a challenge for two reasons. First, it is true that caregivers did the best they could, and their loved one's gratitude is warranted, and so it may seem odd to challenge these facts. Second, when caregivers carry a significant amount of self-blame, simply put, these responses can bring relief. In other words, caregivers can be tempted to accept the reassurance at face value because it can soothe their pain. However, it is crucial that caregivers resist the temptation to do so, at least at first. Instead, caregivers are prepped to validate their loved one's inclination or impulse to reassure, and then reassert their apology similar to as follows:

> Scenario 2: "Simon, I get why you would try to reassure me. You've seen me locked in my own guilt, and I can imagine that's been really hard for you to witness. In your shoes, I would do the same. But I'm not letting you protect me from your pain anymore, and I'm certainly not going to let you take care of mine! I am well supported, and this is for you. And so I will say it again: I am so very sorry. I should have protected you from the conflict, and I should have helped you to manage your pain with healthy coping strategies. From now on, I am going to be there for you in a better way."

Regardless of the circumstance, it is our experience that when the intervention is completed using the steps outlined here, it is likely to be experienced as deeply validating because it communicates a commitment to attend to old pain and to allow for two truths: A loved one can feel pain and gratitude at the same time. In fact, many of our clients have expressed that even when their caregivers apologized for an event that occurred when they were an infant, it still felt validating and in many cases it opened the door for them to share with their caregiver their personal narrative of pain. Caregivers have also found this process helpful throughout the treatment process, particularly when they make "mistakes" or struggle to improve the ways in which they relate to their loved one.

Marker for the End of the Intervention

Most often, loved ones will respond to the validation of their reaction and the reassertion of the apology with surprise and relief. Should the loved one remain steeped in resentment after a first iteration, caregivers may need to deliver the apology again, with time in between. In a subsequent attempt, caregivers try to capture other nuances of the idiosyncratic injuries—and always from the good house. Should the loved one maintain a stance of anger, denial, or reassurance after repeated attempts, caregivers can rest assured that although they didn't observe a shift in their loved one, it is likely to have been felt. Emotion processing can occur even when there are no apparent verbal or nonverbal signals. However, it is still recommended that caregivers explore with the therapist whether they experienced some difficulty with adhering to the steps as scripted. If there were issues with implementation—for example, caregivers ask for forgiveness rather than communicate an apology—they can circle back with their loved one to acknowledge the misstep and try again. Whether or not the resistance to the apology was related to a technical issue, a genuine attempt to "try again" can be incredibly healing for a loved one. Caregivers' persistence and commitment to the process communicates that they are determined to attend to these old family wounds in a manner that is validating to their loved one.

Expected Outcomes

In addition to a strengthening of the caregiver–loved one relationship, typical outcomes of the therapeutic apology include an unburdening of the pain of self-blame for all involved. Moving through this family-based process of unearthing and tending to old wounds can lead to a reversal of emotion-avoidant dynamics in the family and an increase in the family's self-efficacy with managing emotional distress. Loved ones learn experientially that the caregiver can support them in processing their most painful emotions and memories, thus making it more likely that they will turn to their caregiver to cope rather than to symptoms. Finally, and across each of the contexts described here, the process of the apology nearly always leads to a deep and experiential knowing of the truth that blame is a futile exercise— whether self- or other-blame—and that all parties involved did the best they could to navigate the challenges of life. In fact, it bears repeating that caregivers should not be guided to deliver an apology to their loved one if they don't have an implicit understanding of "the big picture"—that is, that in the context of intergenerational trauma and cultural influences, they are not to blame. Similarly, and perhaps most importantly, it is our strong belief that treating therapists cannot guide caregivers through this work unless they are themselves firmly rooted in the spirit of no blame. We have seen firsthand the negative consequences that can occur when well-intentioned therapists inadvertently engage in caregiver blame, especially in the context of this psychotherapeutic process. In these instances, clinical supervision is essential before supporting the caregiver to engage in this powerful intervention. Finally, given that the relationship is the vehi-cle for change in EFFT, any efforts to strengthen the bond can lead to a parallel strengthening of the healing power of caregiver efforts, and thus we consider them to be a worthwhile investment.

Additional Considerations

When preparing to enact a therapeutic apology, caregivers are supported to view the apology as a gift that they give to their loved one with no expecta-tion for anything in return. They are reminded that within this framework, it is best that they resist the temptation to offer rationales for their choices, behaviors, or the unfolding of events (e.g., "I'm sorry that I wasn't there for you. I was overwhelmed with the business and your little brother's extra needs"). Although grounded in truth and despite caregivers' best inten-tions, loved ones are likely to experience rationales as invalidating. Parents involved in the process are also taught that an I-apology is more potent than a We-apology (on behalf of both parents, for example) and that they should only apologize for their own actions. This is because each caregiver will have played a different role in the unfolding of events, and therefore a combined apology does not capture the uniqueness of their experiences. For this reason, both parents craft their own apology, even if they are to be delivered to their child at the same time. Similarly, when a family event had a negative impact on all members, parents are encouraged to create unique apologies for each of their children to capture their idiosyncratic impact, whether due to their developmental stage, temperament, individual needs, or other factors.

It is not uncommon for some caregivers to share with us that they are unsure of the relevance of the intervention given that they have already apologized to their loved one for various family life challenges in the past, sometimes with little success. In these cases, caregivers are invited to reen-act the past apology to the best of their ability with the therapist. Most often, we are able to help them identify that one of the steps was missing or incom-plete; the apology was thwarted by the blast, denial, or reassurance; or the undertone of the caregiver's apology was one of shame. These caregivers are guided to rework the apology, practice its delivery with the therapist, and consider delivering it again. In other instances, once caregivers experience the power of the apology, they are motivated to identify other potential inju-ries to harness their healing power. Again, caregivers are supported to follow their instincts in this regard, with the knowledge that they can consult with the therapist to determine the appropriateness of next steps.

Methods of Delivery

In this chapter, we have illustrated a method of delivery whereby caregivers work with the therapist to coconstruct an apology and enact its delivery in session with an empty chair. Then, if appropriate, they may share it with their loved one at home or with the support of the therapist in a dyad session. The method of delivery has evolved over time as caregivers have taught us over and over again how capable they are with the right kind of support and skills practice. Early in the development of EFFT, the method of teaching and delivering the apology involved multiple individual sessions with the loved one to identify and understand his or her pain. The therapist then worked individually with the caregiver(s) for a few preparatory sessions, sharing (with consent) the content of the sessions with the loved one, supporting caregivers in their reactions, and preparing them for a joint session in which the therapist would facilitate the process. Over time, and with the development of the EFFT caregiver workshop (Lafrance Robinson et al., 2016), some caregivers began reporting that after having learned about the intervention, they were delivering the apology on their own—and often with great success. It became clear to us that there was a subset of caregivers who did not require the extensive preparatory work to identify and work through family pain. As a result of the workshop, they also carried a lot less shame and self-blame, making them more confident to lead the intervention in the home setting. As such, we concluded that caregivers could make attempts to deliver the apology, and if for some reason it did not go well, they could go back, address the rupture, and try again, or they could deliver the apology in a facilitated dyadic session for extra support. In addition, we began to see that by restricting the delivery of the intervention in session with a therapist, there was an inadvertent message that caregivers were not capable of doing it on their own and that if they struggled, it could cause permanent harm. This inadvertent message went against the core tenets of the EFFT model, which underscore caregiver empowerment and the belief that "it's not what happens, it's what happens next."

Each of these factors together led to a radical change in the delivery of the intervention. We began introducing caregivers to the process in a group setting where they are taught the steps of the apology and associated rationales. They are then supported to write an apology using the framework as outlined. A few of the participants are provided with opportunities to practice in front of the group, receiving live feedback from the facilitators and their peers. The other group members benefit from vicarious learning and processing as they reflect on the ways in which what they observed could help to inform their process. Caregivers are then encouraged to deliver an apology to their loved one on their own, provided they feel ready and it makes sense to do so.[6] Using this structure, many caregivers facilitated therapeutic apologies with incredible results—again causing us to deepen our belief in caregivers. On the second day, those who struggled were provided with opportunities to brainstorm ideas to increase the effectiveness of the intervention and to process any possible blocks before making a second attempt (see Chapter 5). Thus, the method of delivery of the apology is now flexible and determined in collaboration with the caregivers in light of their perceived readiness and their goals. Regardless of the approach used, the most important element of the intervention involves communicating to parents and caregivers the firm belief that they are not to blame, and that you, the therapist, are honored to move through this process alongside them to support their family in healing.

Surrogate Apologies

There are some instances where therapists may encourage caregivers to apologize to their loved one on behalf of a parent or caregiver who is estranged or even deceased. For example, a father apologized to his son on behalf of his mother who suffered a stroke and therefore couldn't participate in his life in the ways he'd wanted and needed. The anger he felt toward his mother felt unjust and the suppression of his pain fueled his anxiety and depressed mood. His father, who had previously felt incredibly helpless, experienced tremendous relief when he could actively support his son in recovering from the ongoing losses in this way. He delivered a heartfelt apology on behalf of his wife, and from a deep place of knowing she'd want the same for her son. The effect was inspiring.

Likewise, we've witnessed deep healing when foster and adoptive parents have apologized to their children on behalf of their birth parents to honor the relationship and support the release of old hurt, shame, and anger. Therapists can also offer apologies to their clients on behalf of parents, caregivers, or partners in the same way. One psychologist in EFFT supervision shared that she hesitated to share an apology with her client on behalf of her deceased father who had been very abusive. Not only was she concerned about her client's potential for dysregulation, she also worried the client might experience her as invalidating, even defending the abuse. In line with the principle of transparency, the psychologist shared her concerns with her

---

[6]As noted earlier in the chapter, some apologies are delivered imaginally for the purpose of releasing caregiver self-blame and may not be appropriate or necessary to share with their loved one.

client, who agreed to participate in the intervention. Not only was it incredibly healing, the client shared that despite the hardships she suffered, she had always believed that deep down, her father loved her but couldn't allow herself to access this inner truth. The client reported the intervention as the most healing component of the therapy.

SUMMARY

This intervention involves a specifically constructed apology from caregiver to loved one to facilitate the transformation of family pain. The apology is rooted within a no-blame framework and provides an opportunity for deep healing in the face of the reality that many loved ones and caregivers blame themselves and that this self-blame can interfere with well-being. When caregivers respond to their loved one by validating their pain, shouldering some of the burden, and acknowledging challenging events, misattunements, losses, and conflicts, the relationship with their loved one is strengthened, and previously unmanageable emotional experiences and memories are processed in a healthy manner. This caregiver support also leads to an increase in loved ones' feelings of confidence in coping with painful emotions on their own or with the support of others, thereby reducing the need for symptoms.

Some caregivers and therapists have asked the question "Why ask parents and caregivers to take responsibility for their loved one's pain when mental health issues are no one's fault?" This is especially relevant given that one of the pillars of EFFT is that caregivers are not to blame. The answer is that whether on the surface or hidden, many caregivers and their loved ones feel toxic shame and obstructive self-blame. As discussed in Chapter 2 on emotion coaching, for emotional experiences to run their course, they must be processed, regardless of whether they are deemed to be reasonable or reflect the "truth." In other words, the only way to quiet the inner critic of the caregiver or loved one is to attend to the underlying pain (Greenberg, 2008). The EFFT apology is structured to transform this pain, engendering a process of forgiveness, whether of the self, other, or both. This is especially relevant given the emerging research suggesting that the ability to forgive is related to better mental health, including lower levels of anxiety, depression, and anger and a better ability to cope with stress and adversity (Toussaint, Worthington, & Williams, 2015). In fact, one of the unintended yet very moving outcomes we've observed over the years is the enthusiasm with which caregivers take this on—not only with the affected loved one, but with others in their family, leading to stronger, healthier relationships overall.

CLINICIAN'S CORNER

Therapeutic apologies have been one of the most effective interventions I've used for moving a family toward recovery *together*. When 17-year-old Amy first came to see me, she had essentially severed ties with both her parents. Her father was in recovery from alcoholism, and in the darkest parts of his addiction, he was abusive toward Amy and her mother. Although this was incredibly painful, Amy shared that her deepest hurt was with her mother, who after having left her father, reconciled with him once he began treatment. Amy experienced this as an invalidation of her trauma, and she felt betrayed. After I worked for months with Amy and her mother separately, Amy's mother delivered a heartfelt apology to her daughter and deeply validated her feelings. Amy didn't accept the apology at first, but it did start a process of relationship repair. Today, Amy and her mother have a strong relationship. Her parents continue to heal their marriage, which Amy now supports. She was even able to rebuild her relationship with her father, who eventually participated in the therapy and also engaged in his own relationship repair work with his daughter. This occurred despite the fact that Amy often shared that she did not want her parents in her life. For a while, Amy's parents believed her, even thinking at times that it was the best option to prevent further damage. As therapy progressed, they learned at a much deeper level—and so did I—that children do in fact want to repair ruptures with their parents, no matter their size. They may say they want nothing to do with their parents, and some might mean it, but it's certain that they don't *want* to mean it.

—Psychologist

5

WORKING THROUGH CAREGIVER BLOCKS

The biggest thing that I took away was that under these circumstances, fear is completely normal and understandable but also very paralyzing. So I'm much more aware of needing to work through the fear of somehow making it worse.

—Caregiver

As noted throughout this manual, the primary aim of emotion-focused family therapy (EFFT) is to assist carers in supporting the behavioral and emotional health of their loved ones. However, it is well established in the literature that caregivers can experience strong emotions in reaction to their loved one's struggles (Holt, Jensen, & Wentzel-Larsen, 2014; Kyriacou, Treasure, & Schmidt, 2008; Scarnier, Schmader, & Lickel, 2009; Stillar et al., 2016). Although these emotional reactions can be primary and adaptive, they sometimes reflect conditioned responses that are based on childhood experiences, sociocultural learning, and trauma. In fact, in times of stress, the emotional signals related to caregivers' default modes can become the

http://dx.doi.org/10.1037/0000166-006
Emotion-Focused Family Therapy: A Transdiagnostic Model for Caregiver-Focused Interventions, by A. Lafrance, K. A. Henderson, and S. Mayman

principal guide for their responses in the moment (Bechara, Damasio, & Damasio, 2000). A father once shared that he would back off from discussing potentially sensitive subjects with his depressed daughter when she became quiet or tearful. He was raised in a family where vulnerabilities were not discussed openly (sociocultural influence), and his own sister had attempted suicide as an adolescent (trauma). Therefore, he had developed a fear response to signals of sadness and withdrawal. When faced with his daughter's pain, he would become paralyzed and quickly provide reassurance and distraction. In other words, he was reacting automatically from learned cues relating to what he had learned was dangerous or painful in the past (Greenberg, 2010).

When evoked in these ways, carers can lose connection to their caregiving instincts and become "blocked" from accessing previously acquired knowledge and skills, potentially leading to reactive, rigid, or otherwise ineffective response patterns (Siegel, 2010). This is particularly problematic because a major goal of EFFT is to equip carers with advanced caregiving skills to support their loved one's recovery from mental health issues. For example, it is common for carers to come up against blocks when they attempt to support their loved one with behaviors or respond with validation to their loved one's feelings. A caregiver may become blocked in her attempts to set boundaries when her loved one yells angrily in response. A spouse or partner may struggle to validate her loved one's shame relating to symptom patterns when he fears doing so will deepen or reinforce his pain. A parent may become paralyzed with fear, completely incapable of rational thought, in response to his son's hopeless despair. In these instances, as such, a significant focus in EFFT involves guiding parents and caregivers to recognize and work through their *blocks*—that is, any problematic attitude or behavior fueled by emotion, particularly when they arise in the context of their role as agents of healing. We've found that the emotional states most likely to negatively influence caregiver attitudes and behaviors include fear, shame, helplessness, hopelessness, and resentment. These states lead most often to denial, avoidance, criticism, rejection, defensiveness, other-blame, and accommodating and enabling behaviors. Guided by this framework, caregiver blocks are not regarded as markers of unmotivated or uncaring carers; rather, they are understood as attitudes and behaviors that regulate their distress. Block work is focused work to support caregivers to attend to and move through the emotional states preventing them from engaging in the tasks of therapy to interrupt problematic patterns of relating to their loved one and optimize the caregiver's supportive efforts.

COMMON BLOCKS TO ADVANCED CAREGIVING

Caregiver blocks in the behavior coaching domain are often reflected in carers' resistance with regard to their involvement in treatment more broadly, as well as with the implementation of specific behavioral interventions. For example, caregivers may resist the facilitation of exposures in the context of an anxiety disorder, or behavioral activation in the context of depression, for fear of causing their loved one too much distress. They may instead deny, minimize, or accommodate and enable their loved one's symptoms. Caregivers may also struggle to set limits around their loved one's behavior or hesitate to challenge their loved one to engage in new health-focused behaviors in case their efforts are rejected or their loved one withdraws. They may even present with reactive hostility and criticism toward their loved one for not respecting the house rules or for failing to take proper care of themselves. In the emotion-coaching domain, the most common blocks relate to the skill of validation, where caregivers struggle to tolerate their loved one's pain, fearing that their efforts will lead their loved one to sink into their sadness, hopelessness, or shame, never to resurface. Other caregivers may resist the "apology" for fear that engaging in this intervention could open the door for other-blame or give reason for their loved one to harbor lifelong resentment toward them.

Regardless of the nature of their involvement, we cannot emphasize strongly enough that carers—from all walks of life and circumstance—will struggle to actively support their loved one when they fear the distress associated with their actions could lead the loved one to fall deeper into symptoms (e.g., depression), withdraw, or, worse, attempt suicide. In these instances, the paralyzing fear is exacerbated by the harshness of caregivers' inner critic who convinces them that they will be to blame should such outcomes occur. Therefore, when caregivers present as disengaged, unmotivated, or even defiant in response to treatment recommendations, the EFFT clinician assumes that they are gripped by a powerful fear (whether conscious or not) that their engagement could lead to "something worse" for which they will be "to blame." With respect to blame, and as discussed in Chapter 4, this volume, it is our experience that most caregivers experience some level of self-blame in the face of their loved ones' difficulties. This self-blame can be easily triggered and become overwhelming, leading to patterns of defensiveness or withdrawal, self-referential expressions of pain or blaming others in an attempt to diffuse the intensity of their suffering.

In addition to fear and self-blame, carers may also present with hopelessness or helplessness, leading them to act out in unhelpful ways. For instance, in the absence of skills, a distraught wife desperate to convince her husband to engage in treatment for posttraumatic stress disorder may resort to threats or other coercive techniques that may further compound the problem. Others may find themselves blocked by resentment toward their loved one, family members, or even the clinician or team. Fueled by feelings of help-lessness and shame, resentment is most likely when caregivers' best efforts to support their loved one were seemingly underappreciated, outright rejected, or ineffective.

It is important to note that the likelihood of these and other manifesta-tions of caregiver blocks increase in accordance with the caregiver's level of exhaustion. When caregiver blocks are intensified by fatigue, the clini-cian supports caregivers to develop a clear plan to help them maintain their own mental and physical health. Such a plan includes specific and manage-able goals to promote self-compassion and self-care because doing so will increase carers' confidence in their role and protect them from burnout, especially if they are already feeling vulnerable or have a history of illness.

WISDOM IN BLOCKS

Although it is clear that unprocessed or maladaptive carer emotion can lead to problematic response patterns in the face of a loved one's suffering, it is also true that within almost every block, there are pearls of wisdom and a foundation of love. For example, some level of caregiver fear or resistance may be appropriate depending on the state of a loved one's current mental health. The fear of a mother who is reluctant to implement exposure exer-cises with her son who has a history of suicidality is not wholly maladap-tive. It is also fueled by the deep love she has for him. The goal is thus to transform the unprocessed emotion driving the reluctance to engage a loved one to access the caregiver's wisdom and love, which can then guide the treatment implementation. With this mother, the clinician would work with her to allay her paralyzing fears regarding her role in the treatment using the strategies discussed in this chapter. Guided by the wisdom of her fear and the love she has for her son, the mother would then be coached to inte-grate the skills of emotion coaching before, during, and after the exposure exercise to increase the tolerability of the intervention. She would also be guided to increase supervision for a period of time in order to identify and act upon potential signs of distress in her child, should they arise. In other words, in EFFT, clinicians work collaboratively with caregivers to help them to extricate themselves from the paralyzing hold of the block in order to find a new path forward that is informed by the wisdom of their instincts and the love they have for their loved one.

PROCESSING CAREGIVER BLOCKS

When an EFFT clinician suspects that a block may be interfering with a carer's sense of empowerment or engagement in a loved one's recovery, the clinician works to support the processing of these problematic states and associated attitudes and behaviors through psychoeducation, self-assessment tools, emotion coaching (i.e., clinician to caregiver), experiential skills practice, and caregiver block chair work. Identifying and processing caregiver blocks throughout treatment helps carers regain access to the wisdom of their caregiving instincts, frees them to implement their new advanced caregiving skills, and reconnects them to their authentic desire to support their loved one to move toward health and adaptive functioning (Strahan et al., 2017). That being said, these interventions require varying levels of comfort and skill with the underlying principles of EFFT and the techniques and tools themselves. As such, we encourage clinicians new to the model to begin by exploring the utility of targeted psychoeducation, self-assessment tools, the emotion-coaching framework, and experiential skills practice before moving on to the more advanced method of targeting caregiver blocks using chair work.

Psychoeducation

Psychoeducation is essential to normalize the fears and other emotional obstacles that will surface for carers on the challenging journey to recovery. In line with the EFFT pillar of transparency, clinicians introduce the concept of blocks during the assessment phase or early in treatment, as needed, noting that they are likely to occur within each member of the family and even among members of the treatment team. Using a tree metaphor, caregivers are taught that blocks are rooted in fear, shame, hopelessness, helplessness, or resentment and that they can manifest in various ways (see Figure 5.1). The clinician then provides examples of the blocks most likely to arise within the caregiver based on the loved one's symptoms or clinical history (or both) and encourages the caregiver to identify those with which he or she can relate. When the blocks emerge in session, the clinician simply refers to the tree metaphor to move the discussion from surface-level attitudes or behaviors (e.g., belief that the loved one is feigning symptoms)

FIGURE 5.1. The Tree Metaphor

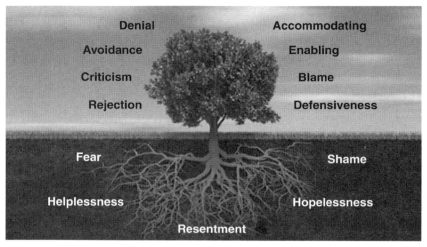

to the emotional roots of the block (e.g., helplessness, shame). Likewise, when coparents are critical about one another's problematic patterns, this metaphor can guide them to conceptualize each other's behavior in a more empathic way, leading to more productive discussion and problem-solving.

In some cases, we have observed that psychoeducation alone can increase carers' awareness of the impact that their emotion blocks have on their ability to feel compassionate toward their loved one, to feel confident in themselves, and to be able to engage in tasks that promote their loved one's physical and emotional well-being. This nonpathologizing process of discovery can also improve the working alliance, which in turn increases the caregiver's trust in the clinical team. Anticipating the emergence of blocks—whether they manifest attitudinally or behaviorally—also empowers the caregiver to ask for help in working them through, rather than dismissing them or being overtaken by fear, shame, or resentment and going "underground" should they arise.

Self-Assessment Tools

Self-assessment tools help carers and clinicians identify current or potential blocks that may interfere with treatment. The following self-assessment tools are used within the context of EFFT: (a) the New Maudsley method's animal metaphors (Treasure, Smith, & Crane, 2007) and the Caregiver Styles Self-Reflection Tool, (b) the Caregiver Traps Scale, and (c) the Relationship

Dimensions Scale. The use of these tools also serves to normalize the presence of blocks for caregivers because they were developed in consultation with parents and caregivers supporting their loved one with a mental health issue and represent common reactions to such involvement.

Animal Metaphors

To aid in the process of identifying, understanding, and depathologizing the expression of emotion blocks, carers are presented with the New Maudsley's animal metaphors (Treasure et al., 2007). The animal metaphors were first developed to illustrate common emotional and behavioral response patterns in which caregivers tend to engage when supporting a loved one with an eating disorder. They have since been adapted for use among caregivers with loved ones suffering from behavioral challenges, mental illness, or physical health issues.

The first set of animal metaphors is used to illustrate emotional response styles carers may exhibit in the face of their loved one's struggles. Included in this set are the jellyfish, the ostrich, and the St. Bernard. The caregiver is first introduced to the jellyfish and the ostrich, which represent the two extremes of emotional responsivity. On one end of the continuum is the jellyfish, who can be a bit wobbly and whose emotions tend to overflow. On the other end of the continuum, the ostrich avoids seeing, thinking about, and dealing with emotions and instead focuses on practical ways of supporting the family. Caregivers are then invited to identify with the animal (jellyfish or ostrich) that is most representative of their emotion-coping style when faced with stressful situations that involve their loved one. Finally, caregivers are presented with the St. Bernard, a dog trained for avalanche rescue missions in the Alps. We encourage parents and carers to strive to emulate the St. Bernard in times of stress because these animals are highly regarded for being reliable, calm, consistent, and providing warmth and companionship on the road to safety (Treasure et al., 2007).

The second set of animal metaphors is used to illustrate common caregiving styles in the face of their loved one's struggles. Included in this set are the kangaroo, the rhinoceros, and the dolphin. Like with the first set of animal metaphors, the caregiver is first introduced to the kangaroo and the rhinoceros, which represent the two extremes on this dimension. The kangaroo tends toward overprotection, carrying a loved one in its pouch to shield it from life's challenges, including failure or pain; the rhinoceros charges in with logic, attempting to convince or control the loved one to behave in the way it believes is most practical. Caregivers are then invited to identify with the animal (kangaroo or rhinoceros) that is most representative of their caregiving style when faced with challenging situations involving their loved one. Finally, caregivers are presented with the dolphin, animals known for the way in which they support their offspring, guiding them by leading the way, swimming alongside, or supporting from behind as needed. It represents the optimal balance of care and control in caregiving; caregivers are thus encouraged to move from the kangaroo or rhinoceros position toward the dolphin position, particularly in times of stress.

The two sets of animal metaphors provide a convenient, easily learned, and nonthreatening approach to discussing problematic caregiving patterns in sessions and within the family unit. They can be used therapeutically in various ways. First, clinicians can invite caregivers and coparents to identify their dominant animals in times of stress, whether in an individual session, a family session, or group setting. In one caregiver workshop, a mother exclaimed with laughter that she was "a jellyfish with a pouch," setting the stage for her peers to reflect on their own patterns. Loved ones are also invited to provide feedback regarding their carers' styles using the same framework, doing so in a playful manner and in a way that reinforces the process of attending to and transforming these potentially problematic patterns. To accompany this exercise, we've developed a tool that supports caregivers to self-reflect on their dominant styles to facilitate change (see Appendix E).

Caregiver Traps Scale

It is our experience that many parents and caregivers involved as collaborative partners in care do not always spontaneously communicate their treatment-engagement fears to their clinical team for fear of judgment or because the fears are simply outside of their awareness. The Caregiver Traps Scale provides clinicians with a tool for quickly assessing the presence and strength of a number of caregiver fears relating to their role as active agents of change in their loved one's treatment. The scale was developed over the course of several years on the basis of common concerns expressed by parents recruited to support their child's recovery from an eating disorder.[1] It has since been validated for use with this population (Lafrance, Strahan, & Stillar, 2019) and adapted for caregivers of loved ones with various mental health issues (see Appendix F). The general scale lists 14 potential fears associated with behavior coaching and symptom interruption.

Sample items from this subscale include the following: "I worry about putting strain on my couple relationship," "I worry about pushing my loved one

---

[1]Because of this, we've found that the measure itself normalizes the presence of such concerns, decreasing possible guilt or shame and therefore increasing the likelihood that caregivers will bring them to the treatment team or clinician for support.

'too far' with treatment (leading to depression/running away/suicide)," and "I worry about being blamed or being to blame." Seven-point Likert scales accompany each item, with higher scores reflecting a greater level of concern.

Using the Caregiver Traps Scale to bring awareness to caregivers' underlying fears normalizes their presence and is perhaps the simplest way to reduce their impact. We recommend a review of individual items, taking note of relative extremes. Some caregivers will endorse few items and at low levels, whereas others will endorse a great number of items at high levels. Regardless of the response pattern, relative elevations are considered significant and provide a road map of potential vulnerabilities that may require attention. In fact, we've found that the fears endorsed may simply represent the range of actual fears the caregiver feels comfortable discussing further, and at the level of intensity indicated. For this reason, and because progression in treatment can reveal new fears, we encourage its repeated administration.

Once fears are identified, the clinician can also offer the caregiver appropriate emotional and practical support. For example, if a father is anxious that his engagement in therapeutic interventions will lead to feelings of resentment in his other children, the clinician could provide him with opportunities to practice responding with validation to sibling reactions.

With regard to caregiver fears relating to suicidality, many caregivers fear that their involvement in their loved one's recovery from mental health issues could lead them to become overwhelmed with distress, even suicidality. Thus, it may be necessary to work with carers to create a safety plan as part of working through blocks. As such, when caregivers endorse the item relating to suicidality, similar to students training to become mental health workers, they are taught to identify warning signs (e.g., patterns of isolation, talking or writing about death), ask direct questions about suicidal ideation (e.g., "Are you thinking of killing yourself?"), determine whether there is a suicidal plan (e.g., "Do you have a plan to take your life?"), and assess the means to carry out such a plan ("Where would you get the pills?"). Caregivers are then instructed to create safety in their homes by removing means for suicide such as sharp objects or substances and are taught about one-on-one monitoring if warranted. They are also encouraged to pay close attention to their internal alarm system and involve external supports such as mobile crisis units or emergency services as necessary (see Appendix G for carer handout). The rationale for equipping carers with these particular sets of skills is twofold. First, doing so increases caregivers' effectiveness in ensuring the safety of their loved one in times of risk. Second, equipping them with these skills can reduce caregiver anxiety if they fear their loved one will become suicidal from the stress of the home-based interventions, regardless of risk. In other words, the importance of this set of skills is not only to respond to needs for safety but also to give caregivers the confidence to move forward with behavior coaching with the knowledge that they can manage challenging situations should they arise.

Relationship Dimensions Scale

On the basis of the premise that for every action there is a reaction, carers are provided with the Relationship Dimensions Scale to identify opportunities to initiate small shifts in their relational style with the hope that they will result in parallel shifts in their loved one (see Appendix H). Although it can also be used to support caregivers to identify polarized patterns, its primary focus is on the identification of behavioral goals to create more flexibility in the system. This becomes particularly relevant when, despite the caregiver and team's best efforts, the loved one's symptoms remain firmly entrenched. To do so, the Relationship Dimensions Scale comprises a number of relational styles with two extremes anchoring both ends of the continuum. Example items include *always serious—always using humor, always apologizing—never apologizing,* and *always expressing anger—never expressing anger.* Caregivers are invited to indicate with a checkmark where they fall along the continuum in reference to their interactions with their loved one in the present day. Once complete, the relative extremes are noted, and two to three behavioral goals are set in response. For example, it is not uncommon for families affected by chronic and severe mental health issues to report few if any joyful moments in the home. In these cases, caregivers are instructed to go home and do something silly in front of their loved one. Parents and spouses who have done so have been amazed at the impact of even the smallest gestures. One woman (Patricia) supporting her partner (Natasha) who was struggling with substance misuse placed a banana peel on her head for the duration of a meal. Her partner responded with amusement, but Patricia refused to acknowledge the fruit peel until they cleared their plates. The next day, Patricia shared in a caregiver group that doing so allowed her and Natasha to discuss the pattern that had emerged and make commitments for change. She also reported that Natasha had a much more relaxed evening and resisted the urge to self-medicate before bed.

Homework ideas associated with other items may not be as intuitive at first glance. Many carers don't necessarily see the problem with always apologizing or never expressing anger. In these instances, the EFFT clinician supports the caregiver to explore the energy behind these patterns. Often, caregivers discover that they are expressions of maladaptive self-blame or of anxiety around the expression of anger or conflict in general. Equipped with this new insight, caregivers can commit to sharing what they've learned with their loved one and working together to interrupt these patterns and create new, more adaptive styles of relating to one another. A married couple supporting their adult daughter suffering from depressed mood decided to stage a fight when they realized the extent to which they avoided conflict in the home. They warned their daughter that the fight wouldn't be genuine so as not to scare her, but they committed to transform the family norm, including encouraging their daughter to express anger toward them. Although it was slightly comical, they did report a positive effect that created hope for greater change.

Once parents and carers have noted their responses for each of the items and discussed possible goals in response to their relative extremes, they are then instructed to consider two additional questions: "Are you more sensitive to rejection or disrespect?" and "Are you more comfortable with providing comfort or setting boundaries?" A family-based recovery from most mental health issues requires of the caregiver some capacity to tolerate both rejection and disrespect. Likewise, and particularly in the context of EFFT, caregivers must have some capacity to provide their loved one with comfort when distressed and set appropriate limits around symptom engagement. Through this exploration, caregivers identify their strengths and work on their weaknesses. Doing so can also help caregivers to recognize and move through related blocks, should they arise, with increased ease. Although this tool was initially developed for carers for use in reference to their loved one, we've found it to be useful to address coparenting issues as well. When doing so, parents each complete the tool in reference to the other and discuss ways in which they can work together to increase cohesion and cooperation, leveraging one another's strengths, and supporting each other's underdeveloped capacities.[2]

Together, these self-assessment tools help to identify and normalize the presence of caregiver blocks and begins the process of working them through by bringing them into the caregiver's sphere of consciousness, making them an explicit focus in session, and encouraging caregivers to develop action plans for when they emerge. In our practices, these tools seem most effective when administered in the context of a session where their loved one is not present (to allow for freedom in discussing potential blocks) or a clinician-facilitated group to benefit from the processes of universality and interpersonal learning when participants share with one another their triggers and experiences overcoming their blocks (Yalom, 1995). The environment of unconditional acceptance also strengthens the working alliance

---

[2]This tool has also been used, with positive results, to support loved ones to identify their own polarized patterns in response to their caregivers and significant others.

with the clinician and team, providing a shared language to communicate and collaborate more effectively when working through potentially sensitive problem cycles.

Whether the clinician uses the animal metaphors, the Caregiver Traps Scale, or the Relationship Dimensions Scale, when working with coparents, it is important to note the possibility that they will present with different patterns of responses. In these instances, they can inadvertently reinforce one another's reactions. For example, when more protective caregivers observe a coparent's tougher stance, they are more likely to overcompensate for their partner's behavior by becoming even more protective in response. This process can lead to a vicious cycle and, in more extreme cases, a fracture within the caregiving unit. This is especially risky when the cocaregivers are separated or divorced or when there is already significant tension. When carers are provided with this information, they can identify the caregiver cycles in action, reduce their impact, and work toward a more cohesive approach to responding to their loved one's emotions and behaviors.

Emotion Coaching: Clinician to Caregiver

Clinicians should not underestimate the value of emotion coaching to support the processing of emotional states fueling a carer's block. Regardless of the manifestation of the block, it is important that the clinician deeply validate the caregiver's fear, shame, hopelessness, helplessness, and/or feelings of resentment before supporting them in more practical ways.

Scenario 1

CAREGIVER: I am so frustrated with Jiabao. I swear he is manipulating us all. He only talks about our screw-ups in session. Not a word at home and no indication whatsoever that anything is wrong. I'm convinced he's taking us for ride. It's like he wants to see us suffer. I'm done with this.

CLINICIAN: Lin, I can only imagine how frustrating that must be for you because, among other things, it must feel like he's trying to make sure that I know you're not perfect. I bet that on some level it's kind of embarrassing too if it feels like you're being called to the principal's office week after week. Especially when you don't know what to expect. I can understand you'd be hesitant to validate Jiabao's experiences in case it's a strategy to get attention that you might then reinforce. In your shoes, I might feel really frustrated, and maybe a bit scared. It's probably really hard to know what to do, and who to trust.

I don't blame you for feeling exasperated by it all, especially when the work we do together has not felt productive so far.

Depending on the caregiver's response, the EFFT clinician may need to continue responding with validation. Once the frustrations begin to diffuse, it is time to identify possible emotional needs (reassurance that you also want to avoid reinforcing problematic patterns of behavior) as well as practical needs (a structured plan to experiment with the approach).

Scenario 2

CAREGIVER: With all due respect, Dr. Morales, I don't think that family therapy is the right way to go. We feel strongly that Sophie needs someone to talk to, you know, other than us. We don't want to interfere with the relationship you both have, and, well, we won't always be here for her to lean on, so we think it's best that her recovery is her own.

CLINICIAN: I can see where you're coming from. Since I've been working with Sophie, her symptoms have stabilized. I could imagine that you'd be worried about a decline in her progress if we change the way we do the therapy. You might even feel responsible if it didn't go well. I wonder if you're also feeling anxious that she might resent your involvement? I wouldn't blame you if you did. Things have been tense lately. If I were in your shoes, I'd probably feel the same way.

The clinician follows these attempts to validate the caregiver's concerns with emotional support, perhaps by emphasizing the normalcy of their experience. When the clinician responds in this way, caregivers will feel heard and understood, the intensity of their emotional state will be lessened, and the emotional support will increase their ability to be flexible and to engage with logic and problem-solving regarding how best to proceed. They will also have more emotional capacity to be responsive and attuned to the needs of their loved one.

Experiential Skills Practice

Once caregivers have learned the advanced caregiver skills of EFFT and they can anticipate the blocks they may experience, clinicians engage them in purposeful role-play. Specifically, the clinician embodies an exaggerated version of their loved one expressing anger, shame, even a wish to die to trigger—with their consent—the physiological expression of the block in the caregiver (e.g., heart racing, blank mind). Then, using principles of scaffolding, the clinician coaches the caregiver to respond with validating scripts and provides feedback regarding volume, tone, and body posture, coconstructing the response until it begins to feel more natural. The clinician and caregiver replay the scenario over and again, introducing slight variations to promote a process of generalization. Sometimes the same scenarios will be practiced for the duration of the session or over several sessions. The key to this exercise is repetition because this will facilitate the creation of new neural pathways. Over time, caregivers will develop the flexibility to pivot from impulsive, fear-based, or conditioned reactions to thoughtful responses more likely to be productive. Eventually, the caregiver's default modes of responding to their loved one's painful emotions will be overridden by the new response patterns, even in times of stress (Siegel, 2012).

Another common scenario known to induce blocks involves a loved one who remains silent in the face of carers' attempts for connection. It is particularly disconcerting for a parent to receive minimal or no feedback from their child, given the strength of their neurobiological bond. Parents and caregivers often feel scared, disrespected, or hurt and react from these feeling states, potentially reinforcing problem cycles. To support them to override this block and guided by a carefully constructed script (see Appendix I for carer handout), the clinician and caregiver take turns embodying the loved one and validating his or her silence for a minimum of 5 minutes. This in vivo practice of "speaking into the void" increases caregivers' comfort and confidence in applying the skills of emotion coaching in such an extreme situation, making it less likely that they will freeze or act out their frustration when their loved one presents as dismissive or shut down. When they take the role of their loved one, they also learn experientially that deep listening and emotion processing occurs behind the veil, further reinforcing the use of their newly acquired skills. Whether in response to their loved one's emotional pain or behavioral outbursts, it is our opinion that experiential skills practice is one of the easiest and most effective methods to support the transformation of caregiver blocks that emerge throughout treatment.

Caregiver Block Chair Work

Clinicians of various backgrounds can use psychoeducation, self-assessment measures, the skills of emotion coaching, and experiential skills practice to identify and work through caregiver blocks. In the context of individual and group-based sessions with carers, trained therapists can also use a more intensive psychotherapeutic technique unique to EFFT to support the transformation of behavioral blocks. This technique is referred to as *caregiver block chair work* and is inspired by chair work interventions in emotion-focused therapy (EFT), in particular, the resolution of self-interruptive splits using a two-chair enactment:

> *Self-interruptive splits* [italic in original; arise when] . . . one part of the self-interrupts or constricts emotional experience and expression, "I can feel the tears coming up, but I just tighten and suck them back in; no way am I going to cry." *Two-chair enactment* [italic in original] is used to make the interrupting part of the self explicit. Clients are guided to become aware of how they interrupt and to enact the ways they do it, whether by physical act (choking or shutting down the voice), metaphorically (caging, etc.), or verbally ("shut up, don't feel, be quiet, you can't survive this"), so that they can experience themselves as an agent in the process of shutting down. They then are invited to react to and challenge the interrupting part of the self. Resolution involves expression of the previously blocked experience. (Greenberg, 2010, pp. 34–35)

Adapted for use with carers struggling to support their loved ones, caregiver block chair work differs from this classic EFT intervention in two significant ways. First, self-interruptive two-chair enactments serve to transform patterns of emotional suppression, whereas in caregiver block chair work, the focus is primarily on transforming patterns of behavior. Second, in the context of caregiver block chair work, the caregiver not only experiences an imagined dialogue between two parts of the self to increase awareness of internal processes, they also engage in imagined dialogue with their loved one to harness the power of empathy and love for transformation. The script to guide this intervention is highly directive and linear. It has been developed in this way to increase the likelihood of transformation and as such we strongly recommend its use as outlined. The order of steps, and the ways in which they were constructed, were elaborated to ensure intervention-adherence and lead to optimal processing (see Appendix J for therapist guide). An example of its use in a clinical setting is illustrated below. Interested readers can also review this book's companion video (American Psychological Association, 2020) where the first author (AL) demonstrates the use of this technique with a mother who engages in patterns of over-protection and enabling in response to her son's distress.

Illustration of Caregiver Block Chair Work

Step 1
When initiating caregiver block chair work, the therapist and caregiver work together to identify the target behavior that will be the focus of the work.

THERAPIST: Laura, so from what I understand, there is a part of you that thinks it's a bad idea to implement the tasks of behavior coaching we talked about for your daughter.

CAREGIVER: Yes, I'm definitely scared. Part of me knows it's not helping when I back off, but I'm terrified to push her over the edge.

Once the target behavior is identified (backing off), the therapist positions two chairs facing one another (the "self" and the "other" chair) and invites the caregiver to sit in the "other" chair on the right side of the therapist.

Step 2

In our example, the therapist next invites the mother to picture herself in the chair facing her. She is asked to enact the part of herself that scares her (imagined in the other chair) into "backing off." The therapist supports the mother to make explicit the reasons why supporting her daughter in active ways could lead to negative outcomes for all involved. The therapist is careful to weave in the motivation to avoid the experience of overwhelming emotion if the caregiver doesn't spontaneously do so.

THERAPIST: Laura, it may seem a bit weird at first, but I'm going to invite you to imagine yourself sitting in the chair across from you. Now, I want you to embody the part of you that scares you to get involved. In other words, be the part of you that convinces you to back off.

CAREGIVER: (in the "other" chair, enacting the part of herself that scares her) Laura, do not push her. Do not make her get out of bed and face her day. You can see the pain she is in. If you do, you will push her over the edge. She could cut you out of her life. She could even kill herself. If something bad happens to her, it will be your fault and you will never be able to live with yourself. You will not be able to survive that guilt [low self-efficacy with emotion]. So don't push her. Walk on eggshells. Better yet, just leave things as they are and hope for the best."

(The therapist invites the caregiver to switch to the "self" chair on their left.)

Step 3

The caregiver is now invited to imagine her loved one in the chair facing her (to the right of the therapist). The therapist offers a summary of the content for the caregiver to share with her loved one focusing on the caregiver's problematic behavioral pattern, the rationale to protect the loved one from emotional pain and associated negative outcomes, the rationale to protect herself from emotional pain and associated negative outcomes, and the caregiver's plan to continue enacting the block.

At this point in the intervention, it is not uncommon for some caregivers to begin rising up against their fears. They may even express resolve to support their loved one in a more active way. Although this is a positive development in the processing of the block, caregivers are guided to continue to move through the steps for deeper processing. Others may express reluctance to share this message with their loved one out of guilt or shame. In this instance, the therapist acknowledges and validates the caregiver's experience and offers reassurance that they are not expected to share this content with their loved one in "real" life. Rather, they are engaged in an active process of transformation where (unfortunately) the only way out is through.

CAREGIVER: (in the "self" chair) Ashley, I am not going to push you. I am not going to try to get you out of bed and I am not going to try to get you out of the house with me. I'm too scared that if I do, I will cause you too much suffering, and that in the worst-case scenario—you'll end up taking your own life. If I cause you to suffer or push you over the edge, I will blame myself forever, and I wouldn't be able to cope with the guilt, shame, and pain of having failed you so badly. I would never recover. So, I am not going to push you. I would rather have a sick kid than a dead one.

(The therapist invites the caregiver to switch to the "other" chair on their right.)

Step 4

The therapist now asks the mother to take the role of her loved one and to respond to what was shared from that perspective. If the caregiver-as-loved-one reacts with resignation, relief, agreement, or anger, the therapist allows the "loved one" to express this reaction and then asks her to speak the more vulnerable feelings that are beneath the surface. The therapist then supports the caregiver-as-loved-one to offer validation in response to the caregiver's fears as a form of self-compassion.

CAREGIVER: (in the "other" chair, enacting her daughter) "Well, Mom, it's about time you got it. I have been telling you for ages to leave me alone. I don't want to get out of bed, I sure am not leaving the house and I don't want anything to do with this stupid treatment. It's not going to work anyway. I am glad you've finally come to your senses [agreement/anger].

THERAPIST: Okay, Ashley (speaking to the caregiver-as-loved-one), take a deep breath. Can you share with Mom the downside of the agreement? Can you speak from that vulnerable place hidden underneath the agreement? From that place where you know things to be true, even though you might not ever say it out loud?

CAREGIVER: (again in the "other" chair, enacting her daughter) Mom, when you're too afraid to push me, when you back off, I end up feeling all alone. I feel broken and really scared that I'll be stuck in this vortex forever.

THERAPIST: Can you try to finish this sentence? "Mom, I could understand why you would back from pushing me because . . ."

CAREGIVER: Mom, I can understand why you would back off from pushing me because I yell and scream and because you know how painful it is for me to face my fears. I know it's because you love me. But I guess there is a part of me that wants and needs you to keep pushing me. If you don't, I'm scared that eventually I will have nothing and no one. I can't do this on my own. Please don't let me scare you away.

Finally, the therapist encourages the mother enacting her loved one to share the reasons why she longs for her caregiver to be the one to support her in these ways. This last component is important to harness the power of love to transform the fear fueling the caregiver block.

CAREGIVER: (again in the "other" chair, enacting her daughter) Mom, I want you to keep fighting for me because I trust you. I know you only want the best for me. If anyone can help me through this, it's you. I know how much you love me and I love you more than anyone in the world, even if I don't always show it.

(The therapist invites the caregiver to switch to the "self" chair on their left.)

Step 5

The therapist invites the mother to share what it was like to embody her loved one's experience and respond from that perspective. Caregivers will often express a mixture of sadness and regret for having misinterpreted their loved one's signals, coupled with a deeper understanding of their true vulnerable needs. Paradoxically, caregivers also experience a sense of empowerment to increase their supportive efforts and manage the discomfort that may arise while doing so. The therapist then guides caregivers to imagine their loved one in the opposite chair for a final time, supporting them to respond to their "loved one's" expressed needs, followed by the explicit communication of love and compassion. The therapist will then encourage caregivers to express clearly to their loved one what they will do differently to support them.

CAREGIVER: (in the "self" chair) Ashley, I'm not going to give up on you. I am going to help you get out of bed, and together we are going to get you moving. I will not let your depression and anxiety keep you trapped in this house any longer. I know that you will get mad and tell me to stop, but I will use the tools I've learned to help ease your suffering. We will do this together. I love you too, sweetie and I really feel for you. I really do.

Finally, the therapist in our example guides the caregiver to warn her loved one that she may slip back and once again act on her fears but that she will continue her efforts to support her daughter with renewed confidence and conviction. This component of Step 5 is an inoculation of sorts, in that the therapist prepares the caregiver for the possible setbacks that may occur. Doing so will help caregivers find the strength to keep working toward change even when they reengage with their problematic pattern when feeling scared, frustrated, or hopeless or when they are met with resistance and anger.

CAREGIVER: (again in the "self" chair) Ashley, I will no doubt make mistakes. There will be times when I will want to back off, and when I do push, I won't always do it perfectly. But I promise that I will keep working with you to get through this. Even when I make mistakes or slip up, I will refocus my efforts on validating your pain and getting you out of bed and out of the house.

(The therapist invites the caregiver to switch to the "other" chair on their right.)

Step 6
The therapist invites the caregiver to take on the role of her loved one for a final time to share how it feels to hear their caregiver's intentions for support. It is important to invite the expression of an authentic response and allow for more than one emotional reaction if relevant. As in Step 4, if the caregiver-as-loved-one expresses anger, it is important that the therapist guides the expression of both the anger and the more vulnerable underlying emotions, including relief and gratitude if the caregiver-as-loved-one does not spontaneously do so.

CAREGIVER: (in the "other" chair, enacting her daughter) I feel so relieved. I am so scared; I really do need you to push me. I know I will make this hard, but thank you for fighting for me . . . with me. I love you so much. I am so grateful.

(The therapist invites the caregiver to switch a final time to the "self" chair on their left.)

Step 7

In this final step, the therapist engages the caregiver to debrief from the experience, highlighting insights gained and outlining possible plans for moving forward. If relevant (as in the scenario illustrated here), the therapist reviews with the caregiver the importance of using emotion-coaching skills when supporting behavior change, particularly if resistance is likely or the interventions are expected to lead to distress.

Expected Outcomes

The possible outcomes of this work are many. At minimum, caregiver block chair work facilitates in carers an increase in their awareness of their fear-based patterns. In fact, it is our experience that caregivers often express genuine surprise in response to what they learn via the chair work. In some cases, their newfound understanding of their internal process and their loved one's experience is sufficient to free them from the hold of the block. The caregiver block chair work also helps carers to engage with deep empathy for the loved one, increasing their understanding of their loved one's true needs (that they usually cannot verbalize), further mobilizing caregivers to engage in the tasks of recovery. With this intervention, caregivers can also benefit from an increase in their confidence and skill in working through their own painful emotions, as throughout they are met with the unconditional positive regard and support of the therapist. When caregivers increase their self-efficacy with respect to the processing of their own emotions, they are also better equipped to support their loved one in doing the same.

Further, whereas many negative emotions (e.g., fear, shame, resentment) narrow individuals' focus and flexibility by calling forth specific action tendencies (e.g., withdraw, attack), positive emotions broaden individuals' response repertoires, prompting them to consider a wider range of thoughts and actions. Broadened thought–action repertoires are also the building blocks of personal resources important to caregivers engaging in EFFT, such as resilience, optimism, and creativity (Fredrickson & Branigan, 2005). As such, when caregivers make explicit and deepen the love and compassion for and from their loved one, even if imaginally, they engage this process of psychological "broadening" and benefit from the many positive outcomes that result. Finally, and perhaps most importantly, the personal resources developed during these states of positive emotions are durable, and so even if the block is not fully resolved, caregivers will emerge better equipped to handle what comes as they support their loved one in their recovery.

At the deepest level, caregiver block chair work can lead to a total resolution of the caregiver block. This resolution occurs via a process of transforming withdrawal emotions such as fear and shame with the more adaptive and vital "approach" emotion of love. This mechanism of change is most notable in EFT where an important goal is to evoke maladaptive emotions (fear and shame) not for their good information and motivation, but to make them accessible for transformation (Greenberg, 2017). In time, the coactivation of the more adaptive emotional states (love) along with or in response to the maladaptive emotions facilitates their transformation. The caregiver block chair work intervention was developed to activate this process of change.

The possible outcomes described here can occur over a single session or across multiple sessions. Some carers will even benefit from several iterations of caregiver block chair work focused on the same pattern. With each repetition, expect that new insights and ideas will emerge and more adaptive neural networks will be reinforced, even if at the close of the session, caregivers still seem affected by their fears or present as confused or weary. It may take a few hours or days before they are able to integrate the shifts that occurred. In fact, many supervision clients have shared with us that they thought they'd failed to support a caregiver to process a block using the chair work intervention only to hear the next week that the caregiver had really benefited from the intervention and had engaged in new and positive behaviors to support a loved one.

ADDITIONAL CONSIDERATIONS

It is important to note that although carers can benefit greatly from a course of individual therapy, this work is focused on the resolution of the block to free caregivers from its hold and support them to support their loved one in more productive ways. This is not to discourage caregivers' own personal therapy or resolving of their own issues, which can only serve to benefit the family. However, it is our opinion that caregivers do not need to do so to play a significant role in their loved one's mental health. In fact, recall from Chapter 1 that one of the guiding principles of the work lies in the concept of the one-degree effect. This means that clinicians aim to facilitate a shift in caregivers that corresponds to single degree, knowing that this can be the beginning of an important change over time. Finally, one of the major strengths of the caregiver block module lies in the fact that most of the tools and techniques can be easily integrated within other treatment modalities, whether or not the family is the primary target of treatment. For example, they can be introduced in "family and friends" groups to shape the client's support system to create more favorable conditions for recovery.

SUMMARY

Supporting carers to understand, identify, and work through blocks is a critical component of the EFFT model. Doing so reconnects caregivers to the wisdom of their instincts, frees them from the shackles of fear, and increases the confidence and resolve to support their loved one to make the changes required for physical and emotional health. Although we presented a range of tools and techniques to do so, the list is not exhaustive. In fact, clinicians can think creatively about how else they can support caregivers in this way. For example, any technique that has the effect of regulating the caregiver's nervous system (with humor, movement, music, or the breath) is likely to prove fruitful. If clinicians do not attend to and process caregiver blocks, the caregiver will be gripped by the hold of the block and at increased risk of engaging in therapy-interfering behaviors (Stillar et al., 2016). Unfortunately, these are the behaviors that can lead clinicians to doubt the appropriateness of carer involvement or consider a treatment plan focused on increasing client autonomy from their family. Instead, the EFFT module on caregiver blocks encourages clinicians to conceptualize these therapy-interfering behaviors as emanating from powerful and maladaptive emotions that interfere with caregivers' healthy instinct and empowerment in the face of their loved one's struggles. By actively attending to and validating caregiver blocks, clinicians can facilitate caregivers' reconnection to their inner guidance system and relieve them from emotional pain as well. It can also facilitate a spontaneous rising of the self where the caregiver naturally feels more empowered to take on the tasks of recovery. For this reason, EFFT clinicians and therapists do not assess caregiver capacity for engagement at a single point in time. Rather, they continuously assess for the presence of blocks in need of transformation to uncover in caregivers their potential to become powerful and positive agents of change.

CLINICIAN'S CORNER

Before learning about EFFT and emotion blocks, I had worked with many parents, who despite being motivated to support their child, couldn't seem to carry out the goals we agreed on between sessions. Learning this module helped me better understand parents' fears and emotion blocks and provided me with specific tools to help parents' process these types of blocks, especially the chair work. Although this particular intervention initially brought up my own anxiety, my confidence using it in session has grown through practice and in supervision, where I take the role of my client (i.e., the parent) and my supervisor facilitates the intervention. I find that using the script in session is also helpful because I am not so focused on trying to remember each step, and instead I can stay with my clients and track their experience. In my practice, I've found that helping a parent work through a block using chair work usually brings about a sense of relief and renewed motivation for us both.

–Psychologist

6

WORKING THROUGH CLINICIAN BLOCKS

Clinician block work has completely transformed my practice. It makes me more accountable to myself and to my team, even to my clients. It also offers a light at the end of the tunnel for those of us working with clients and families with complex needs.

—Therapist

As discussed in Chapter 5, carers can experience emotion blocks when supporting their loved one in the recovery of a mental health issue (Lafrance Robinson et al., 2015; Strahan et al., 2017). In a similar fashion, clinicians may find their work with clients affected by their own emotional reactions, which can influence case conceptualization and clinical decisions (Brener, Rose, von Hippel, & Wilson, 2013; Kosmerly, Waller, & Lafrance Robinson, 2015; Lafrance Robinson & Kosmerly, 2015). When clinicians' unprocessed or maladaptive emotions fuel therapy-interfering attitudes or behaviors, this is considered in emotion-focused family therapy (EFFT) to be a clinician block (Lafrance Robinson et al., 2015). As with

http://dx.doi.org/10.1037/0000166-007
Emotion-Focused Family Therapy: A Transdiagnostic Model for Caregiver-Focused Interventions, by A. Lafrance, K. A. Henderson, and S. Mayman

caregivers, clinician blocks are normal and to be expected, regardless of age, years of experience, or extent of training (Greenberg, 2016). It is also essential that clinicians practicing EFFT understand that clinician blocks are not weaknesses, nor are they limitations. In fact, we believe that the capacity to recognize one's own clinician blocks, and the willingness to work through them, are notable strengths. Finally, it is important to note that, as with caregiver blocks, within each identified clinician block, there are pearls of wisdom as well.

Within this module, we encourage clinicians to use EFFT strategies to work with their feelings in response to clinical situations to disentangle their maladaptive or unprocessed emotions from their clinical intuition. They can then use the wisdom within the block to inform how they will be guided by principles of EFFT in treatment delivery. For instance, a clinician may hesitate to engage a father with an abuse history in his son's treatment for fear of causing the client too much distress. Once the clinician's fears are processed, she may realize that although it might not be wise to work with the parent and child in the same room, it could be possible to support the dyad using principles and techniques of EFFT in the context of separate sessions. Identifying and processing clinician blocks helps clinicians to free themselves from fear, regain access to their clinical intuition, and benefit from increased flexibility in the application of the model or in their work more generally.

TOOLS AND TECHNIQUES FOR CLINICIAN BLOCKS

Several markers help clinicians recognize the presence of a potential block, including when (a) they resist carer involvement; (b) treatment progress slows or is stuck; (c) they experience frustration, hopelessness, or exhaustion when working with a client or caregiver; (d) they feel particularly attached to or protective of a client or carer; or (e) they become aware of therapeutic drift (Waller & Turner, 2016)—in other words, they are deviating from standard protocols or avoiding the use of certain clinical interventions (e.g., caregiver block chair work). Once identified, the EFFT model offers a variety of tools to identify and address these common experiences to support the effective delivery of treatment. The process of helping clinicians to identify, understand, and work through clinician blocks can occur via psychoeducation, self-assessment tools, clinician block chair work, and EFFT supervision (with a peer or with a direct supervisor). Similar to the guidance offered in Chapter 5, this volume, we encourage clinicians new to this module to begin by exploring the utility of targeted psychoeducation, self-assessment tools, and peer or directed supervision before exploring the use of the more advanced method of targeting clinician blocks using chair work.

Psychoeducation

According to Rasic (2010), "interactions with children, adolescents, and their families can bring up particularly complex and confusing feelings, which, if unrecognized, can significantly influence clinical judgment and clinician behavior in unpredictable and potentially counter-therapeutic ways" (p. 249). This is especially relevant for clinicians working in the context of high-stakes or treatment-resistant clinical scenarios. In these settings, EFFT clinicians are introduced immediately to the concept of clinician blocks. Like caregivers, they are taught that most, if not all, problematic patterns of relating to clients are fueled by unprocessed or maladaptive emotions, including fear, shame, hopelessness, helplessness, or resentment. EFFT clinicians are also taught to identify the behavioral manifestations of such emotion blocks in themselves and their colleagues. In some cases, we have observed that simply using psychoeducation to bring the impact of blocks into the clinicians' awareness can free them to reconnect with their intuition and resume productive implementation of the treatment model.

Self-Assessment Tools

Self-assessment tools provide a structured method for identifying and processing clinician blocks with a focus on emotional and caregiving styles; emotional reactions to clients and clinical scenarios; and blocks specific to carer involvement. When initiating their own self-reflective processes, it is helpful for clinicians to consider their emotional and caregiving response styles in response to clients and their caregivers. As we do with caregivers, we encourage clinicians to refer to the New Maudsley's animal metaphors presented in Chapter 5 to increase awareness of default modes in times of stress (Treasure, Smith, & Crane, 2007). Clinicians are also encouraged to consider whether their typical response styles are exaggerated in response to others (Treasure, Crane, McKnight, Buchanan, & Wolfe, 2011). For example, when discussing treatment planning for a long-term residential patient, a frustrated team member may take on a rhinoceros stance, fueled by a belief that discharge is the only way to engender the motivation required for recovery. In response, a worried team member, may react with an exaggerated kangaroo caregiving style, and advocate more strongly for increased treatment intensity and duration. These conflicting positions among team members have the potential to further reinforce and polarize each stance, driving potential discord within the team. When clinicians use the language of the animal metaphors in the context of regular team supervision, they are afforded opportunities to identify such patterns and determine whether and how they are influencing decision making and treatment delivery.

In addition to the use of animal metaphors, there are two self-report measures designed to facilitate the identification and processing of clinician blocks. They are the Clinician Traps Scale and the Self-Directed Block Worksheet for Clinicians (these clinician tools can be found in Appendices K and L). The Clinician Traps Scale is a brief 12-item measure on a Likert scale ranging from 1 (*not likely*) to 7 (*extremely likely*). Clinicians rate the extent to which they are likely to feel concerned about scenarios that relate to the client, the caregiver, or the family unit, with sample items including "Being disliked by caregivers/client," "Causing suffering to the caregivers/client," and "Being blamed or being to blame for lack of treatment progress." This tool can increase clinicians' awareness of their tendencies in their overall practice and in specific contexts. It can be used in personal self-reflection, in peer supervision, or with a direct supervisor, with relatively high scores on the measure guiding the focus of the session. We also encourage its use among groups of clinicians or on teams to normalize the process and increase comfort with identifying one's own vulnerabilities.

The Self-Directed Block Worksheet for Clinicians is a self-guided tool designed to support clinicians to process blocks related to carer involvement specifically. In other words, should they doubt the appropriateness of caregiver involvement or feel hopeless about a caregiver's capacity to support the loved one in some way, clinicians can use this tool to work through the block on their own. To begin this process, the first item invites the clinician to identify traits or behaviors in the caregiver that would suggest the individual is incapable of participating in treatment in a meaningful way. The next items support the clinician to identify the potential negative outcomes that could occur with involvement from this caregiver. Clinicians are then guided to broaden their awareness of the emotional processes underlying real and potential problematic caregiver attitudes and behaviors, as well as the impact of their own anticipatory anxiety and avoidance behaviors. The final items guide the clinician to connect with the possible needs of the client regarding caregiver involvement in the loved one's treatment. Like the Clinician Traps Scale, this self-directed worksheet can be used by an individual clinician or in the context of peer and supervisor-led consultations. These three self-reflective assessment tools offer a structure to support EFFT clinicians in their ongoing identification and processing of clinician blocks that will occur throughout their careers as helping professionals.

Clinician Block Chair Work

A powerful method to process clinician blocks involves the specifically constructed clinician block chair work interventions. These techniques allow for the exploration, acceptance, and transformation of blocks by targeting the maladaptive fears, shame, hopelessness, helplessness, and resentment underlying problematic attitudes and behaviors in clinicians. The intervention also supports clinicians to embody their client and carer's experiences and more deeply appreciate the potential outcomes of their therapeutic actions, leading to more thoughtful clinical decisions. Clinician block chair work interventions can be used in peer or hierarchical supervision, dyads, or groups. In fact, it is our experience that clinician block chair work is most powerful when enacted in small group settings because there is great potential for powerful vicarious processing, especially if in the context of a day treatment, inpatient, or residential treatment team working together to support the same clients and their families.

There are many possible markers for clinician block chair work, including blocks that clinicians may experience relating to caregiver involvement or a lack of hope, feelings of incompetence, or resistance related to the implementation of specific treatment tasks (in EFFT or another treatment modality). In all cases, the intervention involves a facilitating therapist who directs the intervention—herein referred to as the facilitator—and the experiencing clinician for whom the intervention is enacted—herein referred to as the clinician. Similar to caregiver block chair work, the elements of this intervention have been carefully designed to support optimal processing of blocks. We strongly advise therapists who use this technique to follow the steps as outlined to increase the likelihood of a positive outcome, as well as to ensure the technique remains appropriate for use in professional contexts. For example, enthusiastic therapists may wish to support the clinician to create a bridge of awareness between their block and early childhood experiences. While doing so could be helpful in a more therapeutic environment, it would require informed consent *and* may not be appropriate in a work setting. The use of clinician block chair work is illustrated with a block relating to caregiver involvement because it is perhaps the most relevant for clinicians new to this model, particularly for those working with older adolescent and adult clients (see Appendix M for facilitator's guide).

Clinician Block Chair Work for Caregiver Involvement

Step 1

When initiating chair work related to resistance to carer involvement, the facilitator supports the clinician to determine whether their block relates to (a) a desire to exclude a caregiver from treatment or (b) feeling hopeless about an involved caregiver's ability to be helpful in treatment. Once clarified, the facilitator therapist positions two chairs facing one another (the "self" and the "other" chair) and invites the clinician to sit in the "other" chair on the right side of the facilitator. Throughout the process, the facilitator is guided by the carefully developed script to ensure intervention adherence.

FACILITATOR: Sarah Jane, I understand you would like support to work through a potential clinical block related to the husband of your client. Is your block related to his involvement in the therapy, or are you feeling rather hopeless about his role in his partner's treatment more generally?

CLINICIAN: Definitely the first one. I am really hesitant to see whether he'd even be open to participating in his wife's treatment. I've heard from my client that he is very critical. I suspect he also meets criteria for narcissistic personality disorder.

(The facilitator sets up the chairs and invites the clinician to move to the "other" chair on her right.)

Step 2

The facilitator then invites the clinician to picture herself in the opposite chair and enact the part of herself that wishes to exclude the husband from treatment. The facilitator supports the clinician to identify the ways in which the husband's involvement could lead to negative outcomes for both the client and the clinician, with a focus on low self-efficacy with emotion.

CLINICIAN: (in the "other" chair, enacting the part of herself that scares her) Sarah Jane, do not invite Hien's husband to join the treatment. He is too critical, and Hien won't be able to handle it. She is too vulnerable—it could make her feel worse. She could even relapse. If that were to happen, you would feel awful. You just wouldn't be able to live with yourself. Besides, you know that narcissism is a major trigger for you [low self-efficacy with emotion—clinician]. Don't even bring up the possibility for his involvement.

(The facilitator invites the clinician to switch to the "self" chair on her left.)

Step 3

In our example, the clinician is now invited to imagine her client in the chair facing her. The facilitator offers a summary of the content from Step 2 for the clinician to share with the client, focusing on (a) the clinician's perspective regarding the carer's involvement, (b) the rationale to protect the client from pain, and (c) the rationale to protect herself from discomfort. Then, the facilitator invites the clinician to tell the imagined client in the other chair that she will act as their surrogate caregiver ("I will be a better caregiver/partner to you"). Although this statement rarely mirrors the clinician's true belief, it serves to facilitate a broadening in perspective for the clinician and evokes an emotional reaction in preparation for the next step.

CLINICIAN: (in the "self" chair) Hien, I'm really sorry, but I don't want to invite your husband to join your treatment. He is too critical and narcissistic. I'm worried you won't be able to handle his harshness and that you might end up relapsing and falling back. If that happened, I would feel awful, and I would never live it down. So I'm just going to pretend like it's not even an option. Besides, as your therapist, I can be a better partner to you in all of this.

(The facilitator invites the clinician to switch to the "other" chair on her right.)

Step 4

The facilitator invites the clinician to imagine herself sitting in the opposite chair, to embody her client and to respond to what was shared from that perspective. If the client expresses resignation, anger, relief, or agreement, the facilitator allows the clinician-as-client to express these reactions and then gently guides her to speak the vulnerable feelings that are beneath the surface. Then, the facilitator supports the clinician-as-client to offer validation in response to the clinician's fear as a form of self-compassion.

CLINICIAN: (in the "other" chair, enacting her client) It's okay, Sarah Jane! We're actually on the same page! I don't want him involved either. He can be a real jerk, and that's no good for me when I'm in this state [relief/agreement].

FACILITATOR: (speaking to the clinician-as-client) Okay, Hien, can you share with Sarah Jane the downside of the relief? From that place

CLINICIAN: (again in the "other" chair, enacting her client) Sarah Jane, even though I share with you how hard things are with Alex, I really do love him, and I need his support. I don't blame you for not wanting to invite him into the treatment. He can be tough, and I've certainly primed you for the worst. But I need you to believe in him and your ability to connect with him. I know he feels really helpless, and you can help him to be the husband that I know deep down he wants to be. Besides, I don't want to leave him, so if you can help us, even just a bit, it will make a real difference.

Next the facilitator encourages the clinician-as-client to communicate the needs they have with respect to the issue of caregiver involvement. The clinician-as-client then expresses to the imagined clinician the reasons why they long for the clinician to be the one to support them in these ways, with a focus on the positive qualities of the clinician and the strength of the therapeutic bond.

CLINICIAN: (again in the "other" chair, enacting her client) If you bring up the possibility of bringing him into treatment, I am going to fight it. I will. But the truth is, I really do believe that his involvement could help me, and so please don't give up. I'm so afraid that I will never feel better and that my marriage will disintegrate. It's important to me that you are the one to help me with this because I really trust you and I know that you really care about me. And you're really good at what you do.

(The facilitator invites the clinician to switch to the "self" chair on her left.)

Step 5
At this stage, clinicians are invited to share what it was like to embody their client's experience and respond from that perspective. Clinicians will often express a sense of surprise or even regret for having overlooked the deeper processes likely at play. Paradoxically, they may also experience a sense empowerment and resolve vis-à-vis their role in facilitating the caregiver's involvement as a therapy ally. Facilitators then guide clinicians to imagine the client in the other chair for a final time, supporting them to share an abridged version of their reaction to the client, followed by the communication of respect and compassion. Facilitators then encourage clinicians to clearly express to the client what they will do differently to

support the client in his or her treatment. It is important that in doing so, clinicians use the pronoun *I* and not *we* (to refer to the treatment team or even the clinician and client) because the use of *we* will diffuse the sense of empowerment and responsibility.

CLINICIAN: (in the "self" chair) Hien, I am realizing I should have encouraged your husband's involvement in some way from the very beginning. Of course, it makes sense to try to recruit him, and in a way that works for you both. I do care about you and have deep respect for you. Next session, I am going to broach the topic and present to you a plan where we can transition from an individual model to a family-based model with individual sessions in between. And I'm going to validate your concerns—as deeply as necessary—as well as provide you with the reassurance that I will treat him with total respect and kindness, even when he shows his prickles. I will also brainstorm with you a plan to manage any challenges that may arise, in particular, if he does become critical or harsh in our dyad sessions. We're in this together, however it goes.

Finally, the facilitator supports the clinician to caution the imagined client that her efforts may be imperfect at times, but that they won't stop trying to find the best path forward in engaging the caregiver. This component of Step 5 is an inoculation of sorts in that clinicians prepare themselves for the possible challenges that lie ahead. It also provides them with the strength to keep working toward positive caregiver involvement even if at times they feel frustrated or hopeless.

CLINICIAN: (again in the self-chair) But Hien, I have to warn you that I am human and my emotions may be evoked at times. It's pretty certain that I will make some mistakes, but I will not let my emotional reactions to your husband stop me from trying to support you in this way.

(The facilitator invites the clinician to switch to the "other" chair on her right.)

Step 6
The facilitator guides the clinician-as-client to share with the imagined clinician in the opposite chair how it feels to hear what was shared. It is important to support the expression of an authentic response and to allow for the possibility of more than one emotional reaction. As in Step 4, if the clinician-as-client expresses anger, it is important that the facilitator guides

him or her to express both the surface reaction as well as the more vulnerable underlying emotions.

CLINICIAN: (in the "other" chair, enacting the client) I'm still really scared, but I am also relieved. I feel some hope, too. I feel like it will give me my best shot for recovery. And it might also strengthen my marriage. Thank you. I really appreciate you. No matter how it goes, I know I can get through this with your support.

(The facilitator invites the clinician to switch to the "self" chair on her left.)

Step 7

In this final step, the facilitator engages the clinician to share how it feels to hear this relief and gratitude from the imagined client. The facilitator and clinician can then review the insights gained as well as any possible plans for moving forward.

Like with the caregiver block chair work, when the behavioral manifestation of the clinician's block and the unintended messages of the clinician's actions are conveyed imaginally to the client in the chair work, it leads to a broadening in perspective for the clinician. Further, by externalizing the fear fueling the block and evoking in the clinician the compassion and respect they feel for and from their clients, a process of transforming emotion (fear) with emotion (compassion) is facilitated. In other words, clinician block chair work supports clinicians by accessing their adaptive emotions and cognitions that were overshadowed by the emotion blocks fueled by their secondary or maladaptive fear. This work also helps clinicians to disentangle their own emotions and needs from those of their clients, allowing them to refocus their attention on what is necessary to support the family to move forward in treatment together.

Supervision

Each of the aforementioned tools and techniques can be integrated within existing supervision models. In addition, we strongly recommend the use of video-based supervision of actual sessions. Memory for clinical content has limitations, especially for the nuances of interest in the context of EFFT. For this reason, supervision that depends primarily on the reporting of session events can be limited, both by the clinician's ability to accurately recount the details of the sessions and the inability of the clinician and supervisor to review and analyze microprocesses in client and clinician interactions (Haggerty & Hilsenroth, 2011). For these reasons, various emotion-focused treatments, including EFFT, are taught, researched, and supervised through the use of video recording and review (Abbass, 2004; Greenberg, 2015). Video supervision can occur in the context of self-, peer-, or supervisor-led consultations in which clinicians and therapists review segments of their EFFT sessions to develop awareness of their strengths and weaknesses in general and with respect to the technical delivery of interventions. Video supervision can also aid in the identification of clinician blocks that could benefit from processing. With advances in technology, clinicians can even use web-conferencing applications for distance supervision (Abbass et al., 2011), complementing local peer-to-peer learning methods and allowing for those within the EFFT community to support one another from around the world.

Supervision Mind-Set and Setting

The various tools and interventions presented do require some degree of cognitive and emotional flexibility, and their use can be optimized by attending to the clinician's mind-set in terms of openness, expectations, and intention as well as their professional setting (Eisner, 1997). Not surprisingly, these self-reflective practices will be most effective when clinicians are feeling calm and curious about their internal processes; compassionate toward their client and caregivers; and are in a supportive clinical milieu of nonjudgment where blocks are recognized as a normal experience in the context of treatment delivery. It is critical for those integrating this module into their practice to cultivate an empathic supportive environment, regardless of the peer or hierarchical nature of the supervisory or team relationships. Further, when engaging with the clinician block chair work specifically, even though the intervention is designed in such a way that it does not cross over into the psychotherapeutic domain, it is possible that the experiencing clinician accesses deeper material than what was expected. For this reason, we also encourage facilitating therapists to initiate a process of informed consent, including professional limits to confidentiality, before commencing the exercise.

THERAPEUTIC APOLOGIES FROM CLINICIAN TO CLIENT OR CAREGIVER

Following the processing of a clinician block, it may be helpful or necessary for clinicians to engage in a process of relationship repair with a client or carer using the structured therapeutic apology discussed in Chapter 4 and

Appendix D. The therapeutic apology from clinician to client or carer can be extremely powerful. For example, clinicians who become aware that they've been avoiding a certain topic of discussion with a carer may find it therapeutically worthwhile to acknowledge having done so with an apology:

> Ali, I have been thinking about our sessions together, and I've realized that, at times, I've been a bit of a kangaroo with you. I haven't been broaching topics that I think could be helpful to your family's healing for fear of upsetting you or pushing you too hard. I realize that, in doing so, I may have been denying you opportunities for deeper healing. I want you to know that I am really sorry. Starting today, rather than making assumptions, I am going to check in with you to see how you are doing and what you feel you can handle from week to week. No doubt, I may slip up from time to time, especially when I sense you are feeling tired or overburdened, but I am committed to resisting the urge to protect you from pain, and I will challenge myself to bring it to you for discussion so that together we can identify the best path forward in our work.

This intervention can repair potential therapeutic ruptures (Elliott et al., 2004; Safran & Muran, 2003), lift client and caregiver shame and self-blame, and model the power of the apology as a healing tool. Clinicians and caregivers who have delivered this type of apology with clients and caregivers have also shared with us the extent to which they felt relief in doing so. They also reported a strengthening of the caregiver alliance in the service of working toward the agreed-on therapy objectives.

SELF-CARE AND PERSONAL THERAPY

It is important to note that clinician blocks can be influenced by events in clinicians' lives, including their emotional state, as well as their own unfinished business with primary caregivers. In other words, clinicians are human too. A strong practice of self-care is extremely important to mitigate the impact of these influences on their professional work (Greenberg, 2016). In addition to physical activity, good sleep hygiene, and the cultivation of mindfulness and other spiritual practices, EFFT clinicians may also derive great benefit from engaging in their own personal therapy. The benefits are many, including tending to their own inner world, increasing awareness of potential blocks, and preventing or addressing compassion fatigue and burnout (Greenberg & Staller, 1981; Macran & Shapiro, 1998; Phillips, 2011; Probst, 2015). Doing so may also support clinicians to untangle their inner world from their clients' struggles, including their stories of trauma. In fact, for these reasons, certified EFFT practitioners make a commitment to engage in supervision or personal psychotherapy (or both) throughout their career.

BENEFITS OF EFFT SUPERVISION AND REFLECTIVE PRACTICES

In our experience training health care professionals across the globe, we've found that the supervision approach to clinician blocks can lead to positive outcomes for all involved (Kosmerly, Penney, Renelli, Miller, & Lafrance, 2018). In a recent study exploring the perceived outcomes of EFFT supervision using the framework described in this chapter, participants noted that this practice contributed to a variety of positive outcomes in their professional and personal lives. In particular, clinicians reported feeling comfortable to process their own blocks, which led to increased skill in supporting caregivers to navigate difficult emotions. Clinicians also learned to reframe "negative" caregiver behaviors in terms of emotion blocks, allowing them to develop more compassion for caregivers as well. The practices also led to enthusiasm for working with what would typically be considered "difficult" or "resistant" families, including carers who are reluctant to engage in treatment, who may criticize or express anger toward clinicians, and who sometimes struggle to follow through with treatment recommendations (Kosmerly et al., 2018). Clinicians reported that they personally experienced higher levels of job satisfaction, decreased feelings of burnout, increased attention to self-care, and greater responsivity to the emotional experiences of their own loved ones (Kosmerly et al., 2018). We have certainly observed and experienced the same in the context of our own practices supervising both novice and senior EFFT practitioners and participating in our own personal therapy, peer supervisions, and self-reflective practices.

SUMMARY

Although supervision has been an integral part of clinical practice within many schools of family therapy, we believe that the clinician blocks module of EFFT offers structured, time-effective, and engaging new ways to support clinicians working with clients across the lifespan and across diagnostic categories. The processing of clinician blocks is an important component of the practice of EFFT across a clinician's career, regardless of level of experience and expertise. As with caregiver blocks, working through a block once does not mean that it won't resurface and require further processing. In fact, some clinicians may need to work through the same block many times over, sometimes within the same context. Although using techniques to process emotion blocks requires commitment and effort on the part of clinician and supervisor or facilitator, the rewards are numerous. Clinicians working within EFFT are able to be less self-critical of their own work, experience less helplessness in the face of clinical challenges, and access a broader range of solutions for their clients. They also benefit from psychological growth that can enrich their personal lives as well. In fact, a major strength of this module of EFFT lies in the fact that clinician block techniques can be integrated within a broad range of treatment modalities, whether or not they are emotion focused or family based.

CLINICIAN'S CORNER

I will never forget the moment I shared with a colleague: "I am a fraud." I had been working with clients and their parents, and teaching professionals for a decade to do the same, grounded in the perspective that caregivers need to be empowered as "agents of change." Yet, in some cases, I was quietly standing in judgment and disbelief of their capability to effectively engage in their loved one's recovery process. I hadn't even considered the concept of the "one degree." I had uttered the phrases "this mom can't do it" and "this family is too dysfunctional" more often than I would like to admit. I was blocked in believing in the capability of some parents. I was blocked about my own capability to support them to support their child, and I hid those blocks beneath conceptualizations and labels. Clinician block chair work nudged me into the muck of the shame and helplessness I felt when faced with those tough clinical situations. I am now more aware of—and at times freed from—those blocks. It has fundamentally changed me as a clinician and as a supervisor. In fact, I have also been humbled supporting other clinicians to move from "avoidant to empowered" within a 40-minute supervision using the chair work technique. The strength that comes from their vulnerability launches them forward and empowers me to remain vulnerable as well.

—Psychologist and clinical supervisor

7 EMOTION-FOCUSED FAMILY THERAPY FOR EATING DISORDERS

Managing family life can be difficult enough without the added stress of supporting a child with an eating disorder. Developing the ability to notice and respond appropriately to emotions—hers and my own—has diffused many stressful situations at the dinner table. It's truly making the difference in her recovery.

—Caregiver

Eating disorders (EDs) are debilitating illnesses that are associated with the highest mortality rate of all mental disorders (Arcelus, Mitchell, Wales, & Nielsen, 2011). In the *Diagnostic and Statistical Manual of Mental Disorders* (5th ed.; American Psychiatric Association, 2013) and the International Classification of Diseases (World Health Organization, 2018), a number of feeding and EDs are listed, including anorexia nervosa (AN), bulimia nervosa (BN), and binge eating disorder (BED). These disorders are characterized by problematic patterns of food intake, low self-esteem and poor or distorted body image (American Psychiatric Association, 2013). EDs are also

http://dx.doi.org/10.1037/0000166-008
Emotion-Focused Family Therapy: A Transdiagnostic Model for Caregiver-Focused Interventions, by A. Lafrance, K. A. Henderson, and S. Mayman

highly comorbid with mood and anxiety disorders, as well as substance misuse (Hudson, Hiripi, Pope, & Kessler, 2007). The lifetime prevalence of EDs is 0.9% for AN; 1.5% BN; and 2.8% for BED in women and 0.3%, 0.5%, and 0.2%, respectively, in men (Hudson, Hiripi, Pope, & Kessler, 2007).

EDs are known to affect every system of the body (Katzman & Findlay, 2011; Mehler, 2018), and the course of the illness can negatively impact one's emotional, cognitive, and social development (Klump, Bulik, Kaye, Treasure, & Tyson, 2009). Although various interventions have been used to treat adolescent and adult EDs with varied levels of success, many individuals affected do not respond to existing therapies, and relapse rates are high (Halmi, 2009, 2013; Hay, Touyz, & Sud, 2012; Zipfel et al., 2014). For these reasons, novel treatment and adaptations to existing treatments are required (Halmi, 2013). As mentioned in the Introduction to this book, emotion-focused family therapy (EFFT) was developed in response to this need, first as an adjunct to family-based treatment for children and adolescents with EDs (Lafrance Robinson, Dolhanty, & Greenberg, 2015) and later as a stand-alone treatment for EDs across the lifespan (Stillar et al., 2016). As such, the application of EFFT is far more nuanced in this treatment context, and therefore, we dedicate this chapter to highlighting its use in EDs. In addition, readers are encouraged to view the following as a detailed and integrated example of the application of EFFT. The lessons we've learned by treating individuals with eating disorders, such as the importance of caregiver involvement, the role of emotion processing in the development and maintenance of mental illness, and the way in which illness severity can increase the likelihood of emotional blocks, are easily applicable across other mental health disorders. It is what EDs have in common with other mental health disorders, rather than the differences that exist between them, that has allowed for such a rapid expansion of EFFT transdiagnostically.

HISTORY OF FAMILY INVOLVEMENT IN EDS

Historically, family factors have been regarded as causal in the development of EDs. For instance, family enmeshment, an emotional style characterized by a lack of personal and emotional boundaries, was often cited as a problem within families of affected individuals (Haworth-Hoeppner, 2000; Minuchin, 1970). In line with this conceptualization of illness, parental blame was a common practice among professionals and treatment frequently involved increasing ED patients' individuation from their families. At its extreme, parents were excluded from treatment or separated from their child for extended periods of time (Munn, Smeltzer, Smeltzer, & Westin, 2010). These practices came to be referred to as *parentectomies* (Harper, 1983). Now various lines of research have confirmed that EDs can develop in a wide range of family contexts and that there is no specific family style that predicts their development (Le Grange, Lock, Loeb, & Nicholls, 2010). In fact, some of the problematic patterns of behavior observed within families of an affected child are now understood as reactions to the presence of a life-threatening and often chronic illness (Whitney & Eisler, 2009).

ED treatment that excludes families (parents, spouses, other caregivers) does not reflect the reality of the lives of many of those suffering. Many individuals with EDs are tightly connected to, and often dependent on, their families. Children, adolescents, and adults with chronic EDs are often delayed in their social or emotional development (or both), which results in needs that differ from their peers. Finally, ED families experience considerable strain as a result of their loved one's illness and can benefit from support to disentangle themselves from the effects of the ED. Families also provide an opportunity to extend treatment efforts beyond the office to effect lasting behavioral and emotional change. As such, in contrast to previous practices, and with the support of parent advocate groups such as F.E.A.S.T (Families Empowered and Supporting Treatment of Eating Disorders), contemporary approaches to ED treatment have evolved to include families as active supports in the recovery process. Recent research outcomes have demonstrated the benefits of carer involvement, including improved outcomes for both those with an ED and their family members (Couturier, Kimber, & Szatmari, 2013; Goddard, Macdonald, & Treasure, 2011; Lafrance Robinson, Dolhanty, Stillar, Henderson, & Mayman, 2016). The most well-known of these family-oriented treatment protocols include family-based treatment (Lock & Le Grange, 2015), the New Maudsley method (Treasure, Schmidt, & Macdonald, 2010), and EFFT for EDs (Lafrance Robinson et al., 2016).

FAMILY INVOLVEMENT IN ED TREATMENT

Family-based treatment (Lock & Le Grange, 2015) is the most widely accepted outpatient family therapy for child and adolescent EDs. It has the most research evidence and has been adapted to more intensive levels of care (e.g., day treatment; Girz, Robinson, Foroughe, Jasper, & Boachie, 2013) and extended beyond childhood and adolescence to support transition age youth (Dimitropoulos et al., 2015, 2018). In its standard form, family-based treatment is a manualized treatment that involves three phases of treatment. Throughout each phase, clinicians and caregivers work together as a multidisciplinary team (Lock & Le Grange, 2015; Lock, Le Grange, Agras, & Dare, 2000). In the first phase of treatment, clinicians focus on empowering carers to take action against their child's ED through a focus on renourishment and symptom interruption in the home setting (Lock et al., 2000). Following steady weight gain and symptom management, clinicians support caregivers to work toward returning control over eating to their child in a developmentally appropriate manner, while maintaining a focus on their physical health. It is also in this second phase that previously set-aside adolescent issues (e.g., puberty, peers, sexuality) thought to influence symptoms are reintroduced into the therapy. Finally, in the third phase of treatment, the team reviews central issues of adolescence, including the development of age-appropriate autonomy, the development of appropriate parental boundaries, and the need for the parents to refocus their caregiving roles in response to their child's evolving needs.

Although the involvement of caregivers in the treatment of children and adolescents has become standard practice, adult interventions are most often individually focused. The New Maudsley method is a noteworthy exception in that carers are systematically recruited as partners in care across the lifespan (Treasure, Schmidt, & Macdonald, 2010). Rooted in part in the cognitive interpersonal maintenance model (Goddard, Macdonald, Sepulveda, et al., 2011; Schmidt & Treasure, 2006; Treasure & Schmidt, 2013), the New Maudsley method uses psychoeducation to support caregivers to identify and transform potential maintenance patterns or traits. Carers are also taught *collaborative care skills*, including the principles and techniques of motivational interviewing, to support change in their loved one. The New Maudsley method also takes into consideration the developmental stage of the affected individual to determine the specifics of carer involvement.

EFFT FOR EDS

It is in part thanks to the developers of family-based treatment and the New Maudsley method that caregivers are now being recruited as treatment allies, closing the book on parentectomies. These treatment models brought essential and novel approaches to the treatment of EDs and were quickly integrated into clinical programs around the world. EFFT was designed to build on the strengths of these approaches and introduce additional components that could benefit sufferers, caregivers, and clinicians. For example, the spirit of Phase 1 of family-based treatment is integrated within the behavior-coaching module in that caregivers are empowered to support the normalization of eating patterns and interrupt ED symptoms. The animal metaphors from the New Maudsley method are incorporated to assist caregivers in the identification of problematic patterns of responses to their loved one's symptoms. Throughout treatment, caregivers are also provided with skills training, and the role of emotion is brought to the forefront with a focus on emotion coaching, therapeutic apologies, and the processing of caregiver and clinician emotion blocks. We believe that EFFT's emphasis on core emotional and relational processes and its transdiagnostic application across the lifespan represent important contributions to the developing field of ED treatment. We urge readers to note, however, that, similar to other models of ED treatment, the EFFT clinician or therapist is not meant to act as a sole treatment provider but rather a member of a multidisciplinary team that, at minimum, includes a medical professional and other allied health and mental practitioners such as a psychiatrist, dietitian, occupational therapist, and others, if relevant.

Caregiver Psychoeducation and Empowerment

Before introducing the modules of EFFT, carers are first provided with psychoeducation on a number of ED-related topics including their causes (e.g., an interplay of risks and stressors, including genetics, temperamental factors, patterns of emotional avoidance, life stressors, sociocultural factors), functions (coping, emotional avoidance), and consequences (physical, psychological, social). Although a full discussion of the psychoeducational content is beyond the scope of this chapter, caregivers should come away with the understanding that although EDs are seemingly about food, weight, and shape, they are complex disorders that serve many functions, one of which is to regulate stress and distress. Our clients with EDs frequently describe the manner in which their symptoms serve to mask and numb their feelings. When they resist the temptation to engage in symptoms, many report experiencing a surge of overwhelming emotion. We therefore encourage caregivers to conceptualize EDs as emotion management disorders, where starving numbs, bingeing soothes, and purging provides relief (Dolhanty & Greenberg, 2007).

We also liken symptoms to *emotion converters*. Whether consciously or not, individuals with EDs convert the experience of emotions such as fear, anger, sadness, and shame to "feeling fat" or to urges to binge, purge, or overexercise. It is as though the narrow focus on weight, shape, and food converts painful emotions into a bodily experience that sufferers can then manage with symptoms. It is for these reasons that we are firm in our belief that ED recovery should involve equal emphasis on symptom management and support to build capacity in the processing of emotions. As such, caregivers are empowered to take on an active role in their loved one's recovery by increasing their involvement in behavior coaching and emotion coaching, including a therapeutic apology if warranted. Given that each of these modules are explained in detail in previous chapters, special considerations related to the application of these modules in the context of EDs are highlighted, along with clinical illustrations.

Behavior Coaching

The value of behavior coaching in EDs cannot be overemphasized. A basic underlying principle of this module, and one that is borrowed from family-based treatment (Lock & Le Grange, 2015), is that for an individual struggling with an ED, food is medicine. Nutrition is essential to prevent, reduce, or reverse medical complications and to support normal cognitive and emotional functioning. If necessary, carers are informed that ED symptoms can be difficult to give up and can prove fatal over time (Reijonen, Pratt, Patel, & Greydanus, 2003; Von Holle et al., 2008) to help mobilize them to regard food as medicine.[1] The behavior-coaching module of EFFT thus involves equipping caregivers with practical meal-support strategies, as well as specific tools to support the interruption of behaviors such as purging, bingeing, and compulsive exercising. Caregivers engage in this "training" in individual or group settings, as if they were clinical staff newly hired in an ED program. The material is delivered using the same methods and techniques used to train hospital staff around the world.

Meal Support
Meal support refers to the act of offering structure, encouragement, and reassurance to an individual completing a snack or meal. It is an incredibly valuable intervention during the renourishment phase of treatment, especially if the affected individual's fear of weight gain is intense, and the temptation to restrict or engage in symptoms is strong. In many cases, meal

---

[1] It is important to inform caregivers of loved ones who have eaten very little over a long period of time that there could be a risk of developing *refeeding syndrome,* a potentially fatal condition in medically compromised individuals. If increases in nutrition occur too rapidly, electrolyte levels such as phosphorous, magnesium, and calcium can drop and cause cardiac, respiratory, or circulatory system failures (Boachie & Jasper, 2011). Thus, it is critical that increases occur slowly and incrementally and with the support of a physician in a position to monitor medical stability and needs.

support can also alleviate the guilt that individuals working toward recovery often experience in response to their harsh inner critic or ED voice. In other words, the involvement of others can serve as a distraction from their critic or allow the individual with ED to eat because they "have to." In its most structured form, carers are involved in preparing and serving meals, including making decisions about the amount and variety of food consumed. That being said, this degree of structure may not be possible for all caregivers or appropriate for all individuals with EDs. As such, in EFFT, the specifics of meal support are developed according to the loved one's chronological and developmental age, stage of illness, and individual circumstances, as well as the needs of the individual's caregivers. For example, caregivers of children or adolescents will be supported to take responsibility for supervision and support during all meals, while caregivers of adults who live away may visit for extended periods of time to offer support or provide meal support via video calls. Regardless of the approach, clinicians should work collaboratively with the family to find ways to help make meals go as smoothly as possible, encouraging them to draw on their caregiving instincts to inform implementation. Following is an example of such an exchange between a clinician and carer:

CLINICIAN: So, you're telling me that you're struggling right now with getting your daughter to complete her meals. What do you think you could change in your approach to help her to eat more?

CARER: Well the eating is so slow, and she seems to take forever. It's like she's not even there during the meal. She's so shut down, and I can tell she's in pain.

CLINICIAN: Of course, it would be hard to push when you see her hurting. I'm wondering if there is anything you could do make the meals a bit easier on her without reducing the amount of food she's expected to eat?

CARER: Maybe if she had some distraction . . .

CLINICIAN: Distraction can be a great way to reduce distress during meals. Any ideas about what might work best for your daughter?

CARER: She used to love documentaries. We used to watch them together all the time. Maybe we can watch TV during meals for a while, to get her mind off the pain.

CLINICIAN: That's a great idea. Anything else that you think might be helpful?

CARER: I don't know . . . I guess I keep thinking back to when she was little and felt sick. She always asked me to rub her back, and it made her feel better. But she's a bit old for that, and things have been pretty tense between us.

CLINICIAN: So you're thinking this could be soothing for her. But it sounds like your gut is also telling you that you might want to check with her to see if that kind of comfort could be welcome right now.

CARER: Yeah, it might be worth asking . . . There are times when she doesn't want to be touched, but not always. Maybe I could invite her to snuggle on the couch as a start, until the worst of it passes.

In this example, the clinician takes care to remind the caregiver of the need for her loved one to increase her caloric intake, while encouraging her to draw on her instincts to individualize the support according to her daughter's unique needs. This collaborative approach instills confidence in the caregivers and serves to recognize the expertise of all members of the treatment team. Should the caregivers struggle to identify possible solutions to the challenges they face, the EFFT clinician offers suggestions from which to choose based on the successes of other families with whom they've worked.

Finally, when supporting a loved one to gain weight, caregivers are encouraged to work on the goals of increasing both the amount and variety of foods consumed. Caregivers must also have a clear understanding of the loved one's "safe" and "scary foods" to work on increasing intake while also reintroducing feared foods. These include those deemed by their loved one as "unhealthy," as research suggests that relapse is more likely when individuals follow a diet limited in variety (Schebendach et al., 2008). To do so, caregivers and their loved ones can work together to develop a fear hierarchy, similar to a process of graduated exposure used to treat specific phobias (Kendall, 1994). Caregivers support the expansion of variety by introducing the least feared foods and moving up to the most feared foods. This allows the affected individual to systematically extinguish fears and develop a more neutral relationship with food. They do the same with respect to eating in front of others, and in different settings, such as at school or in restaurants. Thus, the overarching goal of this phase is to support caregivers to support their loved one to eat without rigid rules about what, when, and how to eat (Satter, 2000).

Bingeing

Episodes of bingeing will naturally decrease in frequency when caregivers encourage the intake of regular meals throughout the day. Eating food at regular intervals stabilizes blood sugar levels and lessens the urge to eat in a chaotic or uncontrolled way. "Trigger" foods can be identified and removed from the loved one's home, knowing that these will need to be reintroduced later in treatment so that normalized eating can occur. Caregivers can also decrease opportunities for bingeing via contact and connection during the times of the day when their loved one feels most vulnerable. In these moments, caregivers can support loved ones to use skills such as urge surfing and distraction techniques to manage impulses to binge.

Purging

Individuals with EDs who purge will greatly benefit from the support of others to break the cycle of behavior, whether they purge through vomiting or other methods. The most common form of behavioral support for purging involves supervision postmeals, including supervision of bathroom use for up to 2 hours. Supervision is usually coupled with support around the management of urges, including efforts to distract the loved one from associated distress. This type of support is best offered in person, although many carers have reported great success using telephone or video calls and text messages.

Caregivers should also be made aware that purging through vomiting can occur in other areas (e.g., in showers and garbage bins), and they are encouraged to remain vigilant of these possibilities. When discussing and addressing purging symptoms, caregivers are guided to maintain a neutral yet supportive stance to create an open line of communication. It is also important to note that individuals who have never purged but who are in the process of being renourished can be at higher risk of *symptom shifting*, especially if they are in distress and desperate for relief. (Symptom shifting refers to a process in which individuals shift their pattern of symptoms—for example, from food restriction to bingeing and purging.)

Problematic Patterns of Exercise

Individuals with EDs who overexercise can put themselves at risk for serious medical issues. These complications can include electrolyte imbalances, injuries, and cardiac events (Attia, 2010). Excessive exercise is also associated with longer treatment duration (Solenberger, 2001). As a result, caregivers of individuals who are medically unstable, underweight, or engaged in compulsive patterns of exercise are guided to support their loved one to cease or reduce physical activity for a period of time. Caregivers may need to provide supervision and distraction in places and at times when the urges to exercise are strongest and be aware of other forms of "activity" that may be occurring (e.g., leg shaking, stomach crunches, and any other excessive movement aimed at burning calories) as these may significantly affect health and weight. Once the return to physical activity has been deemed medically and psychologically safe, caregivers can support their loved one to resume engagement in activities in a way that is separate from the influence of the ED. This might mean that caregivers help their loved ones to participate in new lower risk activities and support them to increase their compensatory nutritional intake, as appropriate.

The Role of Intensive Treatment

Although carers can support their loved one in the home setting as part of outpatient treatment, there are times when their loved one may require a more contained and intensive therapeutic environment due to the severity of the illness or the need for medical monitoring. In these cases, caregivers may need to focus on supporting their loved one to navigate an admission to hospital as a behavioral coaching task. The EFFT clinician may also advocate on behalf of the caregivers to be involved in the partial hospitalization, inpatient, or residential treatment in some way. If this is not possible, EFFT clinicians urge caregivers to recognize the importance of their role leading up to admission and postdischarge. They may also seek the support of an EFFT clinician while their loved one is in treatment to better prepare for the transition to the home environment.

In addition to the techniques already described, several publicly available resources can further inform caregivers' efforts to support their loved one's behavioral recovery from an ED (see Appendix N). Regardless of the strategies employed, caregivers are guided to move flexibly between empathy and encouragement, compassion and firmness, validation and limit-setting when providing meal support and working to interrupt symptoms. To do so, caregivers are also equipped with the skills of emotion coaching to respond to emotions that often arise during the renourishment and symptom interruption phase in a way that is loving and productive. In other words, these modules work together to increase the effectiveness of the behavioral interventions.

Emotion Coaching

There are multiple ways in which emotion coaching can enhance the recovery process for individuals with EDs and their families. As stated in Chapter 2, this volume, this emotion-coaching framework can lead to increases in cognitive flexibility and connection. Therefore, when caregivers attend to their loved one in this way, possible outcomes include a decrease in resistance to ED interventions (including resistance to having their family involved in structured ways) and an increase in the effectiveness of caregiver-led interventions (meal support and the interruption of symptoms). It can also promote a strengthening of the caregiver–loved one relationship, making it more likely that the loved one will seek out the caregiver for support. Most importantly, however, emotion-coaching serves to facilitate the internalization of emotion-processing skills among those with an ED, making it easier for them to resist the temptation to engage in symptoms when experiencing distress. We next describe some of the more practical uses of emotion coaching in the context of EFFT for EDs.

Emotion Coaching and Caregiver Involvement

When carers can empathize and connect with their loved ones' pain and validate their experiences, including their resistance to intervention and support, loved ones will be more likely to trust and accept the support offered by their caregivers. This style of emotional support can also serve as a powerful buffer against an angry ED voice "warning" sufferers not to believe in those trying to help them in their recovery. Among adult clients, resistance to caregiver involvement may be particularly strong because the level of support required often feels developmentally awkward and generates feelings of shame and resentment. Following is an illustration of the power of emotion coaching based on a real-life example of its use in the context of adult ED treatment.

LOVED ONE: I don't want your help, and I don't need it. Please just leave me alone.

CAREGIVER: I don't blame you for not wanting my help. You don't want me to see you hurting, and I can only imagine how much shame you must feel that I even know about what's going on.

LOVED ONE: Seriously, I'm fine, it's going to be fine, and I can figure this out myself.

CAREGIVER: I believe you will be fine. But I also believe that you don't want my help because you're afraid that I will think less of you.

LOVED ONE: No—that's not it. I know you love me, but I also know that you're already stressed out with your own life. We both know your health isn't great, and there's no chance I am going to put even more stress on you. I could never live with myself if you had another heart attack.

CAREGIVER: Okay, I get it now. I can understand you wouldn't want to be burdened with the guilt if something happened to me. And so I don't blame you for trying to push your mom and me away. I didn't realize why until now, and the truth is, I would probably feel the same way if I were you. That being said, I am your dad and I can't stand on the sidelines knowing you are struggling. That would be far worse. Let me make you a promise. I promise that if I feel stressed or worn down, I will take a break to take care of myself. I will even schedule an extra appointment with the cardiologist to reassure you. Sound like a plan?

LOVED ONE: Fine. As long as you keep your promise and we revisit the terms every once in a while.

This exchange illustrates the ways in which the spirit of emotion coaching can serve to decrease resistance to support, even when caregivers' attempts to validate their loved one miss the mark. In fact, inspired attempts, regardless of their accuracy, can convey to loved ones that their caregivers are invested in understanding their perspective, thereby increasing the overall trust between carers and those with an ED. This increased trust and connection often helps loved ones to reveal the fears and motives underlying their treatment refusal or hesitation to involve caregivers in treatment, creating openings for a new path forward.

Emotion Coaching for Meal Support and Symptom Interruption

It is not unusual in the early phases of treatment for loved ones to react to meal support and symptom interruption with uncharacteristic displays of despondence, anxiety, anger, and even violence. We have heard too many reports from parents who described that when they insisted that their child complete a meal, plates went flying. They were not prepared to respond to this level of anger and anguish. As such, it is vital that clinicians teach caregivers emotion coaching strategies so that they can respond effectively to their loved one's reactions that surface before, during, or after meal times. Here is an example of emotion coaching in the context of meal support.

LOVED ONE: (points to a slice of cake) There is no way I am eating that.

CAREGIVER: I thought you might say that. When I put myself in your shoes, I had the exact same thought. You haven't eaten a pastry in ages, and I can imagine that you'd feel terrified of overdoing it. The fear of bingeing is so strong. It feels too risky to even try one bite.

LOVED ONE: I'm serious. There's no chance. I don't ever want to be fat ever again. Don't make me eat this. It's not even healthy.

CAREGIVER: I'm sorry, honey. I understand now how scary it was when things were out of control. I don't blame you for feeling nervous. You've been in this pattern for so long. Remember, you have my support. I will be with you for every bite, and I will stay with you until the urges for symptoms pass. Let's start with the first one.

Collectively, we have more than 40 years of experience working on the front line of ED treatment, providing meal support to people in inpatient and partial hospitalization settings, and supervising other clinicians to do the same. We also have years of experience supporting caregivers of children, adolescents, and adults with EDs in the context of family-based treatment and EFFT. Although we acknowledge that emotion coaching does not yield the desired outcomes 100% of the time, we can say with conviction that, in our experience, this technique is by far the most effective strategy to support sufferers to "eat one more bite." It is a tool we hope will be used more often, and as an alternative to some of the more coercive or punitive practices sometimes employed out of desperation. Although we are in support of firm limits, we believe they must be coupled with the steps of emotion coaching to maximize the effectiveness of meal support and symptom interruption strategies and to minimize distress for all involved.

Emotion Coaching for Cognitive Symptoms of EDs

We have found that for clinicians and carers alike, it can be extremely difficult to resist the urge to reassure, correct with logic, or ignore ED-related comments. Individuals with EDs often express the desire to be sick, to never eat again, or even to die. These statements are incredibly hard to validate for caregivers because they can provoke strong fear reactions. When supporting caregivers to respond to these types of statements, it is important to underline that validation is separate from agreement. Using the structure of emotion coaching, caregivers might respond to their loved one who expresses a wish to remain ill forever in the following way:

> Of course you want to be sick. Everything inside you tells you that being sick makes it so that you are deserving of our affection. I can imagine that you'd be terrified to be well again, just in case you lost our love and support.

Although their loved one's pain won't be resolved, the validation efforts will make it so that they are more receptive to support, whether emotional (e.g., reassurance) or practical (e.g., setting limits regarding the completion of a meal).

Carers can also use the steps of emotion coaching to respond to loved one's expression of body image disturbances, whether the loved one is emaciated, in the normal weight range, overweight, or obese. The following illustrates a possible exchange between a woman struggling with an ED and her husband:

MICHELLE: I'm not going out today. I feel so gross. I can't show anyone this fat, disgusting body.

AHMED: I can only imagine how hard it is to feel so uncomfortable in your own body. Like you want to climb out of your own skin to escape the feeling. I could see how you might feel like there's something wrong with you or that you might feel scared about how others might see you.

MICHELLE: Yes! I don't want to go!

AHMED: I get it. The eating disorder is convincing. It must be so heavy to have to carry that burden all day, every day. It sounds exhausting.

MICHELLE: It is exhausting. I am exhausted, and I just don't know who to trust.

AHMED: No wonder you feel conflicted. I know we can get through this feeling together. I'll tell you what, why don't we snuggle up on the couch and watch a show, and we'll try again in 30 minutes. Let's take some pressure off of you.

MICHELLE: Okay. Thanks, love.

Although it takes practice, this type of exchange will be far more effective than typical responses to "I feel/look/am fat," which usually involve reassurance or attempts to correct the individual's experience of her or his self. We remind carers that in EFFT, "fat is a feeling" and a projection of negative affect onto the body. Therefore, the caregiver is guided to attend to the loved one's surface feelings (e.g., feeling fat), followed by the validation of deeper experiences of vulnerability or emotional pain.

Therapeutic Apologies

As discussed in Chapter 4, therapeutic apologies is a module in EFFT that is applicable when self-blame is high in either the sufferer or the caregiver.

Individuals with EDs typically report an extremely strong self-critic making this intervention especially relevant. The ED self-critic often takes the form of a powerful, even abusive, internal voice (Dolhanty & Greenberg, 2007) that convinces sufferers that they are fat, ugly, and unworthy—and, in more extreme cases, that they are better off dead. The intensely negative emotions that result serves to fuel the guilt and shame so many sufferers already experience for the pain "they are causing their family." Many sufferers blame themselves for having developed the ED in the first place, especially if they recall a turning point in their lives when they "chose" to restrict or purge the first time. In these instances, a therapeutic caregiver-led apology can be used for lifting this self-blame to reduce its impact on help-seeking behaviors and treatment progress.

We also encourage the use of this intervention as a means of strengthening the carer–loved one relationship. Whether or not the relationship is or has been under strain, doing so will maximize the healing power of caregivers' supportive efforts. As readers will have noted several times throughout this manual, EFFT uses the relationship between carers and their loved ones as a vehicle to effect change. The stronger the relationship, the more impactful caregivers' efforts will be and the more their loved one will benefit from the carers' behavioral and emotional support. In light of the extent to which EDs are known to be treatment-resistant, we believe that it is worthwhile to invest in strengthening even the healthiest of relationships to optimize the healing potential of caregiver-led interventions in the various domains of recovery.

Although this module is powerful in the treatment of EDs, we do caution the EFFT clinician to take great care with its implementation. We have observed high levels of self-blame in many parents of children with EDs (Stillar et al., 2016). This propensity for caregiver self-blame is due in part to a long history of parent blaming within the ED field, which may still influence professionals and families today. Additionally, EDs usually develop and flourish in secrecy, often leaving caregivers feeling shame about not having noticed the early signs of illness progression. Others may have encouraged "clean" eating, influenced by a culture flooded with messages about "health," and therefore feel responsible for their loved one's obsession with food and weight. This is especially true when caregivers have struggled with disordered eating or an ED themselves. As such, if not sufficiently prepared, caregivers may respond to the proposal of a therapeutic apology with hurt, defensiveness, or even more self-blame. For this reason, and to ensure maximum therapeutic benefit, EFFT clinicians must take great care in conveying the spirit of no blame in which the intervention is firmly rooted, supporting caregivers to work through any painful feelings that may arise. This process serves to prepare them to deliver the apology, as well as healing the deep roots of their own pain. In fact, and as noted in Chapter 4, only once carers can connect with some level of self-compassion and self-forgiveness for not having been "perfect" can they deliver an effective therapeutic apology delivered from their "good house." The process of the therapeutic apology can take time, but we've found it to be an incredibly worthwhile process to free both the sufferer and the caregiver from the grips of self-blame, among other positive outcomes.

Caregiver Blocks

Carers are often faced with the very real fear of medical complications and, in more extreme cases, the death of their loved one. Not surprisingly, these and other emotional reactions can lead caregivers to "walk on eggshells" or resist engagement in behavior or emotion coaching in case the distress causes their loved one to withdraw, reject further support, or give up on recovery altogether. Carers can also fall into unhelpful patterns in which they accommodate ED symptoms (e.g., buying low-calorie foods, avoiding the reintroduction of feared foods in their loved one's diet) so as to avoid these feared consequences (Treasure et al., 2008). These findings highlight a need to identify these and other fears prior to the onset of caregiver-based interventions as they could lead to treatment-interfering behaviors and their transformation could improve outcomes. In response to this need, and in collaboration with parents of children struggling with an ED in a hospital-based program, I (AL) developed the Caregiver Traps Scale for Eating Disorders (CTS–ED) to assess caregiver fears specifically related to their involvement in providing home-based meal support and symptom interruption.[2] One hundred and twenty-four parents of adolescent and adult children with ED participated in a validation study to examine its psychometric properties (Lafrance, Strahan, & Stillar, 2019). Exploratory factor analysis revealed one component, and the scale yielded high internal consistency. The measure was positively correlated with a measure of accommodation and enabling of ED symptoms and negatively correlated with a measure of parental self-efficacy with respect to their helping role. Although it has been used clinically for several years, the results of this study confirm that the CTS–ED can be a valuable tool to target and transform potential fears to improve outcomes. In addition to

---

[2]The Caregiver Traps Scale, described in Chapter 5, was adapted from this tool.

the CTS–ED, we recommend that ED clinicians consider integrating the other tools and techniques developed to transform emotion blocks outlined in Chapter 5, in particular, caregiver block chair work, as they too were initially developed for use in the context of ED treatment.

Clinician Blocks

It is well established that working as a clinician in the field of EDs can be emotionally challenging (Franko & Rolfe, 1996; Golan, Yeruslavski, & Stein, 2009; Thompson-Brenner, Satir, Franko, & Herzog, 2012; C. S. Warren, Schafer, Crowley, & Olivardia, 2013). Two theoretical models have emerged that explore the influence of clinician factors on the delivery of ED treatment in the context of individual and family-oriented therapies. They include the iatrogenic maintenance model of eating disorders (Treasure, Crane, McKnight, Buchanan, & Wolfe, 2011) and the therapist drift model (Kosmerly, Waller, & Lafrance Robinson, 2015; Tobin, Banker, Weisberg, & Bowers, 2007; Waller, 2009; Waller & Turner, 2016). The developers of these models posit that clinicians, like carers, can find themselves engaging in avoidant or otherwise unhelpful practices when supporting individuals and their families (Treasure et al., 2011; Waller, Stringer, & Meyer, 2012). According to Waller (2009), clinicians may also resist pushing clients for behavioral change when it results in making the client (and, in turn, the clinician) uncomfortable. This can lead the clinician to engage in negotiations around treatment recommendations or to downplay the severity of symptoms to avoid conflict. Positive emotions can also hamper clinical judgment because they may mislead and distract from important clinical information and cues. For instance, clinicians may become enthusiastic about minor changes in a client's course of treatment, which can distract focus away from some of the more serious issues still requiring attention.

In 2015, ED professionals were surveyed with respect to their perception of the influence of emotions on clinical decisions (Lafrance Robinson & Kosmerly, 2015). Clinicians from various disciplines who were engaged in the treatment of child and adolescent EDs were randomly assigned to complete one of two surveys. The first survey assessed clinician perspectives regarding the negative influence of emotions on their own clinical decisions ($n = 143$), and the second survey assessed clinician perspectives of the same with respect to their colleagues ($n = 145$). Both groups endorsed this phenomenon to some degree, although participants were about twice as likely to endorse the negative impact of emotion among their colleagues. The specific treatment decisions thought to be affected fell within three categories: decisions regarding food and weight, decisions regarding the involvement of the family in treatment, and decisions regarding autonomy and control. Decisions related to the involvement of the family were perceived to be the most emotionally charged—in particular, the involvement of a critical or dismissive parent. Clinicians' responses indicated that certain client states and fears fueled problematic clinical practices on the part of the clinician (Kosmerly, 2014). Specifically, clinicians reported that the client states that were most likely to negatively influence their decision making included expressions of anger, hopelessness, and flat affect. They were most influenced by their own fear of potentially alienating the client (i.e., arousing a hostile or negative emotional reaction, causing the family to disengage from treatment) and feelings of incompetence. Clinicians reported that their most frequent reactions included focusing on another less emotionally arousing topic; overemphasizing minor improvements in the client; and rationalizing, negotiating, or bartering with the client. Follow-up research was conducted among 16 family-based therapists who participated in a semistructured interview (Penney, 2018). Transcripts were analyzed using thematic analysis. Results revealed that the tone of therapist–client interactions and the level of family resistance affected clinical decision-making the most frequently. In fact, every one of the therapists shared that in response to critical or angry parents, they were more likely to deviate from protocol in some way, including advocating for premature discharge. Results also revealed that impact of therapist emotion on clinical decisions could be mitigated via engagement in self-reflective practices and working as part of a treatment team.

Common Clinician Blocks in the Treatment of EDs
We do not believe that the experiences of the clinicians and therapists described in this chapter are unique. In fact, when the stakes are high, as they are in the treatment of EDs, emotions run high as well. The emergence and expression of clinician blocks in these settings are normal, and ED clinicians are supported to increase their awareness of the potential blocks most common to their practice. For example, family therapists may hesitate to enlist caregivers as recovery allies when they present as hostile or in denial or when a caregiver struggles with an ED, substance use disorder, or personality disorder. Similar to the common caregiver blocks in ED treatment, the medical risk associated with ED symptoms can also lead clinicians to be blocked by a tremendous fear of losing a client to death, including being held responsible in some way. These blocks can lead clinicians to avoid working with some clients (or all clients with EDs), blame other health care professionals for lack of treatment progress, or adhere rigidly to treatment protocols.

When a clinician's personal beliefs about food, nutrition, weight, and shape stand in contradiction to the central messages of ED recovery that "all foods fit and variety in nutrition is key" they can also interfere with important aspects of recovery, such as the reintegration of high-calorie foods. There are numerous other blocks that clinicians may experience in the context of ED treatment: They may perceive the individual with the ED as manipulative rather than sick; clinicians may avoid bringing attention to certain ED symptoms, such as laxative use or bingeing or purging (to prevent from shaming the client but also because it can be uncomfortable to discuss the more private features of these symptoms); and they may hesitate to confront their clients about potentially undisclosed symptoms for fear of causing offense and losing their trust. For these reasons, we encourage ED clinicians to maintain a routine of self-reflection and self-care, as well as to engage in regular supervision (peer or otherwise) or personal therapy to identify and work through blocks as they arise.

SUMMARY

Similar to EFFT for general mental health, there are three main areas of intervention in EFFT for ED. They include supporting carers to (a) increase their involvement in supporting their loved one with meal support and symptom interruption; (b) provide structured emotional support to respond to reactions that arise in response to the behavioral interventions and to attend to the emotional processes fueling ED symptoms; and (c) initiate a therapeutic apology for the healing of family wounds—whether related to relational injuries, the burden of self-blame, or to upgrade the relationship and therefore the impact of caregiver interventions. The associated skills in each of the modules are designed for use in person, over the telephone, or even by text or e-mail. Caregivers are then taught to combine these three sets of skills to increase their effectiveness and are provided with opportunities to practice in session. Should a caregiver struggle to engage in any of the aforementioned tasks, the EFFT clinician supports the caregiver to move through these impasses using the tools and techniques outlined in Chapter 5 on caregiver blocks. Similarly, EFFT clinicians who specialize in EDs are also very aware of the increased vulnerability for the emergence of clinician blocks when working with EDs and integrate within their practice a structure for ongoing processing of potentially problematic attitudes, emotional reactions, or behaviors.

CLINICIAN'S CORNER

I spent nearly 10 years working as a psychologist in a hospital-based program treating children and adolescents with eating disorders. We adhered largely to principles of family-based treatment and I thought at the time that I was a clinician who believed in parents and their healing power. I felt as though I addressed emotion with my patients and had taught parents to do the same, but at times, I felt some deeper processes were lacking in my approach. When I first learned about EFFT, it was as though a piece of the puzzle that I didn't even know I was missing finally fit into the picture. I felt that I now had a holistic framework from which to conduct my work. I had practical ways of helping them understand the illness and address both behaviors and emotions. As I deepened my training and practice and went on to become a supervisor and trainer, I continued to experience the benefits and also the challenges of this approach. Working through my own blocks is not something I always look forward to, but I have never engaged in that work without deriving some benefit. When I left the hospital and went into private practice, I extended my focus to include general mental health issues across the lifespan. Tools and techniques from EFFT are now integrated within every case I see in one way or another. I am definitely a better therapist today because of it.

—Psychologist

8

FREQUENTLY ASKED QUESTIONS AND FUTURE DIRECTIONS

Psychologists and social workers had tried different therapies with my daughter with little success. My family has now had the good fortune of benefitting from EFFT. We have a long way to go, but from the beginning it improved our communication, and her symptoms decreased. Our daughter still needs lots of support from therapists, doctors, and her school to supplement what we're doing, but we feel empowered and her behaviors don't feel as scary.

—Caregiver

This concluding chapter addresses frequently asked questions about the model with respect to its origins and theoretical foundation as well as its application in specific settings. We then introduce a number of exciting developments within emotion-focused family therapy (EFFT) that extend the approach for those individuals who struggle with an eating disorder and a comorbid substance use disorder, as well as emotion-focused applications in school settings and in health care more broadly.

http://dx.doi.org/10.1037/0000166-009
Emotion-Focused Family Therapy: A Transdiagnostic Model for Caregiver-Focused Interventions, by A. Lafrance, K. A. Henderson, and S. Mayman

FREQUENTLY ASKED CLINICAL QUESTIONS

My client refuses carer involvement. What can I do?

It is important for clinicians to understand that when clients refuse caregiver involvement, it does not preclude them from offering services to the caregiver separate from the individual work with the client. However, when doing so, they must not share with caregivers any of their client's personal health information without consent, consistent with laws regarding client confidentiality in their jurisdiction. In fact, the caregiver workshop was developed so that carers could learn skills to support their loved one regardless of their involvement in treatment. As such, the content does not depend on the clinician or caregiver having any specific information regarding the loved one's difficulties. In addition, when a client refuses to involve their parents or partner in their therapy, EFFT therapists can engage their clients in therapeutic interventions to resolve this type of block, including a specific version of chair work related to client resistance to caregiver involvement.[1] Doing so uncovers the low self-efficacy with emotion that typically fuels this block and thus provides an avenue for its transformation. Some clients resist caregiver involvement for fear of judgment (and the associated experience of shame and anger), whereas others do not want to burden their loved ones, especially if they are prone to strong feelings of guilt. Working through these emotional states can then lead to the client agreeing to caregiver involvement in some way, whether in session or separately.

How do I engage caregivers who decline an invitation for involvement in their loved one's treatment?

When caregivers express reluctance to involvement, the EFFT clinician first uses the model of emotion coaching to name and validate the emotions fueling their resistance. The clinician also validates the myriad of reasons why the caregiver might feel this way: "I can imagine you wouldn't want to be involved in your daughter's treatment if you fear that doing so could negatively affect your already strained relationship" or "I don't blame you for not wanting to engage in this work given your experiences the last time your son was in the program." Then, the EFFT clinician offers emotional support in the form of reassurance and an offer for a trial session, for example. Seasoned EFFT clinicians have described doing so with positive results, even by voicemail and email.

---

[1]The description of this intervention falls outside the scope of this book. Influenced by caregiver block chair work, it is taught as part of the advanced EFFT training.

My client's caregiver is on the verge of burnout. How can I ask the caregiver to do more?

We believe, as do others, that what is most detrimental to the mental health of a parent or caregiver is to witness a loved one's suffering, and feel helpless or ineffective in the face of it (Monin, 2016). As such, in EFFT, we do not want the caregiver to "do more." Rather, our goal is for them to "do different." In other words, we support caregivers to replace existing strategies with evidenced-based tools and techniques that are more likely to lead to positive outcomes and will therefore be self-reinforcing. That said, when caregivers are exhausted and depleted, regardless of the reason, we have learned that it is critical to prioritize self-care to protect them from burnout and support them to recharge and reenergize. For example, in some cases, we build in self-compassion meditations in session to ensure they benefit from opportunities to reconnect to themselves with loving kindness.

Does EFFT work with all clients?

The simple answer is no. Although more research is needed to identify variables related to positive outcomes, we would be remiss to suggest that we always succeed in supporting families using this model. This indicates a need for the EFFT community and the treatment community at large to continue researching new tools and techniques to better serve families. That said, we have been humbled too many times to count by parents and caregivers who have exceeded our expectations with respect to their capacity to acquire behavior and emotion-coaching skills, take the lead in the facilitation of therapeutic apologies, and work through blocks with insight and awareness. As such, and as a rule, we are not "first to leave the table" in that we continue working with carers who are willing to offer their loved one support or who are significantly involved in their loved one's life. We offer them support, knowing that the fruits of our collective efforts will reveal themselves in time. When we aren't able to bring them into session, we honor caregivers by bringing them into the client's individual therapy imaginally, highlighting their strengths and communicating the love they have for their loved one, whether or not they are able to do so in "real life."

What are the considerations for caregiver involvement when caregivers are suspected of being verbally or physically abusive or highly symptomatic?

In EFFT, the protection of the most vulnerable individual (the loved one) is paramount. Although it can be possible to work with highly dysregulated or symptomatic caregivers in separate sessions, there may be complex ethical and legal issues related to ensuring a client's safety and advanced skills are required. In other cases, the most ethical choice for a clinician may be to terminate the therapy or make a referral to another clinician (as per Standard 10.10, Terminating Therapy, in the American Psychological Association's, 2017a, *Ethical Principles of Psychologists and Code of Conduct*).

Are there behavioral or emotional issues for which EFFT is less effective?

Although EFFT is a transdiagnostic treatment approach, this is an area of study yet to be explored. Practitioners of EFFT across a wide range of presenting problems and levels of severity have reported positive results, and most frequently with mood and anxiety disorders, eating disorders, substance misuse, and behavioral issues. We would argue that the model includes components that can be universally helpful, even in the context of personality disorders, mental disorders with an organic basis such as schizophrenia, or medical issues, where those affected can still benefit greatly from increased emotional and practical support. Until research elucidates the efficacy of EFFT across disorders, clinicians should consider a conscious integration of modules to support their treatment efforts.

What is the history of the model?

Initially developed as a family-based treatment for eating disorders, EFFT's focus on the empowerment of caregivers in the behavioral recovery of their loved one was influenced by the works of Ivan Eisler (multifamily therapy for eating disorders; Le Grange & Eisler, 2009), James Lock and Daniel Le Grange (family-based treatment for eating disorders; Lock & Le Grange, 2015), and Janet Treasure (New Maudsley method; Treasure, Smith, & Crane, 2007). Key concepts of motivational interviewing shaped the model's development; in particular, the approach to ambivalence and the emphasis on the role of the interpersonal helping relationship in facilitating change and sustaining healthy behaviors (Miller & Rollnick, 2012). As the name implies, EFFT was also heavily influenced by the role of emotion in mental health and healing, and in particular through the works of Leslie Greenberg and colleagues (emotion-focused therapy for individuals and for couples; Greenberg, 2015, 2017; Greenberg & Goldman, 2008; Greenberg & Johnson, 1988). The contributions of other leaders in the field helped shape the development of EFFT as well. These include John Gottman's model of emotion coaching (Gottman, Katz, & Hooven, 1996), Daniel Siegel's theory and research on interpersonal neurobiology (Siegel, 2010), and Gabor Maté's conceptualization of mind–body health (Maté, 2011), as well as his views on childhood attachment and development (Neufeld & Maté, 2004). As EFFT emerged as a promising practice in the treatment of eating disorders (Lafrance Robinson et al., 2015), it became apparent to those clinicians and families involved that its application extended beyond this scope. EFFT thus evolved into a transdiagnostic approach used to treat mental health issues in children, adolescents, and adult sufferers worldwide.

What's the difference between the EFFT approach described in this clinician manual and emotionally focused family therapy?

Emotion-focused techniques were first developed and researched by Leslie Greenberg (1979). Greenberg and Sue Johnson (1988) then manualized a structured approach to treat couples. Both Greenberg and Johnson continued to support the evolution of separate but related individual and couples models, from which family adaptations later emerged (emotion-focused family therapy by Lafrance and Dolhanty and emotionally focused family therapy by Johnson and colleagues). Although there are differences between them with respect to specific interventions (e.g., the role of clinician and the focus on attachment vs. emotion) because of their common roots, the models also share a number of similarities in terms of theoretical underpinnings, methods of implementation and treatment goals. As such, we encourage readers drawn to an emotion-focused approach to working with families to take advantage of the benefits related to learning both approaches.

EXTENSIONS OF EFFT IN PRACTICE AND IN DEVELOPMENT

A number of variations of EFFT are currently in development and in practice. EFFT practitioners have found that EFFT as a stand-alone treatment, or components of the model, can be flexibly applied to a variety of settings and problems. Although these developments are still in their infancy, and more research is required to demonstrate their efficacy, the extensions provide an exciting opportunity to bring the benefits of EFFT to a broader range of individuals and their families.

EFFT for Concurrent Eating and Substance Use Disorders

EFFT for concurrent eating disorder (ED) and substance use disorder (SUD; C-CARE) is a comprehensive treatment model developed by Katherine Henderson and Shari Mayman in response to the growing need for concurrent treatment for ED/SUD. C-CARE addresses the significant gaps in resources for concurrent ED/SUD by providing an integrated treatment approach that provides clinicians with expertise in both disorders, with a focus on shared underlying emotional processes that drive and maintain symptoms. C-CARE involves four treatment components: C—caregivers; A—across the lifespan, R—recovery coaching, and E—emotion processing. The model is built on the principles of EFFT, integrating techniques and skills from emotion-focused therapy, dialectical behavior therapy, and cognitive behavior therapy. C-CARE was designed to be accessible to clinicians from a variety of disciplines and implemented within agencies serving a diverse range of client populations, including individuals, families, and groups. Like EFFT, C-CARE tools and techniques can be integrated within existing clinical approaches by individual clinicians and teams.

A 3-year grant was obtained to provide C-CARE training for a large community addiction agency in Ottawa, Ontario. Staff completed initial intensive training, followed by 2 years of regular supervision for clinicians selected to become the C-CARE experts within the agency. Clinicians report that the model has strengthened their clinical practice, deepened their therapeutic relationships, and led to a new way to deal with "unmotivated" clients. Preliminary research results from a parent group that integrated the principles of C-CARE are promising (Henderson & Mayman, 2018).

Emotion-Focused School Support

After completing studies in child and clinical school psychology, and informed by more than 10 years working with various school boards, Adele Lafrance sought to increase the involvement of school staff in supporting the emotional health of children and their families in the service of learning. Inspired by her work with EFFT, she created an adaptation for the school setting. Given that a regulated physiology is critical for learning, the primary goals of EFSS include supporting school staff in regulating child and adolescent emotion to facilitate a "return to learning," preventing emotional escalations, and deescalating outbursts in progress. EFSS also includes a module to support school staff to respond to challenging parental dynamics, including those who present to school staff with anxiety, shame, resentment, or criticism. These strategies were developed for delivery during phone calls, parent–teacher meetings or when crossing paths in the hallway. The finale module of EFSS involves opportunities for school staff to identify their strengths and challenges when faced with emotional situations with students, their caregivers and with colleagues, and in a manner that is respectful and compassionate. EFSS can be delivered throughout elementary and secondary schools; however emotional language varies according to developmental age. The model can be introduced to classroom staff directly, through mental health support staff or through a targeted approach with those students and their parents who require more intensive support. Research is currently in progress among teachers who've received training in the approach.

Emotion-Focused Health Care

Illness and the health care environment can increase emotional stress for patients and their families. All health care staff play a role in attending to patient and family emotional needs, whether they have received formal training in this area or not. Inspired by EFFT, Lafrance and child psychiatrist Ashley Miller created an adaptation for health care settings to increase hospital staff capacity to confidently support the emotional needs of patients and their families across mental health and medical units.

We know that a strong therapeutic relationship between patients, families, and health care providers encourages better health outcomes for patients, improves patient satisfaction, and decreases stress for all involved. Therefore, the emotion-focused health care (EFHC) model includes the following modules: (a) recognizing emotion in patients and their families; (b) understanding challenging behaviors, including nonadherence to treatment protocols; and (c) providing emotion-focused support to manage emotional reactions and treatment resistance more effectively. EFHC also includes a module to support health care staff to respond to challenging family dynamics, including those family members who present as highly anxious, angry, or in denial. EFHC also provides a framework for managing highly charged situations on health care teams and reducing the influence of emotion when making treatment decisions. EFHC skills training have been provided to front-line clinical and administrative staff, as well as through mental health support staff as part of system-wide initiatives across North America.

CLINICIAN'S CORNER

As a nurse in a general psychiatry ward, I am exposed to a lot of emotion—from my patients but also their friends and family members. Although I received a lot of training around safety, especially in moments of escalation, I didn't have much in the way of skills to respond to the day-to-day stressors that come up. As soon as I learned the emotion coaching skills, I used them that afternoon to respond to a family's complaint about a discharge protocol. I was so relieved to see that it worked to help them to calm down so that we could explain our decision-making process. Now I use the skills as often as I can remember, and in a variety of situations—responding to pass requests, demands for off-protocol medication, even interpersonal issues between patients. It makes it so that we as a nursing team are more independent on the ward to deal with nonurgent issues in a way that works well.

—Nurse in a general hospital

EPILOGUE

Lessons Learned

PERSONAL REFLECTIONS BY DR. KATHERINE HENDERSON

EFFT has enriched my professional and personal life in ways that I could never have imagined. With its focus on emotion processing and the power of caregivers, it has felt like the key that unlocked me as a psychologist. The focus on emotion has been transformative across all aspects of my professional work. As a clinician, my work with individuals and families is more authentic, vulnerable, and powerful. Being privileged to work with EFFT colleagues has given me the freedom to not only challenge myself to identify my own clinician blocks, but more importantly to process these blocks through chair work, where I can truly *feel* the feelings, (embracing the motto "you gotta feel it to heal it"). Believing fully in the power of caregivers and having a "no blame" stance has helped me support caregivers with compassion and hope. I am always in awe of, and full of gratitude for, the many caregivers and clients with whom I work, who trust me, and share with me their vulnerabilities and strengths. Each of them inspires me to "practice what I teach" in my own life as a parent and a partner. I want to thank my clients for the privilege of working with them and reminding me of the

http://dx.doi.org/10.1037/0000166-010
Emotion-Focused Family Therapy: A Transdiagnostic Model for Caregiver-Focused Interventions, by A. Lafrance, K. A. Henderson, and S. Mayman

power of emotion, compassion, and connection. There is a special group of parents—Shari and I call them the "Bagelshop Group"—who deserve a mention here for their incredible dedication to their loved ones: Thank you for inspiring us with your courage and determination. Finally, personally, EFFT has helped me navigate the adventure of parenting and marriage. Even though my children may still roll their eyes when I start talking about emotions, I have seen firsthand the power of emotion coaching and relationship repair. Although there are always the emotion coaching "fails," I am empowered to know that what happens next is even more powerful.

PERSONAL REFLECTIONS BY DR. SHARI MAYMAN

EFFT arrived in my life at the time as I was becoming a mother for the second time. I saw Adele first speak about this exciting new therapy when I was just weeks from giving birth, and then attended further training with my infant son in my arms. I knew right away this was a developing area that I wanted to be a part of. From that point forward, EFFT has always been situated at the intersection of my professional and personal life.

Being involved in the development of the 2-day caregiver workshop and delivering these regularly is one of the great joys of my work life. Being able to spend two intense days with caregivers who are struggling and offering them a new perspective on their loved one, as well as the hope of going forward with new skills, moves me deeply each and every time. I have a similar reaction when training clinicians in this model—it is so enriching and exciting to see them experience the sudden shift in the way they see caregivers and their healing power. In my work with families in my private practice, one of EFFT's greatest impacts has been in the way I work with parents and caregivers who present as angry or critical. This has always been my professional Achilles heel. EFFT helps me see beneath their anger and gives me concrete ways of working with them more empathically, and therefore more effectively.

On a personal level, I have grown from EFFT's having named and explained experiences I had as a child. Being a super-feeler, I am very familiar with what it feels like to receive misattuned and well-attuned responses from carers (thankfully, there were more of the latter than the former). Now, as a mother of two wonderful boys with some pretty big feelings, I see the other side of things. I recognize how hard it can be to stay true to parenting from an emotional place, even when you practice, teach, and train about its importance regularly. I bring this hard work back into the office every day, and I use it to deepen my practice with the families I serve.

PERSONAL REFLECTIONS BY DR. ADELE LAFRANCE

I can't begin to explain the impact EFFT has had on my life. A firm believer in "walking the talk," I have practiced each of the interventions I've developed with members of my own family. I've stumbled, been overtaken by blocks, and made mistakes. I've also benefited from deep healing—we all have. The framework and techniques have also equipped me to navigate my own personal and professional challenges over the years. In fact, in the later stages of the model's development, I went through a separation and divorce. For a long time, I struggled with how I could be a developer of a family-based model and have "failed" within my own family. The dissolution of my marriage brought forth all kinds of difficulties that I couldn't ignore (although I wished I could!), as well as numerous blocks; some more stubborn than others. A few years later, and thanks to the many principles and techniques of EFFT (including a few therapeutic apologies), I can honestly say that we survived, even thrived. Because of this, I am better able to embody the no-blame spirit of this approach, anchored firmly in the belief that "we do the best we can" and "it's not what happens, it's what happens next." I am so excited to see how EFFT continues to evolve as we heal, learn, and grow together. Finally, I would like to extend my sincerest gratitude to the many clients, colleagues, and family members who've supported the evolution of the model, as well as the coauthors of this manual, Katherine and Shari. Without them, this book would not be. Gros merci!

Appendix A

THE SUPER-FEELER EXPLAINED

What makes a super-feeler?

- Genetics—a super-feeler can be "wired this way."

- Early life experiences can also increase the likelihood of becoming a super-feeler.

- The experience of the super-feeler is most intense in childhood and adolescence because the parts of the brain that help to calm emotion aren't fully developed until adulthood.

What makes a super-feeler unique? Super-feelers . . .

- Can have a keen sense for emotions in their environment

- Can experience emotions very intensely—their own and those of others

Illustration courtesy of Maya Partrick. Printed with permission.

- Can pick up on others' stress and emotions easily

- Can be more sensitive to perceived threat in the environment (this is why super-feelers become more upset when someone raises their voice)

- Can either be explosive or very agreeable

- Can be motivated to manage others to protect themselves from feeling their pain

- Can feel alone as many will struggle to understand their emotional experiences

- Can hide that they are a super-feeler well, mostly to protect others or relationships or out of embarrassment

What happens with super-feelers? Super-feelers . . .

- May try to find ways to reduce pain/avoid emotions, sometimes with unhealthy behaviors

- Because of this tendency to avoid emotions, super-feelers can be vulnerable to developing eating disorders, anxiety, depression, other mental illnesses, and some chronic health issues, especially if they are exposed to significant or chronic stressors

- Will need support from their environment to manage their emotions until they develop the advanced skills to do so (and until their brain completes its development)

- Are likely to succeed in the caring professions (e.g., as social workers, doctors, nurses, psychologists) and might perform unusually well in the world once they learn to manage the emotions they sense and feel

Appendix B

EMOTION-COACHING CHEAT SHEET

First: Start off emotion coaching with a phrase.

Possible sentence starters:

- It seems like maybe . . .
- I'm wondering if . . .
- I imagine you might also be feeling . . .
- I see something in your face that tells me maybe you're . . .

Second: Follow the sentence starter with an emotion label.

Words to describe anger:

- Angry
- Mad
- Fuming
- Furious
- Full of rage

Words to describe sadness:

- Sad
- Blue
- Low

Words to describe fear:

- Scared
- Anxious

- Terrified
- Fearful

Words to describe shame:

- Embarrassed
- Like there's something wrong with you
- Like you're not good enough
- Like you're broken
- Unworthy/worthless
- Undeserving

Other emotional states to watch for and label:

- Lonely
- Hopeless
- Jealous
- Guilty

Third: Complete the sentence with a validating statement.

- And that would be so hard because
- And that would feel just awful because
- And that would so painful because
- And of course you feel _____ because
- Yes, it's (sad, lonely, etc.) when

Appendix C

BEHAVIOR COACHING FOR COOPERATION AND COLLABORATION

Step 1: Check yourself

- Are you calm? Is your expectation reasonable?

Step 2: Connect with your loved one

- "Oh, wow—look at the drawing!" "What's happening in the show?"

- Do this for at least 2 minutes—it will be a great investment.

Step 3: Make the request

- Deliver the command: "Please do X," rather than: "Can you do this?"

- Pay attention to your tone of voice and posture. The way you make the request can evoke different responses from your loved one. Aim for calm confidence.

- Be as concise as possible; resist giving a list of reasons why cooperation is necessary.

Step 4: Validate

- Be prepared for resistance; this is the content that you will then validate using three "because" statements to convey your understanding of their perspective.

- "I can understand why you wouldn't want to ____ because . . . because . . . because . . ."

Step 5: Make the request a second time and set a limit if necessary

Practice example: Your daughter won't stop texting at the dinner table.

1. Check yourself. Are you calm? Is your request reasonable?

2. Connect by inquiring sincerely about her friend: "How is Kayden doing these days? Is he still working at the grocery store?"

3. Make the request "Okay, love, please put your phone away until we're done with dinner."

4. If resistance, validate: "I can imagine you might not want to stop texting because it's been awhile since you've connected. Maybe you're worried he needs your support or that he might not be available later."

5. Make the request again "I'm sorry. I do need you to put your phone away until the meal is done. You can try again after dinner."

6. If your loved one doesn't cooperate, then set a limit or communicate a consequence.

Appendix D

HEALING FAMILY WOUNDS VIA THERAPEUTIC APOLOGY

PREPROCESS—SELF-CHAIR

This experiential activity is meant to prepare caregivers to initiate a therapeutic apology with their loved one to strengthen the relationship, share the burden, or relieve their self-blame, as relevant.

To begin the process, invite the caregivers to sit on your left (in the self-chair) to clarify the event(s) or caregiving style for which they wish to deliver a therapeutic apology. Once clear, invite caregivers to take a breath and to picture their loved one in the opposite chair, as they are today.

Step 1: Self-Chair—Caregiver Communicates the Apology

1. Using the following prompt, invite the caregiver to name the event(s), its idiosyncratic impact, as well as to acknowledge the insufficient emotional support that was available, if relevant:

   I want to talk to you about when _____ and how hard that must have been for you. Especially because _____ (idiosyncratic impact). And I know that you didn't get the emotional support you needed (from me).

2. Guide the caregiver to label and validate the painful emotions and experiences associated with the event. Encourage the validation of at least three emotions or emotional experiences, ensuring there are at least two or three related "becauses" for each statement to deepen the healing.

   I can imagine that you felt SCARED because . . . and because . . .

   I can imagine that you felt SAD because . . . and because. . .

   I can imagine that you felt ASHAMED because . . . and because . . .

   I can imagine that you felt ANGRY because . . . and because . . .

Then, invite the caregiver to validate the pain associated with the experience of these emotions without sufficient support from the caregiver (if relevant).

I can imagine that you also felt really lonely going through all of this on your own/without my support.

3. Support the caregiver to communicate a sincere apology, free of shame, using the hanging sentence:

I am so sorry . . . (for the pain you suffered/that this caused you)

4. Encourage the caregiver to share what he or she "should have done," using the framework of the crystal ball and the benefit of financial and social support resources. Doing so maintains the focus on the fact that all caregivers did the best they could with the resources to which they had access at the time.

   a. "If when your loved one was born you had a crystal ball that could show you the future, what would you have done differently in response to what you saw?"

   b. "Imagine you had access to sufficient financial and social support throughout your loved ones' life, what would you have done differently?"

   (Name of loved one), I should have . . . (asked for a second opinion when the family doctor said you were okay; protected you from _____; helped you to move through the pain when _____ occurred).

Then, invite the caregiver to share with their loved one what change they will initiate to move forward together. Most often, this step will involve a shift in the way emotional pain is dealt with in the dyad or family.

Starting today, I will . . . (check in with you more often; I will ask you how you are really doing; I will validate your fear/sadness/anger/pain.)

Switch the caregiver to the "other" chair on the right.

Step 2: Other-Chair—Loved One Reacts to the Apology

1. Invite the caregiver to take a breath and picture himself or herself in the opposite chair. Guide the caregiver to embody the loved one, as the loved one is today. Then, use the following prompt:

   Be your loved one. (Name of loved one), tell your (mom/dad/etc.) what happens when you hear what has been shared.

2. Encourage the communication of an authentic response (including silence) without making any attempts to guide or correct the expression of the "loved one's" experience. Switch the caregiver to the "self" chair on the left.

Step 3: Self-Chair–Caregiver Validates Loved One's Reaction

1. Invite the caregiver to identify the type of reaction received from the loved one (blast, silent blast, denial, or reassurance). Then, invite the caregiver to take a regulating breath (more than one if necessary). Invite the caregiver to respond to the loved one's reaction with validation (with two or three becauses) followed by reassurance using the following prompts.

   If blast (assume anger): *I can understand why you would be angry because . . . (It probably feels like too little too late . . .) because . . . , because . . . [validation] I am going to own this as long as it takes to work through it. [reassurance]*

   If silent blast: *I don't blame for remaining silent because . . . (You might not trust my capacity to handle your anger . . .) because . . . , because . . . [validation] I am ready and willing to take this on. Seriously. I am stronger than you think, and I've had support to get here. [reassurance]*

   If denial: *I can understand why you would deny the impact of it all . . . (We've avoided talking about the tough stuff in the past, and so it can be really uncomfortable) because . . . , because . . . [validation] I am committed to working this through. I'm not going to give up. [reassurance]*

   If reassurance: *I can understand why you would want to reassure me because . . . (You've seen me hurting in the past and that's been painful for you . . .) because . . . , because . . . [validation] You don't need to protect me or my feelings. I've got this, and I want to do this for you. [reassurance]*

2. Once the loved one's reaction is validated, invite the caregiver to once again communicate a sincere apology, this time with a stronger stance (sculpting her or his body and voice as needed) and using the hanging sentence:

   I am so sorry . . . (for the pain you suffered/this caused you).

3. Then, encourage the caregiver to reiterate what could have been done to prevent the event from occurring or to minimize the suffering associated with the event, as well as what the caregiver will do differently from now.

   I should have _____ and from now on, I am going to _____ and _____.

4. Next, invite the caregiver to share why the intend to make these changes on behalf of their loved one using this prompt:

   Tell _____: I'm committed to doing things differently for you because _____ (I love you so much; I need to be here for you in a different way; this is going to be family's new normal).

5. Finally, support the caregiver to warn the loved one that it won't always go perfectly and that the caregiver will make mistakes but that he or she

won't give up on these supportive efforts. Switch the caregiver to the "other" chair on the right.

Step 4: Other-Chair—Loved One Reacts to the Apology

1. Invite the caregiver to take a breath and to picture himself or herself in the opposite chair. Guide the caregiver to embody the loved one for a final time. Use this prompt:

   Be your loved one. (Name of loved one), tell your caregiver what happens when you hear what he or she has shared this time?

2. Encourage the communication of an authentic response without making any attempts to guide or correct the expression of their experience.

   If the expression is angry, defensive or dismissive, once communicated fully, invite the caregiver-as-loved one to speak the softness and the vulnerability that lies underneath.

   (Loved one's name), if you could speak about what's underneath the anger/ defensiveness/resistance, what would you say?

3. Then, encourage the expression of love and gratitude. Although this may not occur in "real life" (should the caregiver deliver the apology to the loved one), it will prime the caregiver not to take such responses personally or at face value if encountered.

   Switch the caregiver to the "self" chair on the left.

Step 5: Self-Chair—Caregiver Responds to Loved One and Plans for Next Steps

1. Invite the caregiver to take a regulating breath (more than one if necessary). Depending on the reaction, invite the caregiver to respond with validation followed by emotional support and practical support as relevant.

2. Ask the caregiver to tell you (the therapist) how it felt to move through these steps and debrief together, highlighting the possible release of shame and self-blame and the rise of empowerment.

3. Finally, work together to develop a plan for next steps, if needed, including setting goals to follow through on commitments, a second pass to deepen the experience, or starting block work if shame and self-blame remain in an intense way.

Appendix E

CAREGIVER STYLES
SELF-REFLECTION TOOL

- In times of stress, are you more like a jellyfish or an ostrich in terms of your responsivity to your loved one's emotion?

- In times of stress, are you more like a kangaroo or a rhino in terms of your caregiving style?

Illustrations courtesy of Maya Partrick. Printed with permission.

- Reflect on your animal tendencies: How do they make you feel?

- How do they influence your coparent/caregiver with respect to his or her animal models, if applicable?

- What steps would you suggest to a friend if he or she wanted to work toward becoming more like the St. Bernard around emotion or the Dolphin around caregiving?

- What blocks could be helpful to explore in order for change to occur?

Appendix F

CAREGIVER TRAPS SCALE

We have found it is a very normal process for caregivers to struggle with concerns that surface while engaging in the tasks of recovery. How likely are you to feel concerned about each of the following items when supporting your loved one?

Please circle the appropriate number where 1 = *not likely* and 7 = *extremely likely*							
1. I worry about being rejected by my loved one.	1	2	3	4	5	6	7
2. I worry about putting strain on my couple relationship.	1	2	3	4	5	6	7
3. I worry about alienating other family members or significant relationships (besides one's partner).	1	2	3	4	5	6	7
4. I worry that my loved one will be seen as abnormal or mentally ill.	1	2	3	4	5	6	7
5. I worry that my loved one will miss out on normal activities or special occasions.	1	2	3	4	5	6	7
6. I worry that I will do or say something I will regret out of frustration or anger.	1	2	3	4	5	6	7
7. I worry about being unable to follow through with interventions (e.g., in the face of resistance, due to time constraints).	1	2	3	4	5	6	7
8. I worry about causing suffering to my loved one or others.	1	2	3	4	5	6	7
9. I worry about breaking down or burning out throughout the process.	1	2	3	4	5	6	7
10. I worry about coddling my loved one and preventing her or him from becoming independent.	1	2	3	4	5	6	7

(continued)

Please circle the appropriate number where 1 = *not likely* and 7 = *extremely likely*

11. I worry about having to face my own past along the way.	1	2	3	4	5	6	7
12. I worry that my loved one's symptoms will shift (e.g., from cutting to substance use, etc.).	1	2	3	4	5	6	7
13. I worry about pushing my loved one "too far," leading to a worsening of symptoms, withdrawal, running away, or suicide, for example.	1	2	3	4	5	6	7
14. I worry about being blamed or being to blame if it doesn't go well.	1	2	3	4	5	6	7
15. Other:	1	2	3	4	5	6	7

When I am triggered, I am more likely to:

1.   2.   3.

BEHAVIOR COACHING

Family Safety Plan for Self-Harm and Suicidality

It can feel scary to support a loved one who is engaging in self-harm behaviors or experiencing suicidal thoughts or urges. You may avoid discussions, express frustration, or try to convince them not to think or feel that way. When we can broach the topic and help our loved ones work through their painful feelings, the symptoms of self-harm and suicidality can decrease. With the support of a psychotherapist, you can use the steps of *emotion coaching* to do so. In addition to emotional support, creating a safety plan is a key element to support.

Warning signs of self-harm/suicidality (e.g., isolation, consistent low mood):

Risks in the home (e.g., medication, sharp objects):

Plan to eliminate risks (e.g., lock up medications, remove or limit access to sharp objects):

Plan to increase one-to-one monitoring (e.g., sleep in loved one's room, invite trusted family members to offer support while away).

Review

1. If you believe your loved one is engaging in self-harm behaviors or experiencing suicidal thoughts or urges, *seek out professional help or emergency services as appropriate.*

2. Use the strategies of emotion coaching to help your loved one work through the emotions associated with his or her symptoms or distress.

3. Stay with your loved one; offer connection and a sense of safety.

4. Manage risks in the home (sharp objects, medications etc.).

5. Call your local crisis services (get support from a mental health professional).

6. Go to your local emergency department and request crisis support. If your loved one refuses to accompany you, call your mobile crisis team or emergency services.

Appendix H

RELATIONSHIP DIMENSIONS SCALE

A. Indicate on the line where you fall on each of the following dimensions in reference to your loved one.

Always apologizing	Never apologizing
Never expressing anger	Always expressing anger
Always showing vulnerability	Never showing vulnerability
Always offering compliments	Never offering compliments
Never offering constructive feedback	Always criticizing
Always offering comfort	Never offering comfort
Always saying "I love you"	Never saying "I love you"
Never sure what to do	Always "sure" what to do
Blaming self	Blaming others
Intense	Laissez-faire
Anxious to resolve conflicts	Aloof in response to conflicts
Never setting limits	Always setting limits
Always serious	Always using humor
Rushing to fix	Letting them learn the hard way

B. Circle one of the bolded choices in each of the following statements:

1. Are you more sensitive to **rejection** or **disrespect**?

2. Are you more comfortable with **providing comfort** or **setting boundaries**?

C. To move towards the middle on three of the dimensions, I will:

Goal 1:

Goal 2:

Goal 3:

Appendix I

CONNECTING IN RELATIONSHIPS
Validating Silence

When your loved one is shutdown, the silence can be painful for all involved, especially if you interpret their behavior as disrespectful or rejecting. Although your loved one may come across as "wanting space," be assured that there are strong (and often vulnerable) underlying emotions that need attention. The following approach may seem contrary to what common sense would suggest, but it's likely to help your loved one to open up, connect, and seek support.

Step 1

Validate your loved one's silence. Convey that you can understand why he or she is closed to your attempts for connection, and from three perspectives:

a. Validate from your loved one's perspective:

  *"I can imagine why you'd not want to speak to me **because** it can be really uncomfortable to talk to others about vulnerable feelings."*

b. Validate from the perspective of the relationship:

  *"I can understand why it would be hard for you to talk to me about your feelings **because** we haven't always been in the habit of talking about the tough stuff."*

c. Validate from your own perspective*:

  *"I can imagine why you would be silent **because** I haven't always been understanding or accepting of your feelings in the past."*

*This perspective is likely to be the most powerful.

Step 2

Validate the emotional states (anger, sadness, fear, loneliness, hopelessness) that you believe may underlie the silence and shutdown behaviors. Remember: making guesses is better than asking questions.

> *"I can imagine that underneath the silence, you might be feeling angry because . . . , because . . . , because . . . I can also imagine that you feel sadness because . . . , because . . . , because . . ."*

Step 3

Now, you may wish to communicate (a) that there is space for them to build trust, (b) that the loved one can take his or her time, and that (c) there is no pressure for them to engage with you at this time. You may also communicate that (d) you will be there for your loved one no matter what. Meeting silence in this way conveys understanding and respect, and this goes a long way toward maintaining connection, even encouraging your loved one to eventually open up. In fact, we've found that it is difficult for many to remain silent when met with this type of unconditional support.

Appendix J

PROCESSING CAREGIVER BLOCKS USING CHAIR WORK

Step 1: Identify the Block

1. Identify the block or problematic pattern of caregiving with the caregiver. For example, the caregiver may resist setting limits or validating a loved one's anger. Once the problematic pattern is identified, the chairs are set up, and the caregiver is invited to sit in the chair to the right of the therapist (also referred to as the "other" chair).

Step 2: Other Chair—Enact the Block

1. Ask the caregiver to take a breath and to picture herself or himself in the other chair.

2. Instruct the caregiver to "Be the part of you that convinces you to/not to . . ." (e.g., avoid conflict, continue to accommodate to the illness, use criticism to motivate, deny the severity of the problem).

3. If caregivers don't spontaneously describe it, ask them to "Scare yourself that it would be a bad idea for your loved one if you . . ."

   Allow caregivers to move through this step and prompt them if needed with: "What's the worst thing that could happen? Because if you did or didn't, then . . ." (e.g., don't push her to go to school because if you do she will get upset and run away/move in with the other caregiver; he'll get more depressed and become suicidal).

4. Then, prompt the caregiver with the following: "If those things were to happen to your child (e.g., she will deteriorate, or worse—die), how would

that be for you?" End with low self-efficacy with emotion: "and you won't be able to handle that pain."

5. Instruct caregivers to "Tell that part to keep doing what they are doing— in other words, keep _____ (repeat of first instruction; e.g., avoiding conflict, accommodating to the illness, using criticism to motivate, denying the severity of the problem)."

Switch the caregiver to the "self" chair on the left.

Step 3: Self Chair—Caregiver Tells Loved One the Plan

1. Ask the caregiver to take a breath and to picture the loved one in the other chair.

2. Offer a succinct summary of the content from Step 2 for the caregiver to share with the loved one, focusing on the following:

   a. Problematic caregiving pattern

   b. Rationale for the loved one's sake

   c. Rationale for the caregiver's sake, highlighting low self-efficacy with emotion

3. Ask the caregiver to share the summary with the loved one (e.g., "Share with your loved one that you're not going to set limits in case she gets angry and maybe even runs away. If that were to happen, you wouldn't know what to do and you'd feel overwhelmed with fear and self-blame").

Switch the caregiver to the "other" chair on the right.

Step 4: Other Chair—Loved One Reacts

1. Ask the caregiver to take a breath.

2. Ask the caregiver to "Be your loved one. [Name of loved one], tell [caregiver] what happens when you hear that."

*If resignation, anger, relief, or agreement, allow the loved one to express the reaction and then say: If you, the loved one, could speak what's underneath or the downside, what would you say (e.g., Even though I don't always show it, I need you. I can't do this without you. I'm scared.)?

If needed, prompt the caregiver to speak from the healthy part of the loved one that wants to be well.

3. Support the loved one to validate the expression of the caregiver's block. "I can understand why you would back off from the limits you set because I _____ " (e.g., resist them and I can be loud).

4. Ask the loved one to tell their caregiver what he or she needs from the caregiver (if needed, prompt the caregiver to relate the need to the block being processed).

   If related to behavior coaching or setting limits, prompt the loved one to ask the caregiver to incorporate emotional support as well (e.g., I need you to follow through on the set limits as well as supporting me with the big emotions that will undoubtedly follow).

5. Make explicit the need for the caregiver to do this even when she or he opposes the caregiver, makes a fuss, and so on.

6. Deepen the softening, the longing, and the love underlying the emotion or needs. This process of deepening will help the caregiver to soften for the next switch. "Tell your mom why you want her to do this. Why is she the most important to you? Tell her how much and how deeply you love her (e.g., Even though I may not always show it, I love you deeply)."

   Switch the caregiver to the "self" chair on the left.

Step 5: Self Chair—Caregiver Reacts to the Loved One

1. Ask the caregiver to take a breath.

2. Ask the caregiver to tell you (the therapist) what it's like to hear what has been said (e.g., a sense of responsibility, empowerment, or sadness).

3. Support the caregiver to share an abridged version of her or his reaction to the loved one's emotions and needs related to the block, with a focus on the realizations made.

4. Encourage the communication of love and compassion toward the loved one.

5. Encourage the caregiver to tell the loved one what he or she will do differently from now on. Guide the caregiver to be specific and to use the pronoun "I" not "we" (e.g., I am going to make sure I stay calm when we talk about your symptoms; I am going to validate your anger).

   If the block related to behavior coaching or setting limits, invite the caregiver to make a commitment relating to emotional support as well (e.g., I will set the limits and support you with the big emotions that will come).

6. Support the caregiver to warn the loved one that it won't always go perfectly; the caregiver will still act out emotional block at times, but that he or she won't give up (e.g., I know I might lose my temper, back off or make mistakes, but I am determined to keep going).

Switch the caregiver to the "other" chair on the right.

Step 6: Other Chair—Loved One Reacts to Caregiver's Revised Plan

1. Ask the caregiver to take a breath.

2. As the loved one, ask him or her to share with the caregiver how it feels to hear that, encouraging an authentic answer; more than one reaction is possible.

   *Help the "loved one" to express what's underneath (anger, fear, doubt), even though he or she may never share these vulnerabilities overtly (e.g., Thank you, I want to believe things can be different, but they've not gone well before. I'm scared it will be too hard for you or you will get angry with me, but underneath, I feel relief. I really need you. I can't do this alone).

3. Encourage the expression of relief and gratitude (if not spontaneous).

4. Ask the loved one (by name) if there is anything else he or she would like to share with the caregiver.

   Switch the caregiver to the "self" chair on the left.

Step 7: Self Chair—Caregiver Connects With Therapist

1. Ask the caregiver to take a breath.

2. Ask the caregiver to tell you (the therapist) how it feels to hear this from the loved one and debrief together, including the development of a plan for implementation if relevant.

Appendix K

CLINICIAN TRAPS SCALE

It is normal for clinicians to have concerns when making decisions or implementing treatment. How likely are you to feel concerned about each of the following items when making clinical decisions or implementing treatment?

Please circle the appropriate number where 1 = *not likely* and 7 = *extremely likely*							
1. Being disliked by caregivers/client.	1	2	3	4	5	6	7
2. Causing suffering to the caregivers/client.	1	2	3	4	5	6	7
3. Going into an emotion and not knowing how to process it.	1	2	3	4	5	6	7
4. Putting strain on the couple, child-parent, carer-loved one relationship.	1	2	3	4	5	6	7
5. Pushing a caregiver or client "too far" leading to a worsening of symptoms, withdrawal, termination, suicide, etc.	1	2	3	4	5	6	7
6. Making decisions that may be unpopular with, or contrary to the views of, other team members.	1	2	3	4	5	6	7
7. Bringing in a critical or dismissive caregiver, leading to too much distress for the client.	1	2	3	4	5	6	7
8. Having to face my own triggers, vulnerabilities, or wounds along the way.	1	2	3	4	5	6	7
9. Being blamed or being to blame for lack of treatment progress.	1	2	3	4	5	6	7
10. Blaming the client/caregivers for lack of treatment progress.	1	2	3	4	5	6	7
11. Feeling or appearing incompetent or lacking competence	1	2	3	4	5	6	7
12. Other:	1	2	3	4	5	6	7

When triggered, I am more likely to:

1.   2.   3.

Appendix L

SELF-DIRECTED BLOCK WORKSHEET FOR CLINICIANS

1. Identify a "style" of parent/caregiver you've experienced (or heard about through his or her loved one) whom you would hesitate to involve in the treatment process.

    - Critical of their loved one, their partner, the treatment team or of you
    - Dismissive or in denial of their loved one's illness
    - Defensive or overly sensitive about being blamed
    - Emotionally fragile
    - Suffering from a serious mental health issue
    - Hesitant to be involved
    - Busy or overwhelmed with other responsibilities
    - Lives too far away

2. On a scale of 1 to 10, rate the potential for this caregiver to play a positive and supportive role in the loved one's recovery. A lower number refers to a lower level of potential.

    $$1 — 2 — 3 — 4 — 5 — 6 — 7 — 8 — 9 — 10$$

3. Identify three therapy-interfering behaviors that you have heard about, observed, or would expect to observe during the course of a session with the loved one or outside of treatment:

    A. Criticize you
    B. Criticize the loved one
    C. Cancel appointments
    D. Be aggressive in the session
    E. Become blatantly distressed, tearful, or self-blaming
    F. Align with the loved one in opposition to you

    G. Insist that the loved one take the lead or take charge of the symptom interruption

    H. Undermine or devalue therapy or team recommendations

    I. Get angry or blow up in front of their loved one for having symptoms

    J. Give up on supporting loved one in the face of resistance

    K. Agree to engage and then not follow through outside of session

    L. Give up on the possibility of their loved one's recovery

4. In your opinion, what negative outcomes could happen if their loved one were exposed to, or continued to be exposed to, these behaviors:

- Not engage in the therapy
- Become more symptomatic
- Become depressed, suicidal
- Become hopeless about family's potential to "get it" or change
- Become hopeless about their own potential to change
- Devalue the therapy
- Not recover

5. Therapy-interfering behaviors serve to regulate FEAR, SHAME, HELP-LESSNESS, HOPELESSNESS, and/or RESENTMENT in the caregiver.

For each of the three therapy-interfering behaviors that you noted above (Question 3), check the emotions in the caregiver that might be driving the expression of their behaviors. Note which behavior you identified in the blank (A, B, C, etc.), and check *all of the feelings that apply* for each of the identified behaviors.

Behavior ___ FEAR, SHAME, HELPLESSNESS, HOPELESSNESS, RESENTMENT

Behavior ___ FEAR, SHAME, HELPLESSNESS, HOPELESSNESS, RESENTMENT

Behavior ___ FEAR, SHAME, HELPLESSNESS, HOPELESSNESS, RESENTMENT

    a. Criticize you

    b. Criticize the loved one

    c. Cancel appointments

    d. Be aggressive in the session

    e. Become blatantly distressed, tearful or self-blaming

    f. Align with the loved one in opposition to you

    g. Insist that the loved one take the lead or take charge of symptom interruption

    h. Undermine or devalue therapy or team recommendations

    i. Get angry or blow up in front of their loved one for having symptoms

    j. Give up on supporting loved one in the face of resistance

    k. Agree to engage and then not follow through outside of session

    l. Give up on the possibility of recovery

6. What three negative outcomes could happen for YOU as the clinician if you were exposed to, or continued to be exposed to, these caregiver behaviors (observing them in session or hearing about them from your client):

    A. Feel anger toward the caregiver

    B. Dislike the caregiver

    C. Feel incompetent

    D. Feel hopeless

    E. Feel worried for the loved one

    F. Feel ineffective as a clinician

    G. Blame the caregiver

    H. Feel burned out

    I. Feel responsible for the further breakdown of the caregiver–loved one's relationship

7. Picture the loved one in front of you and visualize sharing with them the rating you gave in Question 2 along with the reasons you identified on the sheet for your rating.

    "I think that your caregiver's capacity to be positive and supportive in your recovery is a ___ out of 10 (from Question 2) because I think they will 1. _____, 2. _____, and 3. _____ (from Question 3)."

    a. If the loved one could speak from a place of vulnerability and love for the caregiver, how would he or she react to your statement? What do you see on the loved one's face and in his or her body language in response? How might the loved one be feeling?

       Relief (if relief, which of the other emotions would the loved one be left with?)

    • Sadness

    • Helplessness

    • Hopelessness

    • Fear

    • Anger

    • Shame

   b. What would the loved one want you to know?

   c. What would the loved one want you to do?

8. Reluctance to bring in the caregiver serves to regulate FEAR, SHAME, HELPLESSNESS, HOPELESSNESS, and/or RESENTMENT in the CLINICIAN.

   For each of the negative outcomes you identified in Question 6, check the emotions that might be driving your reluctance to work with the identified caregiver. Check *all of those that apply* for each of the identified negative outcomes.

   Negative outcome __ FEAR, SHAME, HELPLESSNESS, HOPELESSNESS, RESENTMENT

   Negative outcome __ FEAR, SHAME, HELPLESSNESS, HOPELESSNESS, RESENTMENT

   Negative outcome __ FEAR, SHAME, HELPLESSNESS, HOPELESSNESS, RESENTMENT

9. What goals can you set to work through your own feelings of fear, shame, helplessness, hopelessness, or resentment?

10. What goals can you set to respond differently to the caregiver and loved one?

Appendix M

PROCESSING CLINICIAN BLOCKS USING CHAIR WORK–CAREGIVER INVOLVEMENT

Step 1: Identify the Block

1. Identify the block with the clinician. For example, the caregiver may resist setting limits or validating a loved one's anger. The clinician may either (a) wish to exclude the caregiver from the therapy or (b) feel hopeless about the caregiver's ability to be supportive. Once the block is identified, the chairs are set up, and the clinician is invited to sit in the chair to the right of the facilitator (also referred to as the "other" chair).

Step 2: Other Chair–Enact the Block

1. Ask the clinician to take a breath and to picture herself or himself in the opposite chair.

2. Instruct the clinician to "Be the part of you that convinces you to exclude the caregiver from treatment" (e.g., the caregiver is to blame for the problems or lack of progress; the caregiver has no potential for being supportive; the caregiver will make things worse).

3. If the clinician doesn't spontaneously describe it, ask him or her to "Scare yourself that it would be a bad idea for your client to involve the caregiver."

   Allow the clinician to move through this step, prompting if needed with: "What's the worst thing that could happen? Because if you involve the caregiver, then . . ." (e.g., it will upset the client if it doesn't go well; the client's symptoms will get worse).

4. If appropriate, you may also prompt the clinician to be specific about how it could go poorly for the caregiver (e.g., the caregiver will burn out or withdraw from the therapy).

5. Then, prompt the clinician to "Be specific about how it could go poorly for you, the clinician, if those things were to happen (c)" (e.g., the caregiver will reject you; you will look stupid; your team will judge you; your client will feel betrayed if things get worse or you will be to blame). End with low self-efficacy with emotion: "and you won't be able to handle that pain."

Switch the clinician to the "self" chair on the left.

Step 3: Self Chair—Clinician Tells Client the Plan

1. Ask the clinician to take a breath and picture the client in the other chair.

2. Offer a succinct summary of the content from Step 2 for the clinician to share with the client, focusing on the following:
   a. Excluding caregiver from involvement in treatment
   b. Rationale for the client/caregiver's sake
   c. Rationale for the clinician's sake, highlighting low self-efficacy with emotion

3. Ask the clinician to share the summary with the client (e.g., "Tell your client that you are not going to invite her caregiver into treatment because you don't think her caregiver can be helpful and it could be make things worse for everyone. Tell her you are worried that if it doesn't go well, you will blame yourself and you can't deal with that right now").

4. Instruct the clinician to tell the client: "I will be a better caregiver/partner to you."

Switch the clinician to the "other" chair on the right.

Step 4: Other Chair—Client Reacts

1. Ask the clinician to take a breath.

2. Ask the clinician to: "Be your client. (Name of client), what happens when you hear that?"

*If resignation, anger, relief, agreement, allow the client to express the reaction and then say: "If you, the client, could speak what's underneath or the downside, what would you say?" (e.g., Even though I'm scared, I want my caregiver to be involved in some way. *I'm not sure I can do this without her. It scared me to hear you say that).

If needed, prompt the clinician to speak from the healthy part of their client that wants to be well.

3. Support the client to validate the expression of the clinician's block: "I can understand why you would be reluctant to involve my caregiver because I _____" (portray them in a very negative light; I am really struggling right now).

4. Ask the client to share what they need from the clinician regarding the issue of caregiver involvement.

If needed, prompt the clinician to relate the need to the block being processed (e.g., I need you to find a way to see my caregiver in a more positive light/to involve my caregiver/to believe in my caregiver).

5. Deepen the client's need for the clinician to take charge even when he or she opposes (e.g., when you first bring it up, I'm going to resist the idea, but don't take it at face value—there's more to it).

6. Invite the client to tell the clinician why her or she wants and needs this from the clinician specifically, focusing on the positive qualities of the clinician (e.g., I trust you; there's no one else who believes in us the way you do).

Switch the clinician to the "self" chair on the left.

Step 5: Self Chair—Clinician Reacts to Client

1. Ask the clinician to take a breath.

2. Ask the clinician to tell you (the facilitator) what it's like to hear what they've heard (e.g., guilt, sadness, a sense of responsibility, empowerment).

3. Support the clinician to share an abridged version of his or her reaction to the client's emotions and needs related to caregiver involvement, with a focus on the realizations made.

4. Encourage the communication of respect and compassion for the client.

5. Encourage the clinician to tell the client what he or she will do differently from now on. Guide the clinician to be specific and to use the pronoun "I" not "we" (e.g., I am going to invite your caregiver into the therapy; I will

coach your caregiver; I will seek supervision so that I can see all sides of the issue).

6. Support the clinician to warn the client that it won't go perfectly but that he or she won't give up (e.g., I know I will make mistakes, but I am determined to keep working this through on your behalf).

Switch the clinician to the "other" chair on the right.

Step 6: Other Chair—Client Reacts to Clinician's Revised Plan

1. Ask the clinician to take a breath.

2. As the client, ask him or her to share how it feels to hear that, encouraging an authentic answer; more than one reaction is possible.

   Help the "client" to express what's underneath if anger, fear, or doubt, even though he or she may never share these vulnerabilities overtly (e.g., Thank you, I want to believe things can be different but they've not gone well before. I'm scared it will be too hard for me or you, but underneath, I feel relief, I really need this—I can't do this alone).

3. Encourage the expression of relief or gratitude (if not spontaneous).

4. Ask the client (by name) if there is anything else he or she would like to share with the clinician.

   Switch the clinician to the "self" chair on the left.

Step 7: Self Chair—Clinician Connects with Facilitator

1. Ask the clinician to take a breath.

2. Ask the clinician to tell you (the facilitator) how it feels to hear this from the client and debrief together, including the development of a plan for implementation if relevant.

HELPFUL RESOURCES WHEN CARING FOR A LOVED ONE WITH AN EATING DISORDER

Books

(*caregiving—life span*):

Treasure, J., Smith, G., & Crane, A. (2017). *Skills-based learning for caring for a loved one with an eating disorder: The new Maudsley method* (2nd ed.). Abingdon, Oxfordshire, England: Routledge.

(*caregiving—adolescent*):

Lock, J., & Le Grange, D. (2015). *Help your teenager beat an eating disorder* (2nd ed.). New York, NY: Guilford Press.

(*caregiving—child and adolescent*):

Boachie, A., & Jasper, K. (2011). *A parent's guide to defeating eating disorders: Spotting the stealth bomber and other symbolic approaches.* London, England: Jessica Kingsley.

(*self-help—adult; useful exercises for caregivers to use with loved ones*):

Heffner, M., & Eifert, G. H. (2008). *The anorexia workbook: How to accept yourself, heal your suffering, and reclaim your life.* Oakland, CA: New Harbinger.

(*Self-help—adult; useful exercises for caregivers to use with loved ones*):

McCabe, R. E., McFarlane, T. L., & Olmstead, M. P. (2003). *The overcoming bulimia workbook: Your comprehensive step-by-step guide to recovery.* Oakland, CA: New Harbinger.

Meal Support Video

https://keltyeatingdisorders.ca/

Websites

Emotion-Focused Family Therapy: http://www.emotionfocusedfamilytherapy.org
Mental Health Foundations: http://www.mentalhealthfoundations.ca/resources
National Eating Disorder Information Centre (Canada): http://nedic.ca/
National Initiative for Eating Disorders (Canada): http://www.nied.ca
The New Maudsley Approach: http://www.thenewmaudsleyapproach.co.uk
Family-based treatment for eating disorders: http://www.maudsleyparents.org
Families Empowered and Supporting Treatment of Eating Disorders: http://www.feast-ed.org
Kelty Mental Health Resource Centre (Canada): http://www.keltyeating disorders.ca

References

Abbass, A. (2004). Small-group videotape training for psychotherapy skills development. *Academic Psychiatry, 28,* 151–155. http://dx.doi.org/10.1176/appi.ap.28.2.151

Abbass, A., Arthey, S., Elliott, J., Fedak, T., Nowoweiski, D., Markovski, J., & Nowoweiski, S. (2011). Web-conference supervision for advanced psychotherapy training: A practical guide. *Psychotherapy, 48,* 109–118. http://dx.doi.org/10.1037/a0022427

Aldao, A., Nolen-Hoeksema, S., & Schweizer, S. (2010). Emotion-regulation strategies across psychopathology: A meta-analytic review. *Clinical Psychology Review, 30,* 217–237. http://dx.doi.org/10.1016/j.cpr.2009.11.004

American Psychiatric Association. (2013). *Diagnostic and statistical manual of mental disorders* (5th ed.). Washington, DC: Author.

American Psychological Association. (2017a). *Ethical principles of psychologists and code of conduct* (2002, Amended June 1, 2010, and January 1, 2017). Retrieved from http://www.apa.org/ethics/code/index.aspx

American Psychological Association. (2017b). *Multicultural guidelines: An ecological approach to context, identity, and intersectionality.* Retrieved from https://www.apa.org/about/policy/multicultural-guidelines.pdf

American Psychological Association. (Producer). (2020). *Emotion-focused family therapy* [DVD]. Available from https://www.apa.org/pubs/videos

Arcelus, J., Mitchell, A. J., Wales, J., & Nielsen, S. (2011). Mortality rates in patients with anorexia nervosa and other eating disorders. A meta-analysis of 36 studies. *Archives of General Psychiatry, 68,* 724–731. http://dx.doi.org/10.1001/archgenpsychiatry.2011.74

Aron, E. N., & Aron, A. (1997). Sensory-processing sensitivity and its relation to introversion and emotionality. *Journal of Personality and Social Psychology, 73,* 345–368. http://dx.doi.org/10.1037/0022-3514.73.2.345

Aron, E. N., Aron, A., & Jagiellowicz, J. (2012). Sensory processing sensitivity: A review in the light of the evolution of biological responsivity. *Personality* and Social Psychology Review, *16*, 262–282. http://dx.doi.org/10.1177/1088868311434213

Attia, E. (2010). Anorexia nervosa: Current status and future directions. *Annual Review of Medicine, 61*, 425–435. http://dx.doi.org/10.1146/annurev.med.050208.200745

Balbernie, R. (2001). Circuits and circumstances: The neurobiological consequences of early relationship experiences and how they shape later behaviour. *Journal of Child Psychotherapy, 27*, 237–255.

Barr, P. (2015). Guilt, shame and fear of death predict neonatal intensive care unit–related parental distress. *Journal of Reproductive and Infant Psychology, 33*, 402–413. http://dx.doi.org/10.1080/02646838.2015.1043624

Bartels, A., & Zeki, S. (2004). The neural correlates of maternal and romantic love. *NeuroImage, 21*, 1155–1166. http://dx.doi.org/10.1016/j.neuroimage.2003.11.003

Bechara, A., Damasio, H., & Damasio, A. R. (2000). Emotion, decision making and the orbitofrontal cortex. *Cerebral Cortex, 10*, 295–307. http://dx.doi.org/10.1093/cercor/10.3.295

Benham, G. (2006). The highly sensitive person: Stress and physical symptom reports. *Personality and Individual Differences, 40*, 1433–1440. http://dx.doi.org/10.1016/j.paid.2005.11.021

Berking, M., Wupperman, P., Reichardt, A., Pejic, T., Dippel, A., & Znoj, H. (2008). Emotion-regulation skills as a treatment target in psychotherapy. *Behaviour Research and Therapy, 46*, 1230–1237. http://dx.doi.org/10.1016/j.brat.2008.08.005

Berking, M., & Wupperman, P. (2012). Emotion regulation and mental health: Recent findings, current challenges, and future directions. *Current Opinion in Psychiatry, 25*, 128–134. http://dx.doi.org/10.1097/YCO.0b013e3283503669

Boachie, A., & Jasper, K. (2011). *A parent's guide to defeating eating disorders: Spotting the stealth bomber and other symbolic approaches*. London, England: Jessica Kingsley.

Bowen, M. (1978). *Family therapy in clinical practice*. New York, NY: Aronson.

Bowen, M. (1982). *Family therapy in clinical practice* (2nd ed.). New York, NY: Aronson.

Bøyum, H., & Stige, S. H. (2017). Jeg forstår henne bedre nå: En kvalitativ studie av foreldres opplevelse av relasjonen til egne barn etter emosjonsfokusert foreldreveiledning ["I understand her better now": A qualitative study of parents' experiences of their relationship to their children after emotion-focused family therapy (EFFT)]. *Scandinavian Psychologist, 4*, e11. http://dx.doi.org/10.15714/scandpsychol.4.e11

Breines, J. G., & Chen, S. (2013). Activating the inner caregiver: The role of support-giving schemas in increasing state self-compassion. *Journal of Experimental Social Psychology, 49*, 58–64. http://dx.doi.org/10.1016/j.jesp.2012.07.015

Brener, L., Rose, G., von Hippel, C., & Wilson, H. (2013). Implicit attitudes, emotions, and helping intentions of mental health workers toward their clients. *Journal of Nervous and Mental Disease, 201*, 460–463. http://dx.doi.org/10.1097/NMD.0b013e318294744a

Carr, K., Holman, A., Abetz, J., Kellas, J. K., & Vagnoni, E. (2015). Giving voice to the silence of family estrangement: Comparing reasons of estranged parents and adult children in a nonmatched sample. *Journal of Family Communication, 15*, 130–140. http://dx.doi.org/10.1080/15267431.2015.1013106

Cassidy, J., & Shaver, P. R. (Eds.). (2002). *Handbook of attachment: Theory, research, and clinical applications.* New York, NY: Guilford Press.

Chen, E., Brody, G. H., & Miller, G. E. (2017). Childhood close family relationships and health. *American Psychologist, 72*, 555–566. http://dx.doi.org/10.1037/amp0000067

Ciarrochi, J. V., Deane, F. P., & Anderson, S. (2002). Emotional intelligence moderates the relationship between stress and mental health. *Personality and Individual Differences, 32*, 197–209. http://dx.doi.org/10.1016/S0191-8869(01)00012-5

Couturier, J., Kimber, M., & Szatmari, P. (2013). Efficacy of family-based treatment for adolescents with eating disorders: A systematic review and meta-analysis. *International Journal of Eating Disorders, 46*, 3–11. http://dx.doi.org/10.1002/eat.22042

Davidson, T., Stillar, A., Hirschfeld, E., Jago, M., & Lafrance Robinson, A. (2014, October). *Exploring the impact of group-based EFFT, for adolescents with eating disorders, on parental fear, emotional dysregulation and accommodating and enabling behaviours.* Poster session presented at the Canadian Group Psychotherapy Association Conference, Toronto, Ontario, Canada.

Dias, B. G., & Ressler, K. J. (2014). Parental olfactory experience influences behavior and neural structure in subsequent generations. *Nature Neuroscience, 17*, 89–96. http://dx.doi.org/10.1038/nn.3594

Dimitropoulos, G., Freeman, V. E., Allemang, B., Couturier, J., McVey, G., Lock, J., & Le Grange, D. (2015). Family-based treatment with transition age youth with anorexia nervosa: A qualitative summary of application in clinical practice. *Journal of Eating Disorders, 3*, 1–13. http://dx.doi.org/10.1186/s40337-015-0037-3

Dimitropoulos, G., Landers, A. L., Freeman, V., Novick, J., Garber, A., & Le Grange, D. (2018). Open trial of family-based treatment of anorexia nervosa for transition age youth. *Journal of the Canadian Academy of Child and Adolescent Psychiatry/Journal De L'académie Canadienne De Psychiatrie De L'enfant Et De L'adolescent, 27*, 50–61.

Dolhanty, J., & Greenberg, L. (2007). Emotion-focused therapy for eating disorders. *European Psychotherapy, 7*, 97–116.

Doran, G. T. (1981). There's a S.M.A.R.T. way to write management's goals and objectives. *Management Review, 70*, 35–36.

Eaton, K., Ohan, J. L., Stritzke, W. G., & Corrigan, P. W. (2016). Failing to meet the good parent ideal: Self-stigma in parents of children with mental health disorders. *Journal of Child and Family Studies, 25,* 3109–3123.

Eaton, K., Ohan, J. L., Stritzke, W. G., & Corrigan, P. W. (2019). The Parents' Self Stigma Scale: Development, factor analysis, reliability, and validity. *Child Psychiatry and Human Development, 50,* 83–94.

Eisner, B. (1997). Set, setting, and matrix. *Journal of Psychoactive Drugs, 29,* 213–216. http://dx.doi.org/10.1080/02791072.1997.10400190

Elliott, R., Watson, J. C., Goldman, R. N., & Greenberg, L. S. (2004). *Learning emotion-focused therapy: The process-experiential approach to change.* Washington, DC: American Psychological Association. http://dx.doi.org/10.1037/10725-000

Evans, D. E., & Rothbart, M. K. (2008). Temperamental sensitivity: Two constructs or one? *Personality and Individual Differences, 44,* 108–118. http://dx.doi.org/10.1016/j.paid.2007.07.016

Evans-Lacko, S., Takizawa, R., Brimblecombe, N., King, D., Knapp, M., Maughan, B., & Arseneault, L. (2017). Childhood bullying victimization is associated with use of mental health services over five decades: A longitudinal nationally representative cohort study. *Psychological Medicine, 47,* 127–135. http://dx.doi.org/10.1017/S0033291716001719

Extremera, N., & Fernández-Berrocal, P. (2006). Emotional intelligence as predictor of mental, social, and physical health in university students. *The Spanish Journal of Psychology, 9,* 45–51. http://dx.doi.org/10.1017/S1138741600005965

Fernández, M. C., & Arcia, E. (2004). Disruptive behaviors and maternal responsibility: A complex portrait of stigma, self-blame, and other reactions. *Hispanic Journal of Behavioral Sciences, 26,* 356–372. http://dx.doi.org/10.1177/0739986304267208

Foroughe, M., Stillar, A., Goldstein, L., Dolhanty, J., Goodcase, E. T., & Lafrance, A. (2018). Brief emotion focused family therapy: An intervention for parents of children and adolescents with mental health issues. *Journal of Marital and Family Therapy.* Advance online publication. http://dx.doi.org/10.1111/jmft.12351

Franko, D. L., & Rolfe, S. (1996). Countertransference in the treatment of patients with eating disorders. *Psychiatry, 59,* 108–116. http://dx.doi.org/10.1080/00332747.1996.11024753

Fredrickson, B. L., & Branigan, C. (2005). Positive emotions broaden the scope of attention and thought-action repertoires. *Cognition and Emotion, 19,* 313–332. http://dx.doi.org/10.1080/02699930441000238

Ginott, H. G. (1965). *Between parent and child.* New York, NY: Avon Books.

Girz, L., Robinson, A. L., Foroughe, M., Jasper, K., & Boachie, A. (2013). Adapting family-based therapy to a day hospital programme for adolescents with eating disorders: Preliminary outcomes and trajectories of change.

Journal of Family Therapy, 35, 102–120. http://dx.doi.org/10.1111/j.1467-6427.2012.00618.x

Goddard, E., Macdonald, P., Sepulveda, A. R., Naumann, U., Landau, S., Schmidt, U., & Treasure, J. (2011). Cognitive interpersonal maintenance model of eating disorders: Intervention for caregivers. *The British Journal of Psychiatry, 199,* 225–231. http://dx.doi.org/10.1192/bjp.bp.110.088401

Goddard, E., Macdonald, P., & Treasure, J. (2011). An examination of the impact of the Maudsley collaborative care skills training workshops on patients with anorexia nervosa: A qualitative study. *European Eating Disorders Review, 19,* 150–161. http://dx.doi.org/10.1002/erv.1042

Golan, M., Yeruslavski, A., & Stein, D. (2009). Managing eating disorders—Countertransference processes in the therapeutic milieu. *International Journal of Child and Adolescent Health, 2,* 214–227.

Goleman, D. (1995). *Emotional intelligence.* New York, NY: Bantam Books.

Gordon, D. A., Arbuthnot, J., Gustafson, K. E., & McGreen, P. (1988). Home-based behavioral-systems family therapy with disadvantaged juvenile delinquents. *The American Journal of Family Therapy, 16,* 243–255. http://dx.doi.org/10.1080/01926188808250729

Gottesman, I. I., Laursen, T. M., Bertelsen, A., & Mortensen, P. B. (2010). Severe mental disorders in offspring with 2 psychiatrically ill parents. *Archives of General Psychiatry, 67,* 252–257. http://dx.doi.org/10.1001/archgenpsychiatry.2010.1

Gottman, J. (with DeClaire, J.). (1998). *Raising an emotionally intelligent child: The heart of parenting.* New York, NY: Simon & Schuster.

Gottman, J. M., Katz, L. F., & Hooven, C. (1996). Parental meta-emotion philosophy and the emotional life of families: Theoretical models and preliminary data. *Journal of Family Psychology, 10,* 243–268. http://dx.doi.org/10.1037/0893-3200.10.3.243

Gratz, K. L., Weiss, N. H., & Tull, M. T. (2015). Examining emotion regulation as an outcome, mechanism, or target of psychological treatments. *Current Opinion in Psychology, 3,* 85–90. http://dx.doi.org/10.1016/j.copsyc.2015.02.010

Greenberg, L. S. (1979). Resolving splits: Use of the two-chair technique. *Psychotherapy: Theory, Research & Practice, 16,* 316–324. http://dx.doi.org/10.1037/h0085895

Greenberg, L. S. (2002). *Emotion-focused therapy: Coaching clients to work through their feelings.* Washington, DC: American Psychological Association. http://dx.doi.org/10.1037/10447-000

Greenberg, L. S. (2008). Emotion and cognition in psychotherapy: The transforming power of affect. *Canadian Psychology, 49,* 49–59. http://dx.doi.org/10.1037/0708-5591.49.1.49

Greenberg, L. S. (2010). Emotion-focused therapy: A clinical synthesis. *Focus, 8,* 32–42.

Greenberg, L. S. (2011). *Emotion-focused therapy.* Washington, DC: American Psychological Association.

Greenberg, L. S. (2015). *Emotion-focused therapy: Coaching clients to work through their feelings* (2nd ed.). Washington, DC: American Psychological Association. http://dx.doi.org/10.1037/14692-000

Greenberg, L. S. (2016). *Supervision essentials for emotion-focused therapy.* Washington, DC: American Psychological Association.

Greenberg, L. S. (2017). *Emotion-focused therapy: Theory and practice* (Rev. ed.). Washington, DC: American Psychological Association. http://dx.doi.org/10.1037/15971-000

Greenberg, L. S., & Goldman, R. N. (2008). *Emotion-focused couples therapy: The dynamics of emotion, love, and power.* Washington, DC: American Psychological Association. http://dx.doi.org/10.1037/11750-000

Greenberg, L. S., & Johnson, S. (1988). *Emotionally focused couples therapy.* New York, NY: Guilford Press.

Greenberg, L. S., Warwar, S. H., & Malcolm, W. M. (2008). Differential effects of emotion-focused therapy and psychoeducation in facilitating forgiveness and letting go of emotional injuries. *Journal of Counseling Psychology, 55,* 185–196. http://dx.doi.org/10.1037/0022-0167.55.2.185

Greenberg, L. S., Warwar, S., & Malcolm, W. (2010). Emotion-focused couples therapy and the facilitation of forgiveness. *Journal of Marital and Family Therapy, 36,* 28–42. http://dx.doi.org/10.1111/j.1752-0606.2009.00185.x

Greenberg, R. P., & Staller, J. (1981). Personal therapy for therapists. *The American Journal of Psychiatry, 138,* 1467–1471. http://dx.doi.org/10.1176/ajp.138.11.1467

Gross, J. J. (2002). Emotion regulation: Affective, cognitive, and social consequences. *Psychophysiology, 39,* 281–291. http://dx.doi.org/10.1017/S0048577201393198

Haggerty, G., & Hilsenroth, M. J. (2011). The use of video in psychotherapy supervision. *British Journal of Psychotherapy, 27,* 193–210. http://dx.doi.org/10.1111/j.1752-0118.2011.01232.x

Halmi, K. A. (2009). Perplexities and provocations of eating disorders. *Journal of Child Psychology and Psychiatry, 50,* 163–169. http://dx.doi.org/10.1111/j.1469-7610.2008.01983.x

Halmi, K. A. (2013). Perplexities of treatment resistance in eating disorders. *BMC Psychiatry, 13,* 292. Advance online publication. http://dx.doi.org/10.1186/1471-244X-13-292

Hancock, K. J., Mitrou, F., Shipley, M., Lawrence, D., & Zubrick, S. R. (2013). A three generation study of the mental health relationships between grandparents, parents and children. *BMC Psychiatry, 13,* 299. Advance online publication. http://dx.doi.org/10.1186/1471-244X-13-299

Harper, G. (1983). Varieties of parenting failure in anorexia nervosa: Protection and parentectomy, revisited. *Journal of the American Academy of Child Psychiatry, 22,* 134–139. http://dx.doi.org/10.1016/S0002-7138(09)62326-8

Havighurst, S. S., Wilson, K. R., Harley, A. E., Prior, M. R., & Kehoe, C. (2010). Tuning in to kids: Improving emotion socialization practices in parents of preschool children—Findings from a community trial. *Journal of Child Psychology and Psychiatry, 51*, 1342–1350. http://dx.doi.org/10.1111/j.1469-7610.2010.02303.x

Haworth-Hoeppner, S. (2000). The critical shapes of body image: The role of culture and family in the production of eating disorders. *Journal of Marriage and the Family, 62*, 212–227. http://dx.doi.org/10.1111/j.1741-3737.2000.00212.x

Hay, P. J., Touyz, S., & Sud, R. (2012). Treatment for severe and enduring anorexia nervosa: A review. *Australian and New Zealand Journal of Psychiatry, 46*, 1136–1144. http://dx.doi.org/10.1177/0004867412450469

Henderson, K. A., & Mayman, S. (2018, October). *C-CARE: A comprehensive treatment model for concurrent eating disorders and substance use disorders.* Presented at the 6th Biennial Conference of the Eating Disorders Association of Canada, Ottawa.

Henggeler, S. W., Rowland, M. D., Randall, J., Ward, D. M., Pickrel, S. G., Cunningham, P. B., . . . Santos, A. B. (1999). Home-based multisystemic therapy as an alternative to the hospitalization of youths in psychiatric crisis: Clinical outcomes. *Journal of the American Academy of Child & Adolescent Psychiatry, 38*, 1331–1339. http://dx.doi.org/10.1097/00004583-199911000-00006

Hirschfeld, E., Stillar, A., Davidson, T., Jago, M., & Lafrance Robinson, A. (2014, October). *Family involvement in adult eating disorders: A pilot workshop for carers.* Poster presented at the Canadian Group Psychotherapy Association Conference, Toronto, Ontario, Canada.

Holt, T., Jensen, T. K., & Wentzel-Larsen, T. (2014). The change and the mediating role of parental emotional reactions and depression in the treatment of traumatized youth: Results from a randomized controlled study. *Child and Adolescent Psychiatry and Mental Health, 8*, 11. http://dx.doi.org/10.1186/1753-2000-8-11

Hudson, J. I., Hiripi, E., Pope, H. G., Jr., & Kessler, R. C. (2007). The prevalence and correlates of eating disorders in the National Comorbidity Survey Replication. *Biological Psychiatry, 61*, 348–358. http://dx.doi.org/10.1016/j.biopsych.2006.03.040

Hughes, D. A., & Baylin, J. (2012). *Brain-based parenting: The neuroscience of caregiving for healthy attachment.* New York, NY: Norton.

Jensen, T. (2018). *Parenting the crisis: The cultural politics of parent-blame.* Bristol, England: Policy Press.

Jerome, E. M., & Liss, M. (2005). Relationships between sensory processing style, adult attachment, and coping. *Personality and Individual Differences, 38*, 1341–1352. http://dx.doi.org/10.1016/j.paid.2004.08.016

Johnson, S. M. (2004). *The practice of emotionally focused couple therapy: Creating connection* (2nd ed.). New York, NY: Routledge.

Joseph, R. (1999). Environmental influences on neural plasticity, the limbic system, emotional development and attachment: A review. *Child Psychiatry and Human Development, 29*, 189–208. http://dx.doi.org/10.1023/A:1022660923605

Katzman, D. K., & Findlay, S. M. (2011). Medical issues unique to children and adolescents. In D. Le Grange & J. Lock (Eds.), *Eating disorders in children and adolescents: A clinical handbook* (pp. 137–155). New York, NY: Guilford Press.

Keenan, K. (2000). Emotion dysregulation as a risk factor for child psychopathology. *Clinical Psychology: Science and Practice, 7*, 418–434. http://dx.doi.org/10.1093/clipsy.7.4.418

Kendall, P. C. (1994). Treating anxiety disorders in children: Results of a randomized clinical trial. *Journal of Consulting and Clinical Psychology, 62*, 100–110. http://dx.doi.org/10.1037/0022-006X.62.1.100

Klump, K. L., Bulik, C. M., Kaye, W. H., Treasure, J., & Tyson, E. (2009). Academy for Eating Disorders position paper: Eating disorders are serious mental illnesses. *International Journal of Eating Disorders, 42*, 97–103. http://dx.doi.org/10.1002/eat.20589

Kosmerly, S. (2014). *The perceived influence of emotions on clinical decision and practices in child and adolescent eating disorders* (Unpublished master's thesis). Laurentian University, Sudbury, Ontario, Canada.

Kosmerly, S., Graham, H., Dahmer, L., Kostakos, M., Gartshore, A., & Lafrance Robinson, A. (2013, May). *Outcomes of an emotion-focused therapy group for parents of children with eating disorders: An adjunct to family-based treatment.* Paper presented at the Academy of Eating Disorders International Conference, Montreal, Quebec, Canada.

Kosmerly, S., Penney, S., Renelli, M., Miller, A., & Lafrance, A. (2018). *Finding the heart of the matter: Clinician perspectives on supervision in emotion-focused family therapy.* Manuscript in preparation.

Kosmerly, S., Waller, G., & Lafrance Robinson, A. (2015). Clinician adherence to guidelines in the delivery of family-based therapy for eating disorders. *International Journal of Eating Disorders, 48*, 223–229. http://dx.doi.org/10.1002/eat.22276

Kret, M. E., & Ploeger, A. (2015). Emotion processing deficits: A liability spectrum providing insight into comorbidity of mental disorders. *Neuroscience and Biobehavioral Reviews, 52*, 153–171. http://dx.doi.org/10.1016/j.neubiorev.2015.02.011

Kyriacou, O., Treasure, J., & Schmidt, U. (2008). Understanding how parents cope with living with someone with anorexia nervosa: Modelling the factors that are associated with carer distress. *International Journal of Eating Disorders, 41*, 233–242. http://dx.doi.org/10.1002/eat.20488

Lafrance, A., Strahan, E., & Stillar, A. (2019). *Treatment-engagement fears in family-based therapies: Validation of the Caregiver Traps Scale for Eating Disorders.* Manuscript submitted for publication.

Lafrance Robinson, A. L., Dolhanty, J., & Greenberg, L. (2015). Emotion-focused family therapy for eating disorders in children and adolescents. *Clinical Psychology & Psychotherapy, 22*, 75–82. http://dx.doi.org/10.1002/cpp.1861

Lafrance Robinson, A., Dolhanty, J., Stillar, A., Henderson, K., & Mayman, S. (2016). Emotion-focused family therapy for eating disorders across the lifespan: A pilot study of a 2-day transdiagnostic intervention for parents. *Clinical Psychology & Psychotherapy, 23*, 14–23. http://dx.doi.org/10.1002/cpp.1933

Lafrance Robinson, A., & Kosmerly, S. (2015). The influence of clinician emotion on decisions in child and adolescent eating disorder treatment: A survey of self and others. *Eating Disorders, 23*, 163–176. http://dx.doi.org/10.1080/10640266.2014.976107

Larkings, J. S., Brown, P. M., & Scholz, B. (2017). "Why am I like this?" Consumers discuss their causal beliefs and stigma. *International Journal of Mental Health, 46*, 206–226. http://dx.doi.org/10.1080/00207411.2017.1304076

Le Grange, D., & Eisler, I. (2009). Family interventions in adolescent anorexia nervosa. *Child and Adolescent Psychiatric Clinics of North America, 18*, 159–173. http://dx.doi.org/10.1016/j.chc.2008.07.004

Le Grange, D., Lock, J., Loeb, K., & Nicholls, D. (2010). Academy for Eating Disorders position paper: The role of the family in eating disorders. *International Journal of Eating Disorders, 43*, 1–5.

Liss, M., Mailloux, J., & Erchull, M. J. (2008). The relationships between sensory processing sensitivity, alexithymia, autism, depression, and anxiety. *Personality and Individual Differences, 45*, 255–259. http://dx.doi.org/10.1016/j.paid.2008.04.009

Liss, M., Timmel, L., Baxley, K., & Killingsworth, P. (2005). Sensory processing sensitivity and its relation to parental bonding, anxiety, and depression. *Personality and Individual Differences, 39*, 1429–1439. http://dx.doi.org/10.1016/j.paid.2005.05.007

Lock, J., & Le Grange, D. (2015). *Treatment manual for anorexia nervosa: A family-based approach* (2nd ed.). New York, NY: Guilford Press.

Lock, J., Le Grange, D., Agras, W., & Dare, C. (2000). *Treatment manual for anorexia nervosa: A family-based approach*. New York, NY: Guildford Press.

Luecken, L. J., Kraft, A., & Hagan, M. J. (2009). Negative relationships in the family-of-origin predict attenuated cortisol in emerging adults. *Hormones and Behavior, 55*, 412–417. http://dx.doi.org/10.1016/j.yhbeh.2008.12.007

Lynch, T. R., Chapman, A. L., Rosenthal, M. Z., Kuo, J. R., & Linehan, M. M. (2006). Mechanisms of change in dialectical behavior therapy: Theoretical and empirical observations. *Journal of Clinical Psychology, 62*, 459–480. http://dx.doi.org/10.1002/jclp.20243

Macran, S., & Shapiro, D. A. (1998). The role of personal therapy for therapists: A review. *British Journal of Medical Psychology, 71*, 13–25. http://dx.doi.org/10.1111/j.2044-8341.1998.tb01364.x

Madigan, S. (2013). Narrative family therapy. In A. Rambo, C. West, A. Schooley, & T. V. Boyd (Eds.), *Family therapy review: Contrasting contemporary models* (pp. 151–155). New York, NY: Routledge/Taylor & Francis Group.

Maté, G. (2011). *When the body says no: The cost of hidden stress.* Hoboken, NJ: Wiley.

Mehler, P. S. (2018). Medical complications of anorexia nervosa and bulimia nervosa. In W. S. Agras & A. Robinson (Eds.), *The Oxford handbook of eating disorders* (2nd ed., pp. 222–228). New York, NY: Oxford University Press.

Meiser, B., Mitchell, P. B., Kasparian, N. A., Strong, K., Simpson, J. M., Mireskandari, S., . . . Schofield, P. R. (2007). Attitudes towards childbearing, causal attributions for bipolar disorder and psychological distress: A study of families with multiple cases of bipolar disorder. *Psychological Medicine, 37,* 1601–1611. http://dx.doi.org/10.1017/S0033291707000852

Meneses, C. W., & Greenberg, L. S. (2011). The construction of a model of the process of couples' forgiveness in emotion-focused therapy for couples. *Journal of Marital and Family Therapy, 37,* 491–502. http://dx.doi.org/10.1111/j.1752-0606.2011.00234.x

Meneses, C. W., & Greenberg, L. S. (2014). Interpersonal forgiveness in emotion-focused couples' therapy: Relating process to outcome. *Journal of Marital and Family Therapy, 40,* 49–67. http://dx.doi.org/10.1111/j.1752-0606.2012.00330.x

Miller, W. R., & Rollnick, S. (2012). *Motivational interviewing: Helping people change.* New York, NY: Guilford Press.

Minuchin, S. (1970). The use of an ecological framework in the treatment of a child. In J. Anthony & C. Koupernik (Eds.), *The child in his family* (pp. 41–57). New York, NY: Wiley.

Monin, J. K. (2016). Emotion regulation in the context of spousal caregiving: Intrapersonal and interpersonal strategies. In J. Bookwala (Ed.), *Couple relationships in the middle and later years: Their nature, complexity, and role in health and illness* (pp. 281–301). Washington, DC: American Psychological Association. http://dx.doi.org/10.1037/14897-015

Morris, A. S., Silk, J. S., Steinberg, L., Myers, S. S., & Robinson, L. R. (2007). The role of the family context in the development of emotion regulation. *Social Development, 16,* 361–388. http://dx.doi.org/10.1111/j.1467-9507.2007.00389.x

Moses, T. (2010). Exploring caregivers' self-blame in relation to adolescents' mental disorders. *Family Relations, 59,* 103–120. http://dx.doi.org/10.1111/j.1741-3729.2010.00589.x

Munn, R., Smeltzer, D., Smeltzer, T., & Westin, K. (2010). The most painful gaps: Family perspectives on the treatment of eating disorders. In M. Maine, B. H. McGilley, & D. W. Bunnell (Eds.), *Treatment of eating disorders: Bridging the research–practice gap* (pp. 349–364). San Diego, CA: Elsevier Academic Press. http://dx.doi.org/10.1016/B978-0-12-375668-8.10021-X

Neff, K. D., & Germer, C. (2017). Self-compassion and psychological wellbeing. In E. M. Seppälä, E. Simon-Thomas, S. L. Brown, M. C. Worline, C. D. Cameron, & J. Doty (Ed.), *Oxford handbook of compassion science* (pp. 371–386). New York, NY: Oxford University Press.

Neufeld, G., & Maté, G. (2004). *Hold on to your kids: Why parents matter.* Toronto, Ontario, Canada: A. A. Knopf.

Niedenthal, P., & Ric, F. (2017). *Psychology of emotion.* New York, NY: Psychology Press. http://dx.doi.org/10.4324/9781315276229

Nixon, C. D., & Singer, G. H. (1993). Group cognitive-behavioral treatment for excessive parental self-blame and guilt. *American Journal on Mental Retardation, 97,* 665–672.

Paleari, F. G., Compare, A., Melli, S., Zarbo, C., & Grossi, E. (2015, July). Self-blame, self-forgiveness and wellbeing among parents of autistic children. Poster session presented at the 14th European Congress of Psychology, Milan, Italy.

Penney, S. (2018). *Therapists' perceptions of the impact of emotions on clinical decision-making in child and adolescent eating disorders* (Unpublished master's thesis). Laurentian University, Sudbury, Ontario, Canada.

Phelan, J. C., Yang, L. H., & Cruz-Rojas, R. (2006). Effects of attributing serious mental illnesses to genetic causes on orientations to treatment. *Psychiatric Services, 57,* 382–387. http://dx.doi.org/10.1176/appi.ps.57.3.382

Phillips, S. B. (2011). Up close and personal: A consideration of the role of personal therapy in the development of a psychotherapist. In R. H. Klein, H. S. Bernard, & V. L. Schermer (Eds.), *On becoming a psychotherapist: The personal and professional journey* (pp. 144–164). New York, NY: Oxford University Press.

Probst, B. (2015). The other chair: Portability and translation from personal therapy to clinical practice. *Clinical Social Work Journal, 43,* 50–61. http://dx.doi.org/10.1007/s10615-014-0485-2

Rasic, D. (2010). Countertransference in child and adolescent psychiatry—A forgotten concept? *Journal of the Canadian Academy of Child and Adolescent Psychiatry, 19,* 249–254.

Rasic, D., Hajek, T., Alda, M., & Uher, R. (2014). Risk of mental illness in offspring of parents with schizophrenia, bipolar disorder, and major depressive disorder: A meta-analysis of family high-risk studies. *Schizophrenia Bulletin, 40,* 28–38. http://dx.doi.org/10.1093/schbul/sbt114

Reijonen, J. H., Pratt, H. D., Patel, D. R., & Greydanus, D. E. (2003). Eating disorders in the adolescent population: An overview. *Journal of Adolescent Research, 18,* 209–222. http://dx.doi.org/10.1177/0743558403018003002

Safran, J. D., & Muran, J. C. (2003). *Negotiating the therapeutic alliance: A relational treatment guide.* New York, NY: Guilford Press.

Salters-Pedneault, K., Steenkamp, M., & Litz, B. (2010). Suppression. In A. Kring & D. Sloan (Eds.), *Emotion regulation and psychopathology: A transdiagnostic approach to etiology and treatment* (pp. 137–156). New York, NY: Guilford Press.

Satter, E. (2000). *Child of mine: Feeding with love and good sense* (Rev. ed.). Boulder, CO: Bull.

Scarnier, M., Schmader, T., & Lickel, B. (2009). Parental shame and guilt: Distinguishing emotional responses to a child's wrongdoings. *Personal Relationships, 16,* 205–220. http://dx.doi.org/10.1111/j.1475-6811.2009.01219.x

Scharp, K. M., & Thomas, L. J. (2016). Family "bonds": Making meaning of parent–child relationships in estrangement narratives. *Journal of Family Communication, 16,* 32–50. http://dx.doi.org/10.1080/15267431.2015.1111215

Schebendach, J. E., Mayer, L. E. S., Devlin, M. J., Attia, E., Contento, I. R., Wolf, R. L., & Walsh, B. T. (2008). Dietary energy density and diet variety as predictors of outcome in anorexia nervosa. *The American Journal of Clinical Nutrition, 87,* 810–816. http://dx.doi.org/10.1093/ajcn/87.4.810

Schickedanz, A., Halfon, N., Sastry, N., & Chung, P. J. (2018). Parents' adverse childhood experiences and their children's behavioral health problems. *Pediatrics, 142,* e20180023. Advance online publication. http://dx.doi.org/10.1542/peds.2018-0023

Schmidt, U., & Treasure, J. (2006). Anorexia nervosa: Valued and visible. A cognitive-interpersonal maintenance model and its implications for research and practice. *British Journal of Clinical Psychology, 45,* 343–366. http://dx.doi.org/10.1348/014466505X53902

Sepulveda, A. R., Lopez, C., Todd, G., Whitaker, W., & Treasure, J. (2008). An examination of the impact of "The Maudsley Eating Disorder Collaborative Care Skills Workshops" on the well being of carers: A pilot study. *Social Psychiatry and Psychiatric Epidemiology, 43,* 584–591. http://dx.doi.org/10.1007/s00127-008-0336-y

Siegel, D. J. (2010). *The mindful therapist: A clinician's guide to mindsight and neural integration.* New York, NY: Norton.

Siegel, D. J. (2012). *Pocket guide to interpersonal neurobiology.* New York, NY: Norton.

Sloan, E., Hall, K., Moulding, R., Bryce, S., Mildred, H., & Staiger, P. K. (2017). Emotion regulation as a transdiagnostic treatment construct across anxiety, depression, substance, eating and borderline personality disorders: A systematic review. *Clinical Psychology Review, 57,* 141–163. http://dx.doi.org/10.1016/j.cpr.2017.09.002

Smolewska, K. A., McCabe, S. B., & Woody, E. Z. (2006). A psychometric evaluation of the Highly Sensitive Person Scale: The components of sensory-processing sensitivity and their relation to the BIS/BAS and "Big Five." *Personality and Individual Differences, 40,* 1269–1279. http://dx.doi.org/10.1016/j.paid.2005.09.022

Solenberger, S. E. (2001). Exercise and eating disorders: A 3-year inpatient hospital record analysis. *Eating Behaviors, 2,* 151–168. http://dx.doi.org/10.1016/S1471-0153(01)00026-5

Starr, L. R., Hammen, C., Conway, C. C., Raposa, E., & Brennan, P. A. (2014). Sensitizing effect of early adversity on depressive reactions to later proximal stress: Moderation by polymorphisms in serotonin transporter and corticotropin releasing hormone receptor genes in a 20-year longitudinal study. *Development and Psychopathology, 26,* 1241–1254. http://dx.doi.org/10.1017/S0954579414000996

Stillar, A., Strahan, E., Nash, P., Files, N., Scarborough, J., Mayman, S., . . . Lafrance Robinson, A. (2016). The influence of carer fear and self-blame when supporting a loved one with an eating disorder. *Eating Disorders, 24,* 173–185. http://dx.doi.org/10.1080/10640266.2015.1133210

Strahan, E. J., Stillar, A., Files, N., Nash, P., Scarborough, J., Connors, L., . . . Lafrance, A. (2017). Increasing parental self-efficacy with emotion-focused family therapy for eating disorders: A process model. *Person-Centered and Experiential Psychotherapies, 16,* 256–269. http://dx.doi.org/10.1080/14779757.2017.1330703

Tennen, H., & Affleck, G. (1990). Blaming others for threatening events. *Psychological Bulletin, 108,* 209–232. http://dx.doi.org/10.1037/0033-2909.108.2.209

Tennen, H., Affleck, G., & Gershman, K. (1986). Self-blame among parents of infants with perinatal complications: The role of self-protective motives. *Journal of Personality and Social Psychology, 50,* 690–696. http://dx.doi.org/10.1037/0022-3514.50.4.690

Thompson-Brenner, H., Satir, D. A., Franko, D. L., & Herzog, D. B. (2012). Clinician reactions to patients with eating disorders: A review of the literature. *Psychiatric Services, 63,* 73–78. http://dx.doi.org/10.1176/appi.ps.201100050

Titelman, P. (2003). *Emotional cutoff: Bowen family systems theory perspectives.* New York, NY: Haworth Press.

Tobin, D. L., Banker, J. D., Weisberg, L., & Bowers, W. (2007). I know what you did last summer (and it was not CBT): A factor analytic model of international psychotherapeutic practice in the eating disorders. *International Journal of Eating Disorders, 40,* 754–757. http://dx.doi.org/10.1002/eat.20426

Toussaint, L. L., Worthington, E. L., Jr., & Williams, D. R. (Eds.). (2015). *Forgiveness and health: Scientific evidence and theories relating forgiveness to better health.* New York, NY: Springer Science + Business Media. http://dx.doi.org/10.1007/978-94-017-9993-5

Treasure, J., Crane, A., McKnight, R., Buchanan, E., & Wolfe, M. (2011). First do no harm: Iatrogenic maintaining factors in anorexia nervosa. *European Eating Disorders Review, 19,* 296–302. http://dx.doi.org/10.1002/erv.1056

Treasure, J., & Schmidt, U. (2013). The cognitive-interpersonal maintenance model of anorexia nervosa revisited: A summary of the evidence for cognitive, socio-emotional and interpersonal predisposing and perpetuating factors. *Journal of Eating Disorders, 1*, 13. Advance online publication. http://dx.doi.org/10.1186/2050-2974-1-13

Treasure, J., Schmidt, U., & Macdonald, P. (Eds.). (2010). *The clinician's guide to collaborative caring in eating disorders: The New Maudsley method*. New York, NY: Routledge.

Treasure, J., Sepulveda, A. R., MacDonald, P., Whitaker, W., Lopez, C., Zabala, M., . . . Todd, G. (2008). The assessment of the family of people with eating disorders. *European Eating Disorders Review, 16*, 247–255. http://dx.doi.org/10.1002/erv.859

Treasure, J., Smith, G., & Crane, A. (2007). *Skills-based learning for caring for a loved one with an eating disorder: The new Maudsley method*. New York, NY: Routledge/Taylor & Francis.

Uher, R. (2014). Gene–environment interactions in severe mental illness. *Frontiers in Psychiatry, 5*, 48. http://dx.doi.org/10.3389/fpsyt.2014.00048

Uher, R., & Zwicker, A. (2017). Etiology in psychiatry: Embracing the reality of poly-gene-environmental causation of mental illness. *World Psychiatry, 16*, 121–129. http://dx.doi.org/10.1002/wps.20436

Von Holle, A., Pinheiro, A. P., Thornton, L. M., Klump, K. L., Berrettini, W. H., Brandt, H., . . . Bulik, C. M. (2008). Temporal patterns of recovery across eating disorder subtypes. *Australian and New Zealand Journal of Psychiatry, 42*, 108–117. http://dx.doi.org/10.1080/00048670701787610

Waller, G. (2009). Evidence-based treatment and therapist drift. *Behaviour Research and Therapy, 47*, 119–127. http://dx.doi.org/10.1016/j.brat.2008.10.018

Waller, G., Stringer, H., & Meyer, C. (2012). What cognitive behavioral techniques do therapists report using when delivering cognitive behavioral therapy for the eating disorders? *Journal of Consulting and Clinical Psychology, 80*, 171–175. http://dx.doi.org/10.1037/a0026559

Waller, G., & Turner, H. (2016). Therapist drift redux: Why well-meaning clinicians fail to deliver evidence-based therapy, and how to get back on track. *Behaviour Research and Therapy, 77*, 129–137. http://dx.doi.org/10.1016/j.brat.2015.12.005

Waltz, M. M. (2015). Mothers and autism: The evolution of a discourse of blame. *AMA Journal of Ethics, 17*, 353–358.

Warren, C. S., Schafer, K. J., Crowley, M. E. J., & Olivardia, R. (2013). Demographic and work-related correlates of job burnout in professional eating disorder treatment providers. *Psychotherapy, 50*, 553–564. http://dx.doi.org/10.1037/a0028783

Warren, R., Smeets, E., & Neff, K. D. (2016). Self-criticism and self-compassion: Risk and resilience for psychopathology. *Current Psychiatry, 15*, 18–32.

Watson, A. C., Corrigan, P., Larson, J. E., & Sells, M. (2007). Self-stigma in people with mental illness. *Schizophrenia Bulletin, 33*, 1312–1318. http://dx.doi.org/10.1093/schbul/sbl076

Whitney, J., & Eisler, I. (2009). Theoretical and empirical models around caring for someone with an eating disorder: The reorganization of family life and inter-personal maintenance factors. *Journal of Mental Health, 14,* 575–585. http://dx.doi.org/10.1080/09638230500347889

World Health Organization. (2018). *ICD-11 for mortality and morbidity statistics.* Retrieved from https://icd.who.int/browse11/l-m/en

Wrigley, S., Jackson, H., Judd, F., & Komiti, A. (2005). Role of stigma and attitudes toward help-seeking from a general practitioner for mental health problems in a rural town. *Australian and New Zealand Journal of Psychiatry, 39,* 514–521. http://dx.doi.org/10.1080/j.1440-1614.2005.01612.x

Yalom, I. D. (1995). *The theory and practice of group psychotherapy.* New York, NY: Basic Books.

Yarnell, L. M., & Neff, K. D. (2013). Self-compassion, interpersonal conflict resolutions, and well-being. *Self and Identity, 12,* 146–159. http://dx.doi.org/10.1080/15298868.2011.649545

Zipfel, S., Wild, B., Groß, G., Friederich, H.-C., Teufel, M., Schellberg, D., . . . Herzog, W. (2014). Focal psychodynamic therapy, cognitive behaviour therapy, and optimised treatment as usual in outpatients with anorexia nervosa (ANTOP study): Randomised controlled trial. *The Lancet, 383,* 127–137. http://dx.doi.org/10.1016/S0140-6736(13)61746-8

Index

A

Academic functioning, 31, 58
Accommodating behaviors, 27, 65, 82, 134
Adoptive parents, 78
Advanced caregiving skills
  common blocks to, 83–84
  defined, 14
  and emotion coaching, 33
  equipping caregivers with, 82
  implementation of, 85
Affect, flat, 136
Aggression, 31, 58
American Psychological Association (APA), 9
AN (anorexia nervosa), 119
Anger
  capacity to hold, 26
  and caregiver blocks, 90, 94
  and chair work, 97, 99, 11
  and clinician blocks, 117, 136
  and eating disorders, 123, 130
  and emotion coaching, 34–36, 38–40
  and emotion-focused health care, 145
  and forgiveness, 79
  needs associated with, 39, 40
  and therapeutic apologies, 66, 72, 73
  and treatment of eating disorders, 130, 136
  in two-step model of emotion coaching, 40–41
Animal metaphors, 86–88, 107–108, 161–162
Anorexia nervosa (AN), 119
The Anorexia Workbook: How to Accept Yourself, Heal Your Suffering, and Reclaim Your Life (Heffner & Eifert), 185

Anxiety and anxiety disorders
  behavior coaching strategies for, 17, 54
  caregiver anxiety, 60, 89
  and caregiver blocks, 90
  in case example, 59–60
  clinician anxiety, 108
  and eating disorders, 120
  effectiveness of EFFT for, 142
  and emotion-focused health care, 145
  externalization and normalization of anxiety, 57
  fear vs., 34, 39
  and forgiveness, 79
  needs associated with, 39, 40
  and parent blame, 42
  patterns of reactivity and, 54
  prioritization of interventions for, 57
  resistance toward exposures for, 83
  and super-feelers, 32, 152
  and treatment of eating disorders, 130
  worry, 42, 57, 78, 107
APA (American Psychological Association), 9
Apologies, therapeutic. See Therapeutic apologies
Attachment, 5, 25, 30, 142
Attention-deficit/hyperactivity disorder, 54
Autism spectrum disorder, 42
Autonomy, 102, 122, 136
Avoidance
  and caregiver blocks, 82
  in case example, 59
  emotional, 13, 33, 53, 123
  and emotion coaching, 29
  and facing anxiety, 34, 108
  and super-feelers, 32

B

BED (binge eating disorder), 119
Behavioral activation, 52, 83
Behavioral issues, 13, 142
Behavior coaching, 49–61
  case example, 58–60
  for eating disorders, 17, 52, 54,
    124–128
  overview, 17, 49–52
  safety plan for, 165–166
  steps in, 155–156
  targets in, 52–58
  in two-day EFFT caregiver workshop, 23
Betrayal, 66
Binge eating disorder (BED), 119
Bingeing, 126–127
Blame, 63–64. *See also* "No blame"
    principle; Self-blame
"Blast" (therapeutic apologies), 72–73, 76
Blocks, 82. *See also specific headings*
BN (bulimia nervosa), 119
Body image, 119, 132
Brief model of emotion coaching. *See*
    Two-step model of emotion coaching
Bulimia nervosa (BN), 119
Burnout. *See also* Compassion fatigue and
    burnout
  of caregivers, 13, 84, 141
  of clinicians, 116, 117

C

Caregiver blocks, 81–103
  and behavior coaching, 56
  common, 83–84
  overview, 18
  processing of, 24, 85–101, 171–174
  in treatment of eating disorders, 123,
    134–135
  wisdom in, 84–85
Caregiver empowerment and involvement
  and behavior coaching, 50
  client resistance toward, 140
  clinician blocks related to, 106, 110–114
  in emotion coaching, 129–130
  importance of, 5
  overview, 12–13
  and therapeutic apologies, 65, 66
  in treatment for eating disorders,
    123–124
Caregiver-led emotion-focused family
    therapy, 19–22

Caregivers. *See also specific headings*
  collaboration between clinicians and, 15
  defined, 5
  empowerment of, 5
  role of, 4
Caregiver Styles Self-Reflection Tool, 86,
    161–162
Caregiver Traps Scale, 86, 88–90, 163–164
Caregiver Traps Scale for Eating Disorders
    (CTS-ED), 134–135
Carers. *See* Caregivers
Case conceptualization, 105
C-CARE treatment model, 143–144
Certification, 9
Chair work
  and behavior coaching, 56
  and client resistance to caregiver
    involvement, 140
  in family-based therapies, 24
  and integration of EFFT in treatment
    settings, 19
  for processing caregiver blocks, 85,
    94–100, 171–174
  for processing clinician blocks, 106,
    107, 109–114, 181–184
  for therapeutic apologies, 64–66,
    157–160
Clinical decision-making, 105
Clinician blocks, 105–118
  and benefits of supervision, 117
  in other forms of treatment, 24–25
  overview, 18
  and therapeutic apologies, 115–116
  self-care and personal therapy for,
    116–117
  strategies for working through,
    106–115, 181–184
  in treatment of eating disorders, 123,
    135–137
Clinicians. *See also specific headings*
  collaboration between caregivers
    and, 15
  defined, 5
  EFFT certification for, 9
Clinician Traps Scale, 24, 108, 175
Coaching. *See* Behavior coaching; Emotion
    coaching
Cognitive behavior therapy, 24
Cognitive distortions, 24
Cognitive interpersonal maintenance
    model, 122
Collaboration, 15, 50, 53, 126, 155–156
Collaborative care skills, 122

Compassion
  and behavior coaching, 57
  communication of, 99
  deepening of, 100
  self-. *See* Self-compassion
Compassion fatigue and burnout, 116
Compulsive exercising, 17, 127–128
Conduct disorders, 54
Confidentiality, 115, 140
Connecting in relationships
  validating silence, 169–170
Cooperation, 155–156
Coregulation, 30, 35
Couples therapy, 143
Creativity, 100
Criticism
  and caregiver blocks, 82, 83
  and family-based therapies, 24
  overt, 18
Crystal ball metaphor, 71, 158
CTS–ED (Caregiver Traps Scale for Eating
    Disorders), 134–135
Cultural factors, 9, 36, 133

D

Defensiveness, 45, 82, 133
Denial, 73, 76, 82, 145
Depression
  and behavior coaching targets, 52
  and emotional intelligence, 31, 32
  and forgiveness, 79
  resistance toward behavioral activation
    for, 83
  and vulnerability of super-feelers, 152
Despondence, 130
Developmental theories, 142
*Diagnostic and Statistical Manual of Mental
    Disorders (DSM–5)*, 119
Dietitians, 19, 123
Disruptive disorders, 54
Doubt, 41, 42
*DSM–5 (Diagnostic and Statistical Manual
    of Mental Disorders)*, 119
Dyad sessions, 16

E

Eating disorders (EDs), 119–138
  behavior coaching strategies for, 17, 52,
    54, 124–128
  caregiver blocks in treatment of, 123,
    134–135
  caregiver psychoeducation and
    empowerment for, 123–124
  clinician blocks in treatment of, 123,
    135–137
  and comorbid substance use, 120, 136,
    139, 143–144
  effectiveness of EFFT for, 142
  emotion coaching strategies for, 123,
    128–132
  family involvement in, 24, 120–122
  intensive treatment for, 128
  and parent blame, 42
  research on emotion-focused family
    therapy for, 26–27
  resources for helping loved ones with,
    185–186
  and super-feelers, 152
  therapeutic apologies in treatment of,
    123, 132–134
Educators, 19
EFFT. *See* Emotion-focused family therapy
EFHC (emotion-focused health care), 145
EFT. *See* Emotion-focused therapy
Eisler, I., 142
Emotional avoidance, 13, 33, 53, 123
Emotional eruptions, 53, 55
Emotional intelligence, 31, 68
Emotionally focused family therapy, 3n1,
    143
Emotional mastery, 31
Emotional miscues, 36
Emotional needs, 38–39, 93, 145
Emotional support
  and behavior coaching targets, 53
  and caregiver resistance, 140
  in emotion-focused health care, 145
  in five-step model of emotion
    coaching, 40
  in two-step model of emotion coaching,
    41
Emotion-based disorders, 23
Emotion blocks. *See also* Caregiver blocks;
    Clinician blocks; Two-day EFFT
    caregiver workshop
  interventions for transformation of,
    11–12
  in two-day EFFT caregiver workshop, 23
  types of, 18
Emotion coaching, 29–48
  and behavior coaching, 49–50, 53,
    58–60
  and caregiver blocks, 92–94
  cheat sheet for, 153–154

in family-based emotion-focused
family therapy, 22
in family sessions, 45–47
models of, 17, 34–41, 142
overview, 17, 31–32
potential pitfalls with, 47–48
for processing caregiver blocks, 85
and super-feelers, 32–33
teaching skills in, 33–45
and therapeutic apologies, 70
in treatment of eating disorders, 123,
128–132
Emotion converters, 123
Emotion-focused family therapy (EFFT),
11–28. *See also specific headings*
caregiver empowerment and
involvement in, 12–13
core principles of, 4–5, 11–16
extensions of, 143–145
frequently asked questions about,
140–143
key terms in, 5–6
methods for delivery of, 19–26
modules of, 16–19
overview, 3–4
research on, 26–28
website for resources on, 186
Emotion-focused health care (EFHC),
145
Emotion-focused school support, 144
Emotion-focused supervision, 18
Emotion-focused therapy (EFT)
chair work in, 95
for couples, 68
emotion processing in, 17
Emotion processing
development of, 31–32
emotion coaching techniques derived
from, 17
internalization of skills for, 129
and mental health difficulties, 4
overview, 13–14
and therapeutic apologies, 75
in treatment of co-occurring substance
use and eating disorders, 144
Emotion-regulation skills, 30–32
Empathy, 32, 95, 116, 129
Enabling behaviors, 65, 82
Ethical issues, 141–142
*Ethical Principles of Psychologists and Code
of Conduct* (American Psychological
Association), 9

Exercise
compulsive, 17, 127–128
and self-care, 116
Experiential practice
of behavior coaching, 55–56
of emotion coaching, 43–44
and five-step model of emotion
coaching, 37
as principle of EFFT, 4
for processing caregiver blocks, 85,
93–94
Exposures, 24, 83
Externalizing language, 57

F

Families Empowered and Supporting
Treatment of Eating Disorders
(F.E.A.S.T.), 121, 186
Family-based emotion-focused family
therapy, 22
Family-based therapies, 24
Family-based treatment for eating
disorders, 186
Family members, 5. *See also* Caregivers
Family sessions, 16, 45–47
Fatigue, 106, 116
Fear
anxiety vs., 34
and caregiver blocks, 82, 83, 86, 89,
92, 101
and clinician blocks, 107, 109
as common type of emotion block, 18
needs associated with, 39, 40
and treatment of eating disorders, 131
Fear hierarchies, 17
F.E.A.S.T. (Families Empowered and
Supporting Treatment of Eating
Disorders), 121
Feedback, 44, 56
Feeding disorders, 54, 119. *See also* Eating
disorders
Firmness, 116
Five-step model of emotion coaching
components of, 35–40
overview, 17, 34
Flat affect, 136
Forgiveness, 68, 79. *See also* Therapeutic
apologies
Foster parents, 78
Friends, 5. *See also* Caregivers
Frontal lobe, 30

G

Genetics, 30, 151
Ginott, Haim, 31
Good house–bad house metaphor, 41–43,
　70–71
Gottman, J. M., 17, 31, 34, 142
Grandparents, 5. *See also* Caregivers
Gratitude, 74
Greenberg, L. S., 34, 142, 143
Group home staff, 6. *See also* Caregivers
Guardians, 5. *See also* Caregivers
Guilt, 35, 65, 69, 70, 133. *See also*
　Self-blame

H

Health care settings, 145
Health-focused behaviors, 49
Health outcomes, 65
Helplessness
　and caregiver blocks, 83, 92
　and clinician blocks, 107, 109
　as common type of emotion block, 18
　and self-blame, 65
Help Your Teenager Beat an Eating Disorder
　(Lock & Le Grange), 185
Henderson, K., 143, 147–148
Hierarchy of target behaviors, 56
Homework, 90–91
Hope, 26
Hopelessness
　and caregiver blocks, 83, 92
　and clinician blocks, 106, 107, 109
　as common type of emotion block, 18
　and emotion coaching, 31
　and family-based therapies, 24
　and normalizing language, 57
　and treatment of eating disorders,
　136
Humor, 43
Hurt
　capacity to hold, 26
　and therapeutic apologies, 66, 73, 133
Hypothalamus, 30

I

Iatrogenic maintenance model of eating
　disorders, 135
Imaginal exercises, 71
Impulse-control disorders, 54

Individual therapy
　for clinicians, 116–117
　emotion-processing skills in, 30
　and role of EFFT, 25–26
Informed consent, 115
Inpatient staff, 24–25
Intelligence, emotional, 31, 68
Intensive treatment for eating disorders,
　128
Intergenerational trauma, 5, 14, 75
International Classification of Diseases,
　119
International Institute for Emotion-
　Focused Family Therapy, 9
Interoceptive exposures, 24
Interpersonal learning, 91
Interpersonal neurobiology, 142
Isolation, 57

J

Johnson, S., 143

K

Kelty Mental Health Resource Centre, 186

L

Labeling (five-step model of emotion
　coaching)
　overview, 35–36, 153–154
　of shame, 34
Lafrance, A., 144, 145, 149
Legal issues, 141–142
Le Grange, D., 142
Limit-setting, 128
Lock, J., 142
Love, 26

M

Major depressive disorders, 54. *See also*
　Depression
Maté, G., 142
Mayman, S., 143, 148
Meal support (eating disorders), 17,
　124–125, 130, 186
Medical issues, 142
Medical professionals, 19, 123
Meditations, 141
Mental health difficulties, 4. *See also*
　specific headings

Mental Health Foundations, 186
Miller, A., 145
Mind–body health, 142
Mindfulness, 116
Modeling, 30
Modules of emotion-focused family
    therapy, 16–19. See also specific
    headings
  behavior coaching, 17
  caregiver blocks, 18
  clinician blocks, 18
  emotion coaching, 17
  and integration in treatment settings,
    18–19
  therapeutic apologies, 17–18
Mood disorders
  and eating disorders, 120
  effectiveness of EFFT for, 142
Morris, A. S., 30
Motivation, 26
Motivational interviewing, 122, 142
Multicultural Guidelines (American
    Psychological Association), 9

N

National Eating Disorder Information
    Centre, 186
National Initiative for Eating Disorder, 186
Negative reinforcement, 53
New Maudsley method, 86–88, 107,
    121–123, 186
"No blame" principle
  benefits of, 147
  overview, 4, 14–15
  for therapeutic apologies, 75
Nonadherence, 145
Nonjudgment, 55, 115
Nonverbal cues, 35, 36
Normalizing language, 57–58
Nurses and nursing home attendants, 19
Nutrition, 124

O

Observational learning, 30
Obsessive-compulsive disorder
  behavior coaching targets for, 54
  prioritization of interventions for, 57
One-degree effect, 15–16, 102
Optimism, 100
Other-blame, 65, 82

Outcome research on emotion-focused
    family therapy, 26, 28
The Overcoming Bulimia Workbook: Your
    Comprehensive Step-by-Step Guide
    to Recovery (McCabe, McFarlane, &
    Olmstead), 185
Oxytocin, 30

P

Parental self-efficacy, 26
Parent blame, 41–42
Parentectomies, 121
Parents, 4, 5. See also Caregivers
A Parent's Guide to Defeating Eating
    Disorders: Spotting the Stealth Bomber
    and Other Symbolic Approaches
    (Boachie & Jasper), 185
Partners. See Romantic partners
Peer relationships, 31
Personality disorders, 16, 18, 136, 142
Physical activity, 116
Positive reinforcement, 53
Practical support, 41
Prevention parenting, 31, 48
Problem solving
  and caregiver blocks, 86
  in five-step model of emotion coaching,
    39–40
Process research, 27
Progressive muscle relaxation, 24
Psychoeducation
  in emotion coaching, 34
  in family-based emotion-focused family
    therapy, 22
  in New Maudsley method, 122
  for processing caregiver blocks,
    85–86
  in treatment of eating disorders,
    123–124
  for working through caregiver b
    locks, 94
  for working through clinician blocks,
    106–107
Psychologists, 19
Purging, 17, 127

R

Rasic, D., 107
Reassurance, 73–74, 76
Reciprocity, 5

Recovery coaching, 144
Refeeding syndrome, 124n1
Reinforcement, 35, 53, 60
Rejection, 82
Relationship Dimensions Scale
    and caregiver blocks, 86–87, 90–92
    copy of, 167–168
    and use in family-based therapies,
        24
Relationship repair, 66, 115. *See also*
    Therapeutic apologies
Relationship strain, 13, 26, 64, 66, 133
Research on emotion-focused family
        therapy, 26–28
Resentment
    and caregiver blocks, 82, 86, 92
    and clinician blocks, 107, 109
    as common type of emotion block, 18
    and emotion coaching, 35, 45
    and therapeutic apologies, 66, 69,
        74
Resilience, 65, 100
Rewards, 60
Role-plays
    in behavior coaching, 55–56
    in emotion coaching, 43
Romantic partners
    and role in EFFT, 4
    and super-feelers, 32
    as caregiver, 5. *See also* Caregivers

S

Sadness, 34, 38–40, 42, 83, 98, 123
Safe brain, 30
Safety, 141–142, 165–166
Schizophrenia, 42, 142
School settings, 126, 139, 144
Self-assessment tools
    for working through caregiver blocks,
        85–92, 94
    for working through clinician blocks,
        106–109
Self-blame
    and caregiver blocks, 83, 90
    and clinician blocks, 116
    and emotion coaching, 42, 45
    and "no blame" foundation of
        EFFT, 14
    and research on emotion-focused
        family therapy, 26
    and therapeutic apologies, 18, 64–70,
        74, 133

Self-care
    for caregivers, 141
    for clinicians, 116–117
Self-compassion
    and caregiver blocks, 84, 97
    and clinician blocks, 111
    and eating disorders, 134
    meditations for, 141
    and therapeutic apologies, 65, 66, 68
Self-Directed Block Worksheet for
        Clinicians, 108–109, 177–180
Self-efficacy
    caregiver, 27
    and caregiver blocks, 100
    and client resistance to caregiver
        involvement, 140
    and emotion coaching, 32, 44
    parental, 26
    and treatment of eating disorders, 134
Self-esteem
    and eating disorders, 119
    and therapeutic apologies, 65
Self-harm behaviors, 52, 57, 165–166
Self-regulation, 32, 48
Self-stigma, 41
Shame
    and caregiver blocks, 86, 92, 94, 101
    and clinician blocks, 107, 109, 116
    as common type of emotion block, 18
    and emotion coaching, 42, 45
    labeling of, 34
    needs associated with, 39, 40
    and normalizing language, 57
    and therapeutic apologies, 65, 67, 69,
        70, 73
    and treatment of eating disorders, 133
Siegel, D., 35, 142
Silence, 169–170
Silent blast, 72
Skill development and practice, 4, 14,
        43–45, 55–56. *See also* Advanced
        caregiving skills
*Skills-Based Learning for Caring for a Loved
        One With an Eating Disorder: The New
        Maudsley Method* (Treasure, Smith, &
        Crane), 185
Sleep hygiene, 116
Social referencing, 30
Social stigma, 67
Social workers, 19
Sociocultural learning, 81
Stepparents, 5. *See also* Caregivers

Substance use
  behavior coaching targets for, 52, 54
  and eating disorders, 120, 136, 139,
    143–144
  effectiveness of EFFT for, 142
Suicidality
  caregiver fears relating to, 89
  and emotion coaching, 31
  safety plan for, 165–166
Super-feelers, 32–33, 71, 151–152
Supervision
  emotion-focused, 18
  and implementation adherence, 9
  for therapeutic apologies, 75–76
  video, 115
  for working through clinician blocks,
    106–109, 114–115, 117
Surrogate apologies, 78–79
Symptom interruption, 40, 55, 88, 122,
  128, 130–131, 134
Symptom shifting, 116

T

Termination, 142
Therapeutic apologies, 63–80. *See also*
  specific headings
  in caregiver-led emotion-focused family
    therapy, 19
  and clinician blocks, 115–116
  and emotion coaching, 48
  facilitation of, 68–79
  healing strained or estranged
    relationships with, 66–67
  overview, 17–18
  processing caregiver self-blame with,
    64–66
  relieving self-blame in loved ones in, 67–68
  resistance towards, 83
  steps in, 157–160
  surrogate, 78–79
  in treatment of eating disorders, 123,
    132–134
Therapeutic drift, 106, 135
Therapeutic relationship, 116, 145
Therapists
  defined, 5
  EFFT certification for, 9
Therapy, individual. *See* Individual therapy

Therapy-interfering behaviors. *See also*
  Caregiver blocks; Clinician blocks;
  Emotion blocks
  and clinician blocks, 105
  techniques for addressing of, 16
  in treatment of eating disorders,
    134
Thought–action repertoires, 100
Transparency, 15, 78–79
Trauma, 81, 116
  and posttraumatic stress disorder, 84
Treasure, J., 142
Treatment plans, 55, 107
Treatment progress, 106
Tree metaphor, 85–86
"Trigger" foods, 127
Two-day EFFT caregiver workshop
  overview, 22–23
  research on, 28
  and therapeutic apologies, 77
Two-step model of emotion coaching
  components of, 40–41
  overview, 17, 34

V

Validation
  and behavior coaching, 53, 60, 155
  caregiver blocks related to, 83
  different definitions of, 47
  in five-step model of emotion coaching,
    37–38
  of silence, 169–170
  statements for, 154
  in therapeutic apologies, 70–75
  in treatment of eating disorders, 128,
    131–132
  in two-step model of emotion coaching,
    40–41
Video supervision, 115
Violence, 130

W

Waller, G., 135
Wisdom, 84–85
Withdrawal emotions, 101
Working alliance, 86, 91–92

About the Authors

Adele Lafrance, PhD, is an associate professor at Laurentian University and codeveloper of emotion-focused family therapy (EFFT). She is a founding member of the International Institute for EFFT (http://www.efftinternational.org). She is a licensed clinical psychologist with a practice of short-term clinical care and supervision. Over the years, she has taught numerous courses on developmental and clinical psychology with a focus on family-oriented mental health care across the life span. Dr. Lafrance provides EFFT training for clinicians, school boards, and mental health agencies worldwide. She has published extensively in the field and currently supports the research base for EFFT. Dr. Lafrance is regularly interviewed in the media and is a frequent speaker throughout the world. She also develops many practical resources for parents, caregivers, and clinicians that are available on her website free of cost (http://www.mentalhealthfoundations.ca).

Katherine A. Henderson, PhD, is a licensed clinical psychologist and co-director of Anchor Psychological Services (http://www.anchorpsychology.ca). She is also an adjunct research professor in the Department of Psychology at Carleton University, Ottawa, Canada. Dr. Henderson is recognized internationally for her expertise and research in the treatment of pediatric eating disorders. She codeveloped the 2-day EFFT caregiver workshop and Concurrent-CARE (C-CARE), an extension of EFFT for the treatment of concurrent eating and substance use disorders. She provides EFFT and C-CARE training to clinicians and community agencies worldwide and is a frequent speaker within her community on mental health issues. Dr. Henderson lives in Ottawa, Ontario, Canada.

Shari Mayman, PhD, is a licensed clinical psychologist and the codirector of Anchor Psychological Services (http://www.anchorpsychology.ca), a private practice in Ottawa. She is an expert in the assessment and treatment of eating disorders, as well as mood and anxiety disorders. She has significant experience in hospital-based eating disorder programs. Dr. Mayman codeveloped the 2-day EFFT caregiver workshop and Concurrent-CARE (C-CARE), a treatment model for concurrent eating and substance use disorders that is an extension of EFFT. She provides EFFT and C-CARE training to clinicians and community agencies internationally and speaks frequently on topics related to mental health. Dr. Mayman lives in Ottawa, Ontario, Canada.